Poker Tips

Expert Strategy Guide for Winning No Limit Texas Hold 'em

JONATHAN GELLING

Play to Pay Publishing

POKER TIPS THAT PAY

Expert Strategy Guide for Winning No Limit Texas Hold 'em by Jonathan Gelling

Play to Pay Publishing
Post Office Box 455
Farmingville, NY 11738
Visit us at www.PlayToPayPub.com
Visit the author at www.JonathanGelling.com

ISBN: 978-0-9840822-9-2

First Edition 2009. First Printing.

PRINTED IN THE UNITED STATES OF AMERICA

TABLE OF CONTENTS

INTRODUCTION

Have you ever wanted to peer into the mind of the world's greatest poker players: to see, step-by-step, the process they use in thinking about a hand? At any moment, a top-notch poker player must consider his chip position, the strength of his cards, the image he's projecting to his opponents, his read on his opponents' play, the chance of improving his hand, the texture of the board, the likelihood of success if he bets, his overall goals, and dozens of other factors.

While all that may seem daunting, there are simple principles underlying this level of thinking. The elements of winning poker play - courage, patience, discipline and judgment - are the same skills you need to excel in any endeavor. This book will help you develop those qualities in your game.

Playing winning poker requires more study than ever before. Big money tournaments have attracted great attention. Online poker has enabled thousands of players to log experience in a fraction of the time it used to take at card rooms and home games. The state of competitive poker today is captured by our first maxim:

"Everything today is at its greatest peak, especially the art of making one's way in the world. There is more required nowadays to make a single wise man than formerly to make seven sages; and more is needed in dealing with a single person than was required with a whole people in former times."

Thus begins Balthasar Gracian's landmark text, *The Art of Worldly Wisdom*. He could easily be referring to our own era: our struggle to make sense of a hyperactive, globalized, media-saturated world on information overload. Except Gracian was a seventeenth century Jesuit priest.

This man of many apparent contradictions – a cultured son of the nobility, devoted clergyman, and Renaissance intellectual – produced a classic book of maxims for all ages. Gracian's broad personal perspective gave him the insight to see that information alone will never lead to true wisdom, no matter how greatly multiplied.

These maxims have been adapted from the original text of *The Art of Worldly Wisdom*, translated by Joseph Jacobs. Illustrated with step-by-step analysis of dozens of actual poker hands, you'll find this sage advice as timely today as when originally penned.

If you follow the lessons in these pages you will certainly be a better poker player than you are right now. These insights should be digested, pondered over, and refined through the crucible of experience. You'll develop your own winning style that works for you.

Poker is not a game of chance, but a battle of wits. Fortune favors the wise.

Jonathan Gelling
Medford, New York

Chapter One

LIGHTS, CAMERA, ACTION!

It's been fifteen hours now. Fifteen hours of poker these past two days. Fifteen hours surrounded by lights, television cameras, frantic ESPN producers, and hordes of admiring fans. The pressure is intense, but you're too exhausted by now to feel it.

This moment has been four months in the making. That's how long you've waited for this final table to play out, with over $9 million on the line. Four months of practice, anticipation, studying your opponents, and planning your every move. And it's all come down to this.

There were 6,844 players in this tournament when it started July 3, and nine remained by July 14. The final table was then postponed until November. Good for ratings; agony on the players. But poker is not a game for the impatient.

And now, after all this time, it's down to two. You're heads-up for the World Series of Poker Main Event Championship. There is no more prestigious tournament. Besides the prize money, the winner will be an instant household name and immortalized in the annals of poker history, joining the likes of Johnny Moss, Doyle Brunson, Stu Ungar, Tom McEvoy, Johnny Chan, Phil Hellmuth, Dan Harrington and Chris Ferguson on the exclusive list of Main Event Champions.

This is what every player dreams about. And you're within striking distance of your dream. It's so close you can practically taste it.

The break is over, and soon the cards are flying.

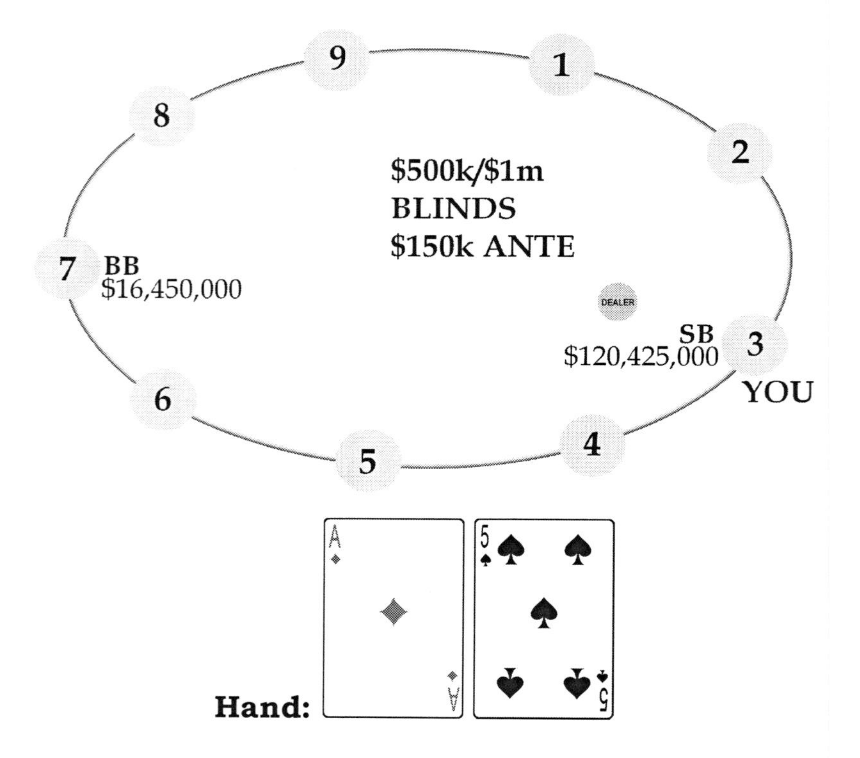

Situation: Heads-up at the final table of the World Series of Poker. You've gained a commanding chip lead over the past two shuffles by hitting some huge hands: a flush and a full house. With the price of poker now $1.8 million, your opponent is down to an M of 9. He's on the ropes – he'll have to move quickly to turn this thing around. You're looking for a knock-out blow.

Analysis: We're first to act with our ace-high. Heads-up, any ace is strong. With an ace in your hand, there's only a 12% chance your opponent has an ace as well. There's also a 5.9% chance of him being dealt a pocket pair.

THE POWER OF ACE-HIGH HEADS-UP

If he doesn't have an ace or a pair, we have the best hand. That means we're at least 88% to have the best hand right now. The better your ace, the more likely you're currently ahead. If you hold AK, you're 94% likely to be out in front – only a pocket pair is beating you before the flop.

The standard play is to raise here. We probably have the best hand, so we want to raise the stakes. We're in position as well, which also argues for building a bigger pot.

But we're looking for a knock-out blow. Although taking down the $1.8 million pot would be nice, we want to position ourselves to earn our opponent's whole stack.

If we limp, he won't expect us to have an ace. We might hit our ace and get action from second or third pair, and earn more money that way.

Or he may assume we're weak and try to raise us off our hand after we limp. We can then spring our trap by coming over the top of his raise. Either possibility might be more profitable than making a standard raise.

Generally, I'd favor raising here, though. Heads-up, you should often raise on the button, with or without a strong hand. But for the sake of deception and mixing up your play, limping is sometimes appropriate.

Action: You complete the small blind of $1 million, and your opponent checks. The pot is now $2.3 million, and it's heads-up to the flop:

Action: He checks.

Analysis: Start your analysis by looking at the good: what hand you have, and what potential it has to improve. Here, we still have the ace-high we started with. We've picked up a wheel draw: a four will give us a five-high straight.

Since as far as we know there are 4 fours remaining in the 47 cards we haven't seen, we have a 4/47 chance of hitting a straight on the turn plus a 4/46 chance of hitting it on the river. We're about 16% to make our gutshot straight draw -- about 8% on each street.

Ace-high and a 16% chance at an inside straight may not sound great. Many players would happily check and take the free card here. Why risk being raised off our draw?

Experienced players generally bet in this spot, however. They know that most flops miss most hands: about two-thirds of the time your opponent will have nothing. Since we likely started with the best hand, we're still in front. A bet here will probably earn us the pot.

We should also pay attention to the relative chip position: we have over seven times as many chips as our opponent. Even if he suspects larceny, there's not much he can do about it without a real hand. His stack is too small to risk a pure bluff.

CONSIDER THE TEXTURE OF THE BOARD: RAGGED OR CONNECTED?

This ragged flop is a great one for our semi-bluff. With just one face-card and two rags, how strong can our opponent really be? If he doesn't have a king in his hand, he's playing a pair of deuces, treys, or nothing at all. Will he come over the top of us with those hands?

Note how different this situation would be if the flop was something like K9T as opposed to K23. Then we'd have no hand, no draw, and our opponent could hold a variety of strong hands and draws. It would make much less sense to bluff in that spot.

Action: You bet $1.25 million. Your opponent considers for about five seconds before smoothly making the call. The pot is now $4.8 million, and you're off to the turn:

Action: He ponders for several seconds before checking.

Analysis: Yahtzee! We've made our straight, and with no flushes possible, only a 56 could beat us. If he has that hand, good luck to him. You're never folding a straight heads-up. We have only one objective now: get all the chips in the center and end this thing. How's the best way to go about doing this?

Do we feign weakness here, trying to trap? Absolutely not! Many new players will automatically play their weakest hands most aggressively, and try to trap with their legitimate hands. They think they're being sneaky with their reverse psychological play. But such a mechanical style is easily exploited.

Always play the situation, not just your hand. There's a time and a place for trapping: when you have a monster, your opponent can't have much, and you won't get action unless your opponent catches up or sees an opportunity to bluff. This is not one of those spots.

Consider the board and the action: we limped in, bet the flop on a board of K23, and now a 4 arrives on the turn. We represented a made hand on the flop, something like a pair of kings, threes, or maybe a pocket pair between kings and threes.

In any event, our opponent will read that 4 as a blank: only a gutshot straight draw (A5 or 56) could have connected with that card. No one ever suspects a gutshot, least of all on a ragged board like this.

Since our opponent can't put us on a strong hand, there's no reason we can't get more value by betting the turn here. Our opponent called on the flop, so he probably has *something*. He may not have a king, since he might have raised earlier – unless he was laying an ill-fated trap for us.

If he called on the flop with a pair of deuces or threes, he may also call a bet here. Maybe he now has two pair (32, 42, 43). Either way he'll probably call, since the 4 seems unlikely to have helped our hand. You should assume your opponent will call on the turn if he called on the flop and a blank comes.

IF YOUR OPPONENT IS DRAWING, GET THE MONEY IN BEFORE THE RIVER

Maybe he has a 5, or an ace, and now has a straight draw himself. If your opponent has some kind of draw, he might call a bet on the flop and turn, but won't if he misses on the river. Get the money in now while the getting is good. There's no worse mistake in poker than handing out free cards.

Action: You bet $2 million into the $4.8 million pot, hoping your opponent has enough of a hand to stick around. He check-raises to $6 million. The pot is now $12,800,000, and it costs you $4 million to call. Your opponent has $8,050,000 remaining in his stack. He has invested more than half his stack, $8.4 million, in this hand.

Analysis: Should we just call here, or set him all-in? Although our opponent appears to have committed himself to the hand, flat calling is probably best here. Unless one of the three remaining fives comes on the river, our hand is relatively invulnerable.

It's possible he's making this big check-raise with a pair and a straight-draw, in which case we'd want to set him all-in here before he misses the draw on the river. But it's more likely he has top pair, two pair, or maybe a set. And he could be making a move -- he's shown a capacity for making huge bluffs at the final table thus far. In any event, it's probably best not to scare him away with a re-raise right here.

He'll have to act first on the river, which is a perfect opportunity for him to fire off his remaining chips. For that reason, we should probably lean towards calling here. Hopefully he'll feel committed to the hand after putting half his stack in, and push all-in regardless of the river.

Action: You call the extra $4 million. The pot is now $16.8 million, and your opponent has just over $8 million left in his stack. Getting over 3:1 to call all-in, it'd be a heroic fold on the river if he checks to us (we'll of course set him all-in). The river brings a blank:

Action: Your opponent goes all-in for his remaining stack, and you quickly call. He turns over his two-pair:

The fatigue is evident as it takes him several seconds to read the board and realize he's beaten. The energy is running a little low after so many hours of grueling play. But it's more than that: he never put you on an ace. Although a 65 was an obvious danger on the turn, he never considered a wheel draw. The turn was a total disaster for him.

As stunned as your opponent is, you're even more speechless. It takes several seconds to process. You're the new World Series of Poker Champion for 2008 - the best in the world. You're a permanent part of poker history.

How did you get here? Was it because you were "lucky" to make a straight when your opponent made two pair? Sure that was fortunate; your opponent didn't make any real mistakes. There's almost no way to get away from two-pair in a heads-up situation, particularly on a non-threatening board like that.

But you also outwitted, outmaneuvered, and outlasted over 6,800 players on your way to the top. And you built a huge chip lead heading into this hand. If you hadn't demonstrated serious poker skills in the hours before this "lucky" hand played out, you wouldn't have had a chance to get "lucky" at all. In the long run, it's not the cards, but the value you extract from your hands.

It's your poker experience, the wisdom you've developed over countless thousands of hands that brought you here. If you play well, you earn the chance to get "lucky."

Chapter Two

KNOW YOUR ODDS!

Maxim 21: To be lucky you must be wise.

There are rules of luck: it is not all chance with the wise: it can be assisted with care. Some content themselves waiting confidently at the gate of Fortune, hoping she'll open the door for them. Others do better, and press forward and profit by their clever boldness, reaching the goddess and winning Her favor through action and accomplishment. In truth there is no umpire in this world, there is merely virtue and insight; there is no luck or ill-luck except wisdom and the reverse.

Maxim 31: Select the lucky and avoid the unlucky.

Ill-luck is generally the penalty of folly, and there is no disease so contagious to those who share in it. Never open the door to a lesser evil, for other and greater ones invariably slink in after it. The greatest skill at cards is to know when to discard; the smallest of current trumps is worth more than the ace of trumps of the last game. When in doubt, follow the suit of the wise and prudent; sooner or later they will win the game.

There are some players who blame "bad luck" for their losing poker play. In truth everything is governed by the law of cause and effect; it's only the countless unseen and unknown factors that combine to produce seemingly random results. As a poker player, you should not concern yourself with these factors, or be discouraged when Fortune turns against you.

You will have runs of "bad luck" which you will remember in great detail. But you will also have games where “good luck” seems to bend all the cards to your will. You’ll probably discount how “lucky” you were to get strong hands at all the right times. You shouldn’t pay attention to where the cards happen to fall.

These random fluctuations in the distribution of starting hands will not make you a winning player. You must make wise decisions with whatever cards you happen to hold. By exploiting your position, chip stack, and opponents’ weaknesses, you can tilt the odds in your favor with or without help from the cards.

If you always *take the odds*, you will come out ahead over time. Just as a casino makes money over the long run by enjoying an edge -- however slight -- if the odds are on your side you’ll eventually make out well.

Here are the key probabilities every poker player should know by heart, and how they should influence your playing decisions:

Odds of being dealt a particular pocket pair:
0.45% or 220:1 against

Odds of being dealt ANY pocket pair:
5.9% or 16:1 against

The message here is clear: if you sit around and wait for AAs, you’ll be waiting an average of 220 hands between play. You’ll quickly run out of money, and worse still, aces can lose upwards of

20% of the time. Clearly, waiting around for a big hand and shoving all your chips is not a winning strategy.

But also note that being dealt a pair is itself a somewhat rare event, and a valuable opportunity that shouldn't be passed up. At a ten-handed table, there's a 59% chance any single player will be dealt a pair. The odds of another player also being dealt a pair would then be roughly 29% (59% x (5.45% x 9), representing the odds of one of the other nine players being dealt a pair other than the one you have, though two players having the same pair is also a remote possibility).

The odds of the other pair being greater or lesser than your own would depend on the specific value of your hand, with half the pairs less than 8s and half greater. So if you had a pair of 8s pre-flop, the chance an opponent has a bigger pair would be 14.5% (or 5.9:1 against). Even a lowly pair of deuces has a 71% chance of being the best hand before the flop at a full, ten-handed table.

Make no mistake: any pair is a pretty powerful hand before the flop.

If you're playing short-handed or heads-up, you can go to war with any pair. Even at a full table, you can play most pairs very aggressively under the right circumstances.

Odds of flopping a set or better with a pocket pair: 11.8% or 7.5:1 against

Of course, when you do flop a set you'll have a well-disguised hand that could capture your opponent's entire stack if he's unlucky enough to hit his hand at the same time.

Given the huge potential pay-off, you should at least call any standard raise with a pocket pair, if: (1) you can do so without committing more than 10% of your chips; (2) your opponent is aggressive and has at least 10x the amount of his raise behind him (so he can pay off your investment); *and* (3) your table is not so aggressive that you're likely to get re-raised before the flop -- it helps to be in late position as this will reduce the number of potential re-raisers.

Delay a few moments before flat-calling the original raiser with a small pocket pair, to give the impression that you considered re-raising the raiser: this will help discourage an aggressive re-raise from late position, i.e. a squeeze play.

This illustrates the power of a pocket pair: it can be played either aggressively as a made hand before the flop, or used conservatively for its set potential, if you can see a cheap flop.

Odds of flopping flush draw with two suited cards:
11.74% - 10.9% for flush draw, 0.84% flush

Odds of flopping straight draw with connectors:
11.75% - 10.45% straight draw, 1.3% straight

If you start with a suited connector between 54 and QJ (avoid playing 32 or 43 because of the limited straight draws), you have a 23.5% chance of flopping some type of draw.

Note that it is in fact the dual draw potential of these hands that makes them valuable to play *in position*; many beginning players make the mistake of routinely calling with any suited cards (e.g. K3 ***suited!***), unsuited connectors, and one or two-gappers of any stripe (e.g. J9, 96).

If you find yourself playing these hands -- except on the button or out of the blinds -- please stop! Without both the flush and straight draw potential you simply won't flop big enough, often enough, to make these hands profitable. You need to flop a draw nearly a quarter of the time to make money on these hands. Remember: even if you flop a draw, you'll still end up missing two-thirds of the time.

If you call with an unsuited connector, you'll flop a draw or better less than 12% of the time and hit your straight less than 5% by the river. You're 19:1 against making a big hand – vs. 9:1 with the suited connector. The hand simply isn't profitable enough to play in most positions.

The second most common beginner's mistake with these hands is to go broke with them when they flop top pair. If you flop a pair of jacks with your JT and are re-raised on the flop or turn, you almost certainly do NOT have the best hand. There may be a small chance that you do, but it's unlikely, and you should proceed on the assumption that you're beat.

Suited connectors are primarily drawing hands: with these hands you *really* do not want to get married to top pair. You're looking for that 10% chance of making a big hand, semi-bluffing with a draw, or taking down uncontested pots with these hands when your opponent misses. You shouldn't appear weak, but you should proceed with extreme caution if you don't make your hand or at least a draw to a big hand.

There's an important corollary to the principle that we should only play cards that are both suited *and* connected. Just as we need both the straight and the flush draw possibilities to make these hands profitable, we shouldn't be overly concerned about facing a particular draw (unless we're in a multi-way pot with four or more opponents). Many players – no doubt burned from a painful experience or two – have learned to fear the flush. This presents our first principle for study:

DON'T FEAR THE FLUSH DRAW (LESS THAN 5% PER OPPONENT)

Let's consider the dreaded flush draw. Before the flop each of our opponents has a 5.9% chance of being dealt two hole cards of matching suit. If the board is showing two of a single suit, a flush draw is possible. However, it's now less likely any of our opponents has that draw because there are only eleven cards of that suit remaining.

In other words, the board has provided us valuable information about our opponents' likely holdings: telling us it's less likely they're four-flushing. How unlikely? Reducing the pool of available cards of a particular suit from thirteen to eleven represents a reduction of over 15%. The probability is reduced even further because it's a dual selection (two hole cards are dealt) from the smaller pool of available cards of that suit.

When you do the math, this reduces the chance of a flush draw from 5.9% (the odds of being dealt *any* two cards of a suit) to *less than 5% per opponent* (the odds of being dealt two cards of a suit matching the other two on board).

While we need to keep a flush draw in mind (especially in a large multi-way pot), don't be obsessed with the possibility:

A flush draw is unlikely with few players and only two of a suit on board! Many amateurs are irrationally terrified of flushes – don't be that guy.

Odds of flopping pair or better with unpaired hole cards (e.g. AK): 32.4%, better than 2:1 against

It's twice as likely the flop did *nothing* to help your opponent. If he started with AK and felt good about his hand before the flop, he won't love it after the flop more than two-thirds of the time. You can put a lot of pressure on him when he misses, even if you missed the flop as well!

If he started with a pocket pair, he has a made hand, but he's 7.5:1 against flopping a set and likely to see overcards out there. If he's beat, his hand is only 8% to improve by the river. How much will he really want to invest in that spot?

Most hands are *not* going to improve on the flop, so this is a good time to pounce on weakness. He raised pre-flop from early position and is leading out on a 9-high board? Test him with a raise if he'll fold ace-high. Or to mix things up, simply call the flop and try to take it away on the turn.

Odds your opponent has a big pair (AAs, KKs, QQs, JJs) or AK: About 3%, or 33:1 against

This is the mathematical foundation of the *Kill Phil* theory of poker, based loosely on David Sklansky's "Tournament System for Beginners." This theory recognizes that large all-in bets before the flop can effectively eliminate the skill factor in no limit hold 'em.

Before the community cards are dealt, even the best hole cards (besides AAs) enjoy a relatively modest advantage over other poker hands. For example, while AAs are at least 80-20 favorites, KKs are just 70-30 against any hand with an ace. AK is roughly 60-40 against any two unpaired cards (except a dominated ace like AQ, but even this best-case scenario leaves AK a mere 70-30 favorite). AKs vs. QQs is a coin flip, with a slight edge to the queens.

If you're a smart, experienced player, you know that you can do better than risking all your chips as a slight favorite. You'll therefore avoid making these gambles, hoping to keep the stakes low and outmaneuver your opponents after the flop. This is the basis of the *Kill Phil* theory:

"PHIL" DOESN'T WANT TO PLAY FAST AND LOOSE FOR ALL THE CHIPS!

Strong, tight players don't want to get into 50-50 -- or even 60-40 -- confrontations for all their chips. How strong must they be to call an all-in from a player they respect? Many need a big pair (at least jacks) or AK, and there's only a 3% chance of a tight player being that strong. If he also calls with AQ, that's 4.2% of all hands he may have been dealt. In short, a tight opponent probably can't call a huge pre-flop all-in move.

This is particularly true if the tight player is raising in position. As more players fold, the number of possible hands at the table decreases. Many players will raise near the button with marginal hands if the table folds around to them.

This presents a perfect opportunity to steal a raise from a *tight* player who will lay the hand down. Stealing a raise is twice as profitable as stealing the blinds. Selective aggression in these spots can make the difference between placing in the tournament and busting out on the cusp.

Just be sure you're really up against a "Phil" when making this move. Do *not* try this against a loose calling station who thinks the object of the game is to see as many flops as possible. The results will be disappointing.

DON'T FEAR THE HIDDEN SET (5% vs. ENTIRE TABLE)

There's only a 5.9% chance of any particular player being dealt a pocket pair. At a nine-handed table, there's only a 53% chance *any* of the players will be dealt a pair, and a 47% chance that a player other than you will have a pair. It's possible some of the weaker pairs may be folded in early position, and the odds of flopping a set or four of a kind are about 11%.

If you work out the chance of a player at a full table being dealt a pair, playing it, and flopping a set, that will all happen about 5% of the time. This is not a negligible possibility, but 19:1 against is fantastic odds in a game like poker. If you're unwilling to bet all your money getting odds of 19:1, you need to forget about gambling. Find another hobby, because bad things happen often in poker, where the best you can hope for before the flop is to get your money in pair over pair, as a 4.5:1 favorite.

If you'd bet it all on AAs vs. KKs at 4.5:1, you should gleefully bet an opponent hasn't flopped a set at 19:1. It's a rare thing that you should fear a hidden set, and you should be skeptical that any particular hand is a "5% moment."

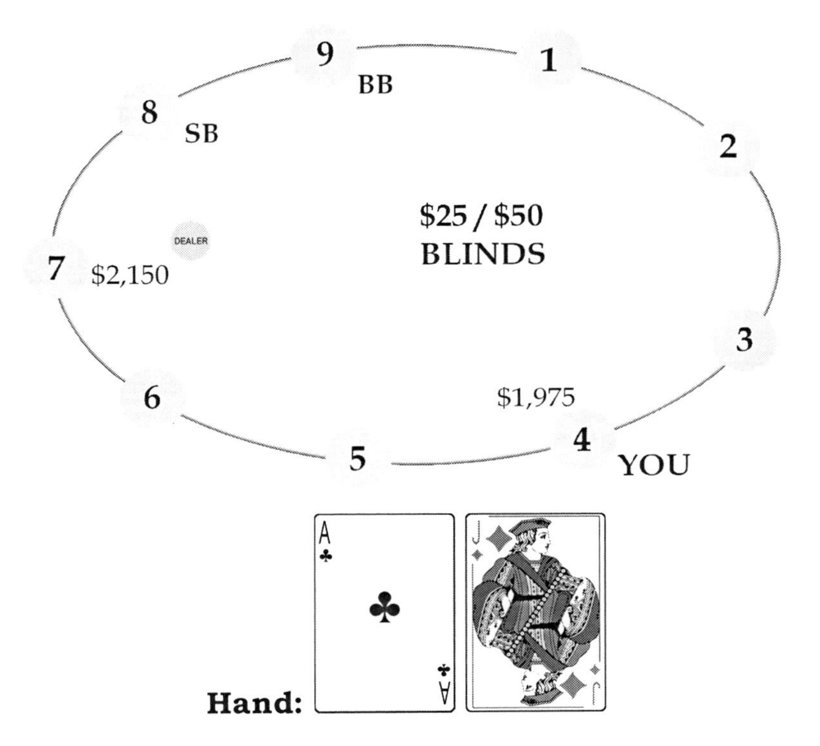

Situation: Mid-stages of a single table online sit and go tournament. The button has been somewhat loose in the early going, but also pretty aggressive. He's shown an ability to fold in the face of danger, however. We'll have to tread carefully against him.

Action: Everyone folds to you in middle position, and you make a standard raise to $150. It's folded around to the button, who calls. The blinds both fold. The pot is now $375, and it's heads-up to the flop:

Analysis: Top-pair, top-kicker: this is exactly what we're hoping for when we play big cards like AJ. Unfortunately we'll only hit our hand about a third of the time. With that in mind, it's important not to be too tentative when we are lucky enough to make something. We'll assume we're ahead unless and until our opponent gives us very good reason to think otherwise.

Action: You make a standard continuation bet of $200, and the button ponders for a few seconds before calling. The pot is now $775, and you're off to the turn:

Analysis: The deuce of hearts completes any flush draws that called on the flop. But basically this card changes nothing: it's unlikely to have suddenly given your opponent two-pair (even a somewhat loose opponent wouldn't call with a hand like 32 or J2, on the button or otherwise), and it didn't complete any inside straight draws our opponent may have made an ambitious call with.

Many players will still get a little nervous right here. Getting burned by one too many flush draws over the years creates painful memories. But in poker you can't be obsessed over worst-case scenarios: you have to play the odds. A lot of what we call "suck-outs" in poker are 5% probabilities. A lot of bad things will happen 5% of the time *over the long run*, but you need to play each hand for the 95% likeliest scenario.

Since we're up against only one other opponent who called a pre-flop raise on the button, we shouldn't dwell too long on the possibility he's suited in hearts. We know from the 5% rule that it's 19:1 against that scenario.

Moreover, although many players will greatly widen their starting hand requirements on the button, Seat 7 has shown himself to be a strong and tough opponent. He didn't call our raise with two random suited cards: he probably has some high cards, a small pair, or a drawing hand like 98, JT, QJ, etc. With the jack of hearts on board, the number of playable suited drawing hands he could be holding is much lower.

Why did he call the flop? A flush draw is probably one of the *least likely* explanations for his play. An aggressive player with a flush draw on a jack-high flop would likely have raised us: unless we had a big pair or exactly AJ, an early position raiser like us is unlikely to have connected with that board.

So what else could he have? Second pair is the likeliest possibility, with our opponent holding something like 87 or 97 suited. Our continuation bet is signaling that we either made a pair of jacks or are holding a big pocket pair: our opponent would rightly be skeptical that we had either hand. But he might just call our bet, not wanting to invest too much money with second-pair, weak-kicker.

Our opponent could have a couple of overcards, like AQ, AK or KQ, and simply called because he doesn't believe our bet and/or intends to try to take the pot away on the turn. This is a possibility, but a loose, aggressive opponent might have re-raised with AQ or AK in position before the flop.

It's also possible he has a weak jack, maybe J9 or JT, and is flat-calling with top-pair, weak-kicker because he wants to limit the size of the pot. Hands like JT and QJ suited are primarily *drawing hands* (i.e. you're looking to make a straight and/or flush draw), and you're in a potentially messy situation when you hit top pair with those.

On the one hand, you don't want to fold top-pair too easily; on the other, you don't want to invest too much against an early position raiser who is likely to hold premium cards. You always have to worry about your kicker with medium drawing cards.

The final, unlikely possibility to keep in mind is some type of inside straight draw, with something like a 54, 98, T9, or T8. These hands are really unlikely, but should always be in the back of your head as a distant possibility to worry about.

The conditions to justify playing an inside straight draw have to be perfect: (1) the betting has to be relatively low as a percentage of your stack; (2) you'd like multiple opponents in the pot to reduce the cost of drawing and to maximize the chances you'll get paid on your longshot draw; and (3) if you're lucky enough to hit your hand, *it has to be the nuts*. You should never call with an inside straight draw against a single opponent, with heavy betting, on a paired or suited board. No skilled opponent would have called with an inside straight draw in this spot.

From this analysis, we see that our opponent's likeliest holding is second-pair, or possibly a weak jack. With that in mind, we want to get more money in the pot because we're ahead right now. And although we're not worried that our opponent had a flush draw on the flop, we should be worried that *he may now have a flush draw with three suited cards on board.*

Action: You bet $400, and your opponent waits several seconds before calling. The pot is now $1,555. You have $1,225 left in your stack, and your opponent has $1,400 left in his. Notice how the pot now exceeds either of your stacks: with no limit betting, a single hand can easily escalate into an all-in confrontation. The river brings the king of clubs:

DON'T FEAR THE MIRACLE RIVER CARD

Analysis: That would seem to be a damaging card, but it's not too worrisome. Yes, we no longer have top-pair; but poker is a relative game. That king only hurts us if it helped our opponent. Since he called healthy bets on both the flop and turn, there's only one hand he could be holding that would be helped by that king: KJ. Other possibilities, like K7, K3 or K2, are unlikely beyond the micro-stakes tables.

Your opponent didn't call two rounds of heavy betting without having *some kind of made hand*, especially on the turn. He wasn't sticking around with some kind of random king hoping for a miracle.

And even if he was sticking around hoping to catch something, you can't guard against that. If your opponent needs a miracle card on the river, *you did everything right in the hand except win.*

Sometimes blind luck will carry the day; you can't and shouldn't worry about that simple truth.

Although that king probably didn't hurt us, there's still an outside chance our opponent really did make his flush on the turn or has been roping us along with a hidden set (another one of those distant 5% possibilities to always keep in mind). But in either case we were behind long before the river.

We thought we were ahead before, and with the river being a blank, nothing has changed. But we generally shouldn't lead out with a bet here.

Why not? Well, the pot is now larger than our remaining stack. Although we're pretty sure we have the best hand, it's only one pair. Any bet would commit us completely to the pot, and that's too much risk to take with one-pair (if we don't have to).

Does that mean we're check-folding this hand? Of course not! We're checking with the intention of automatically calling any normal bet. If our opponent goes all-in after we check, then we'll have to stop and reconsider the hand. But if our opponent is planning an aggressive all-in move as a river bluff (which is usually something only a crazy aggressive opponent would try), any bet we throw out here is unlikely to stop him without also committing us to the pot.

If we throw out a tiny probe bet of $100-$300, we're signaling weakness and possibly enticing a huge all-in response. So the best move we have is to check to our opponent and see what he does. We probably can't get away from the hand at this point; but we're hoping to avoid committing our entire stack to this pot.

Avoiding an all-in shouldn't be too difficult. If our opponent really has a very strong hand (either a made flush or a hidden set), then he wants to earn some chips from it. The only bet that can scare us away is an all-in move. Given the flop and turn action, we've indicated we have *some* kind of hand and are likely to call any normal bet he might make.

Since he should expect us to call any half- or two-thirds pot bet with ease, why would he go all-in and risk not earning any additional chips? It is true there are some players who make a habit of unexpectedly going all-in when they have the nuts. They hope to be called because of how suspicious their bet looks. It doesn't take long to identify such opponents.

But most players are savvier and try to extract maximum value from each and every hand. Missing just one additional bet on a few big hands can make the difference between a winning and losing session. It's a mistake to swing for the fences when you can win the game with a base hit.

In fact, we should be fairly suspicious of an all-in move here. That king would only help our opponent if he's holding KJ; but *he also knows that the king probably didn't help us*, unless we're holding KJ. KJ is not a standard raising hand from early-mid position; an all-in move could well be a bluff trying to capitalize on our "weak" check and "fear" of the king.

An aggressive opponent will reason: "If he liked a jack-high board on the flop and turn, will he really want to risk all his chips with what could be second pair after the king on the river?" But again, poker hands are relative; a card is only bad for us *if it helped our opponent*. For the same reason that the king didn't help us, it probably didn't help him. Don't be afraid to look him up if he tries to exploit our check on the river.

Action: You check, and after several seconds of delay your opponent checks behind you. You turn over your cards, and your opponent shows:

Your ace-kicker beats his queen-kicker, and you scoop the pot.

Analysis: We had our opponent out-kicked from beginning to end. Notice he checked behind us rather than risking another bet in an uncertain situation. He followed a basic rule that we'll discuss later: there's no reason to bet a medium-strength hand on the river. His pair of jacks, queen-kicker might have been good enough to win the pot; there was no reason to invest more money to see the showdown.

This hand also illustrates the dangers of playing a drawing hand for its pair potential. Kicker problems abound with hands like JT, QJ, KQ, KJ, etc. You should never get too excited when they fail to produce a solid draw.

Note that if the river had been a queen, our opponent would have made two-pair. When you see JT, QJ, or KQ on board, be very careful of likely two-pair possibilities. KJ didn't frighten us nearly as much, because it's less-played.

Chapter Three

VALUE HANDS BY THEIR PROFIT POTENTIAL

Maxim 27: Prize intensity more than extent.

Excellence resides in quality not in quantity. The best is always few and rare: much lowers value. Even among men giants are commonly the real dwarfs. Some reckon books by the thickness, as if they were written to try the brawn more than the brain. Extent alone never rises above mediocrity: it is the misfortune of universal geniuses that in attempting to be at home everywhere, are so nowhere. Intensity gives eminence, and rises to the heroic in matters sublime.

Maxim 34: Know your strongest suit.

Know thyself and your preeminent gift; cultivate your talent and you will assist the rest. Everyone would excel in something if he knew the best place to start. Notice in what quality you and your situation surpass, and start from there. In some prudence excels, in others strength or courage. Most do violence to their natural advantage, and thus attain superiority in nothing. Time is better spent working with one's strengths than in fiddling with weakness. Your strongest suit will yield the greatest results.

Maxim 142: Do not stubbornly fight an opponent who has the upper hand.

You begin the fight already beaten. With bad weapons one can rarely win. It was astute in the opponent to seize the better side first: it would be folly to come lagging after with the worst. 'Tis the common failing of the stubborn that they lose sight of the truth by contradicting it, and the useful by quarrelling with it. The sage never places himself on the side of passion, but stays on the wise and prudent course. If the enemy is a fool, he will inevitably find the wrong way. Thus the only way to drive him from the better course is to take it yourself, for his folly will cause him to desert it, and his obstinacy will be his undoing.

Some books on Texas Hold 'em include extensive charts on exactly which hands should be played from which positions. Occasionally these charts are made more complex by offering tighter or looser styles of play in response to table conditions.

This book will not follow the conventional wisdom of "starting hand requirements", for three reasons: (1) there are many factors beyond showdown potential and seat position to account for in selecting starting hands; (2) the mathematical models they rely on are based on a limit betting structure that fails to account for the much greater upside potential in no limit hold 'em (i.e. you can earn the entire stack of one or more opponents in every no limit hand); and (3) a table-based mechanical approach makes one too easy to read.

Instead hands should be judged by their ***profit potential under the circumstances***. In theory the tables are supposed to take profit potential into account, but they overestimate big starting hands and underestimate the profitability of draws in a no limit betting environment. When you're playing for all the marbles each and every hand, you can afford to make some speculative gambles if the price is right. At low stakes, do not assume a standard raise will clear out all the trashy hands.

Here are some general guidelines to consider in starting hand selection:

1. Big cards (AK, AQ, AJ, KQ) have big showdown equity but little potential to profit from the flop.

Too many people go broke with AK and AQ because it is such a treacherous hand. When it wins, you've usually made a small raise at the pot, hit your ace, king, or queen, gotten respect for exactly the hand you represented, and made a small profit. Occasionally a continuation bet bluff will also lead to a small win. Or you might play a small pot down to the river and win with ace-high or one pair.

When it loses, however, you can either get raised off a continuation bet bluff (which will cost you both a pre-flop raise *and* a post-flop bet) or, in the worst-case scenario, lose much of your stack if you flop big but your opponent flops bigger. These hands win a lot of small pots fairly often, but lose disastrously, and miss the flop more than twice as often as they hit.

What differentiates big cards from other unpaired hands, like QJ, JT, or even a lowly 32 or 43? ***While they lack much of the straight or flush draw potential (unless suited)***, they do have *showdown equity*. That's the key to these hands: the mechanical charts rank them so highly because they are 60-40 favorites over most hands (or roughly 50-50 vs. most pairs) *if they see the showdown.*

In limit hold 'em, you only need to call a few small, fixed bets to guarantee you see the river. In no limit hold 'em, in contrast, it could cost you everything. At any moment, your opponent could put you to the ultimate test for all your chips. With this in mind, unpaired high cards can be very tricky to play. Unless we hit our hand right on the flop or guarantee a showdown with an all-in pre-flop move, their potential is more theoretical than practical.

So how do we play them? The answer is a bit contradictory: both very cautiously and very aggressively. We need to play these hands very cautiously if we're in a ring game or the low-blind phase of a tournament where it's too risky to get married to them. And if these hands see a flop, we should play them softly, not looking to build a huge pot without good reason to think we're ahead.

On the other hand, where possible, we should jam the pot with these hands pre-flop to force out cards that have superior profit potential *if they can see a cheap flop.* When the blinds rise to 7-10% of average stack size or more, or we're short-stacked in a cash game, err on the side of pre-flop pot commitment. Don't fool around with small raises and let a drawing hand stick around. Go for the jugular and flush out drawing hands that can bluff or semi-bluff us after the flop.

2. Pocket pairs are your strong suit, and should be folded only in the face of a big re-raise.

Perhaps misled by the mechanical tables of starting hand requirements set out in much of the poker literature (largely parroting Sklansky and Malmuth, who designed them for ***limit hold 'em***), many players undervalue "small" or "medium" pairs. I can't think of the number of times I've heard the inane commentary that "medium pairs are the toughest hands to play in no limit hold 'em." Malarkey!

Yes, they can face tough decisions, but high cards are often forced to fold when they're still the best hand, earn little when they connect, and lose a lot to sets or drawing hands that get there. In contrast, pairs are a favorite over all high cards and possess overwhelming profit potential. You have a made hand before the flop, and while you're unlikely to improve your hand, you don't necessarily need to.

Many players are absolutely giddy when they stare down and see AK or AQ, suited or otherwise, and fairly nonplussed about looking down and finding a pair of 2s. My reaction is precisely the opposite: I almost dislike being dealt a hand like AK or AQ, particularly in a position where I have to open-raise and all but announce the strength of my hand.

Big cards are usually "must-play" hands, but they have by far the *least* profit potential of all *playable* hands -- in fact, unplayable oddball hands are often worth more if you get in free and make a hand.

The pair of deuces are more likely to be the best hand at the table pre-flop, don't need to connect with the flop to still be best, can be played aggressively pre-flop (or not), and can garner an opponent's entire stack with a well-concealed set. I would take one pocket pair over three ace-kings. Make no mistake: pairs of any rank are the strongest, most profitable starting hands in *no limit* Texas Hold 'em, period.

How to play them? I generally hate limping from an early position with small pairs, since that just screams "weak hand." Instead, if I'm first to open, I'll raise just as though I had AK. This provides multiple ways to win: (1) your opponents can fold to the early position raise (usually thought to represent great strength by textbook players) and scoop a small pot; (2) you can get called and represent top pair if an ace or face card hits; (3) you can hit a set and win big money if an opponent makes a hand; (4) you can bet at a ragged board and represent an over-pair; or (5) you can value bet a really ragged board and win a fair bit of money against a tight, aggressive opponent who gets out of line with ace-high. That's a lot of ways to win -- and a lot of pure profit potential.

If someone has raised before you, call a standard (or even somewhat oversized) raise if it's less than 10% of your stack, but never flat call a strong re-raise. A re-raise is a sign of great strength, and you don't want to risk getting involved in a situation where you could be dominated. Domination (pair over pair) is the pocket pair's greatest fear.

The rule of thumb is that a raise may be a bluff, but a re-raise seldom is. Even if you suspect theft it's not worth it to find out, and you don't want to get caught in the middle of a bidding war with two players without a premium pocket pair (AAs, KKs, or QQs, and even queens may be folded).

If you have a small or medium pair and your opponent's raise is more than 10% of your stack, I wouldn't favor just calling too often unless it's part of a move to take the hand away on the flop (which you'll remember is more than twice as likely to miss your opponent if he has two unpaired hole cards). If you're short-stacked, or this is a short-handed situation, don't hesitate to take your pocket pair to war. It's unlikely there's a bigger pair out against you, and if you get action from a couple of overcards at least you're a slight favorite.

3. Don't fall into the trap of playing unsuited connectors, one or two-gappers suited or otherwise, or suited cards (even weak suited aces) unless you're playing in position, in a big pot with several other players, or at a discount out of the blinds.

Drawing hands do best in multi-way, unraised pots, played in position so you know how much it will cost to draw. Unlike with high cards, drawing hands want to see more players in the pot, to make drawing cheaper and to maximize the chances of getting paid off.

Not all drawing hands are created equal. Realize that you're speculating with these hands. As with any speculative investment, you want to be sure your winners occur with enough frequency, and provide sufficient yield, to compensate for all the losers (which will be the vast majority of such bets).

There's a well-known curve that occurs with Texas Hold 'em players. When we first start playing the game, we're much too loose, overvaluing weak aces and a variety of suited cards with little real profit potential. We usually lose a lot of money with this approach, and this causes us to study the game, read about starting hand requirements, and tighten up substantially.

This style of play is usually good enough to win at the lower levels, and our winning streak encourages us to play more and more hands, based on our supposed superiority over our opponents.

At the same time, we may begin to move up in stakes or play multiple tables. Gradually, our winning edge declines, we become too loose, too aggressive at the wrong times, allow our attention to become distracted by the multiple tables, or generally become complacent and thus play losing poker again. Hopefully we learn to tighten up before the downward spiral leaves us blaming online poker sites, "cheaters", or the cruel, foul poker gods themselves.

Here's an important point: no matter how great your hand-reading skills, no matter how aggressive your playing style, no matter how perfect your post-flop judgments and decisions, ***if you start with inferior cards you are giving your opponents an edge***. The worse the hand, the lower the return on your investment (equity) will be. If your opponents are sufficiently competent, you don't have to give them much of an edge to end up with a negative return on equity.

Don't be the guy who brings a knife to a gun fight.

Here are the four keys that will give your opponents an edge and *cost you money*: (1) you start with bad cards with little upside potential; (2) you play the hand out of position; (3) you telegraph information about your hand, allowing your opponent to make optimum decisions; and (4) you fail to earn money, or worse yet fold, when you have the best hand, or bet or call when you have the worst hand. Of these four mistakes that cost you money, ***by far the easiest mistake to avoid is playing bad cards with negative profit potential***.

We saw in the odds section above how unsuited connectors, one or two-gappers, or suited cards without *both* straight and flush draw potential are "unlucky"; such hands are less than 12% to flop a draw and only 5% to make a big hand by the river.

It's true you'll still make a pair or better 32.4% of the time as well, but then you're playing the hand not for its drawing potential but for its high card value.

Even if you flop a pair with these lower-ranked cards, how much will you then like your hand? You'll often be playing second or third pair without a very strong kicker. Playing these lesser hands is NOT justified based on their drawing strength alone, without one of the following:

- **You're in position** - Never underestimate the power of that button! I would often play unsuited connectors and perhaps suited one-gappers on the button against one or more of the right opponents. I may be giving up some edge on my starting hand strength, but I'll make up for it by getting to act last after the flop, when I've seen how the betting goes relative to my own hand.
- **It's a huge, multi-way pot** - Pot odds are always your friend! If you're getting paid 3:1 to see the flop, why not call along if there's a reasonable chance you won't get raised out of the pot? Calling with 3:1 odds, you'll only need to win 25% of the time to make a profit on the hand, and it's more likely you *will* win that often because your hand has at least some potential to make a monster by the river. It will also be cheaper to draw in a multi-way pot as there are several people who may be calling bets with you. Again, you're giving up edge on your starting hand requirements, but you're being paid by the pot (i.e. given odds) to do so.

- **You're in the blinds** - Any hand is worth a free check, and a hand with *any* drawing potential is worth a half-bet from the small blind. A hand with significant drawing potential is worth calling another big blind if the pot's been min-raised. And a one-gap suited connector or unsuited connector (or better) is worth a min-raise call out of the small blind. This is a case where the pot is laying you odds to see the flop, and you should use your best estimate of whether its profitable to play it out, given the particular drawing hand and number of opponents you're facing. Remember, with drawing hands, we want to see more players involved in the pot so we can draw more cheaply and get paid off if we eventually hit.
- **Suited aces close to position** - Ace-high has great *showdown potential* and high card value. That is to say, it's *not* strictly a drawing hand. You don't want to fall in love with every ace, but it may be playable on or near the button, even in a raised pot. With this type of hand, you really don't mind if you play it heads-up or in a large multi-way pot, but adjust your expectations accordingly. The more players in the hand, the less your ace is worth (with your kicker problems) and the more you're looking to connect on your flush draw.

4. **Most other cards are unplayable based on their hand strength alone.**

Most hands other than those outlined above (i.e. big cards, pairs, suited connectors and the occasional suited ace) are generally unplayable based on their own potential strength. Of course, you will sometimes need to move at a pot with any two cards. Also, you might lower your standards and call a very loose, aggressive player with a weak, unsuited ace in position.

If you're playing short-handed you're much less interested in card strength. Short-handed play is like a game of chicken with a lot of head-on collisions. But at a full table, you don't want to invest too much with other types of hands, unless the circumstances are favorable for some kind of move.

When you consider how profitable it is to play a hand in a given situation, rather than playing hands based solely on their "strength", you'll improve your results at the table. There are many times when "strong" hands like AK and AQ are easily folded. And complete garbage is often much more profitable than a real hand. When you're playing with trash, it's easier to get away from real danger.

Some hands are simply more profitable than other hands overall. But the situation is more important than the absolute strength of your cards or how playable they are. Pick your cards according to the spots you find yourself in.

Chapter Four

PICK YOUR SPOTS

Maxim 59: Start slowly and finish well.

You ought to think of the finish, and attach more importance to a graceful exit than to an early applause. 'Tis the common lot of the unlucky to have a very fortunate outset and a very tragic end. The important point is not the vulgar early applause - nearly everyone has a shining moment or two - but the general feeling at exit. Few in life are felt to deserve an encore.

Maxim 78: Only fools rush in.

Fools rush in through the door; for folly is always bold. The same simplicity which robs them of all attention to precautions deprives them of all sense of shame at failure. But prudence enters with more deliberation. Its forerunners are caution and care; they advance and discover whether you may also advance without danger. Every rush forward is guarded with a watchful eye. Be prepared to retreat in the face of true danger, no matter how promising the beginning.

THE RIGHT OPPORTUNITIES WILL COME

Often, inexperienced players rush into a game looking to get some early "action." They're willing to limp into pots with a wide variety of hands because of the low blinds in a cash game and during the early stages of a tournament. From their perspective, it's worth a few dollars to splash around and try to make something happen. It's exciting, and maybe they'll get lucky and quickly double up. This is what I like to call the "slot machine" theory of poker.

The problems with this approach are numerous: (1) you'll be entering pots with marginal cards and will face a lot of difficult decisions (e.g. top pair, weak kicker or some sort of weak flush draw) after the flop; (2) when one person limps, there's a strong tendency for many other players to limp in right behind them, and it's very difficult to play in a multi-way pot without making a monster hand - which is unlikely because you're entering with marginal holdings; (3) you haven't had a chance to gauge the other players to determine whether they're tight or loose, passive or aggressive, competent or completely random - you'll be left playing the cards and the situation without a good read on your opponents.

In poker, as in any competitive game, you profit when you hold some competitive advantage over your opponents. By jumping right into the early action, you're doing little more than buying a lottery ticket and keeping your fingers crossed. You're throwing your money away on a longshot, and this rush for "action" quickly cuts into your bottom line.

Another factor to consider, for tournaments only, is the need to avoid a big early confrontation. In a cash game you can take your chances on any hand where you think you're a favorite. This is because you're equally invested in every hand that you play, as the forced betting (the blinds) are the same from beginning to end. The object of a cash game is to maximize value from each and every hand, so *any advantage, no matter how slight, is profitable and should be exploited.*

Of course, if you've just sat down at the game and have no real read on your opponent, playing a big pot is probably ill-advised. But if you feel good about your chances, even if you think it's a 52-48 situation, you take those odds if your bankroll can afford the risk.

The object of a tournament, however is to outlast all your other opponents. You don't make money unless you survive longer than most of the other players at the table. As such, swinging for the fences on an early bold gamble is generally just too risky, unless the other players at the table are clearly superior to you in experience and ability (in which case you'd favor gambling over letting skill become a factor). But generally, it's simply not worth it to risk your entire tournament on coin toss situations at the very beginning, *even if you believe that you're a modest favorite.*

In a tournament, *some slight advantages can be unprofitable, as they negatively impact your goal of surviving and advancing.* Of course, if some fellow goes all-in before the flop and you're holding AAs, then you call and take your chances. But in situations where you're holding a single pair and the stakes are still low, you can get away from the hand and live to fight another day.

You want to be conservative and wait for situations that present a clear and decisive advantage, until the blinds get too high and you make aggressive moves to compensate. Start slowly and you'll have the chance to finish well.

DON'T INVEST TOO MUCH, TOO EARLY IN A RISKY SPOT

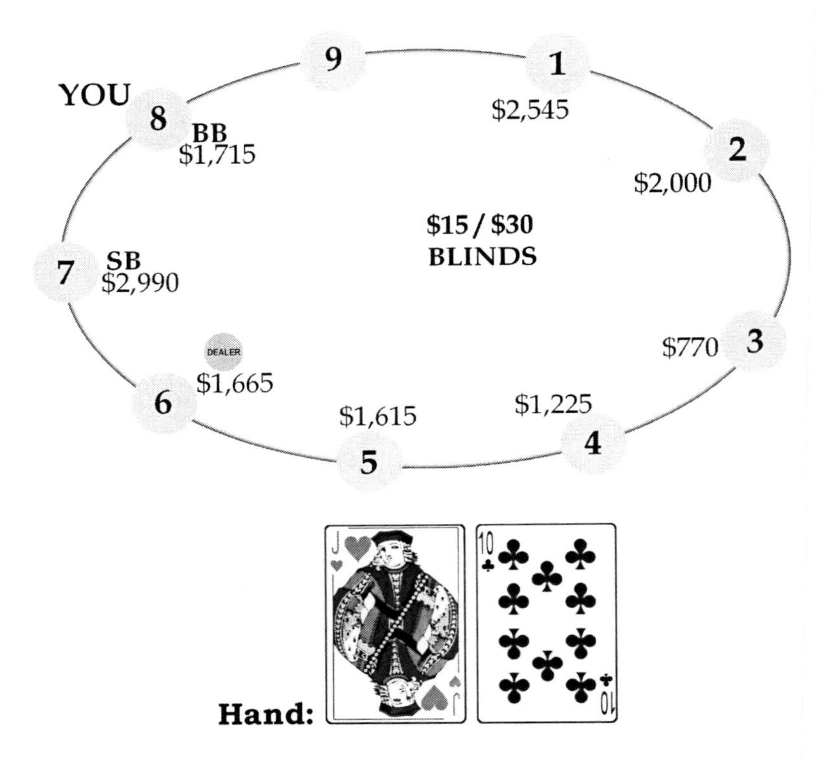

Situation: Early stages of a single table online sit and go tournament. The action has been fairly loose and aggressive thus far, and one player has already been knocked out. You're in the big blind.

Action: Players 1, 2 and 3 all fold. Player 4 limps for $30. Player 5 folds, the button calls $30, and the small blind completes. You have a very playable little drawing hand so you love the multi-way action. You should check. If you were considering making a move at this pot before the flop against the crowd of limpers, note that you shouldn't do it when you're holding a hand like JT, where you really want to see a flop.

Instead, you should get aggressive against limpers from the big blind either when you have a legitimate hand or complete trash. When you get a free look with some kind of drawing hand in a multi-way pot, take it and see if you can make something big happen. You check, the pot is now $120, and four players see the flop:

Analysis: Well, top pair is a good flop. We probably have the best hand, but that isn't the end of the analysis. Note this was an unraised pot with three other opponents in a low-blind situation. That means they could be holding practically anything, especially the button and small blind. That flop is also very scary, as it's rife with straight and flush draws (indeed, anyone holding a 98 has flopped a straight and will be lying in wait for action). And those middle cards are exactly the type of hands that could have limped into this pot.

We shouldn't feel too confident about our top-pair, jack kicker, but we also need to test the waters and not give any free cards to something like an inside straight draw if some fellow is holding a lone 8 or 9. I'd bet out about 3/4 of the pot here most of the time, but if I felt sure that the button was an aggressive, position player I would strongly consider check-raising.

Action: The small blind checks. You bet $70, Seat 4 calls, and the button and small blind both fold. The pot is now $260, and your heads-up to the turn:

Analysis: You really didn't want anyone to call your bet on the flop, but on the bright side, you're in a heads-up situation. Your opponent limped from middle position and smooth called the flop. He could have had a flush draw, second or third pair (perhaps something like A7, A6, 75 or 65 - in which case he just made two pair), a pair and some sort of inside straight draw (T9 or 87), or even be slowplaying a made straight. It's also possible he has top pair with a decent kicker, although it's strange he wouldn't have raised with that hand on such a dangerous board with action still behind him.

To quickly summarize: we have absolutely no idea where we stand in the hand, and that 5 of spades has created many more dangerous possibilities for our pair of tens with a medium kicker. When you reach this point in the hand, you need to step back and keep the broader strategic perspective in mind: yes, this hand started out kind of promising, and we thought we had the best of it.

But at the end of the day, given how the hand is going, how much do we really want to keep investing in this pot? Ask yourself, "Could I earn more by cutting my losses and waiting for a better opportunity?"

I would generally favor checking here, but I'd take a second stab a strong minority of the time, hoping to represent two pair or perhaps a made flush in this spot. And I'd be prepared to jettison the hand in the face of resistance.

Action: You actually bet $100 into the pot, and your opponent raises you to $250. The pot is now $610 and it costs you $150 more to call.

Analysis: That was a weak bet given the pot, intended to give the impression that you had semi-bluffed on the flop, made your flush on the turn, and are now trying to extract what you can out of your opponent. That may seem reasonable, but I'd generally favor a larger bet here of at least $150 to make it clear that you're serious about the hand.

Your small bet has allowed your opponent to make a cheap, fairly minimum raise, which indicates one of two things: (1) either he has a strong made hand, like a straight, flush or two-pair, and is just roping us along; or (2) he has little if anything, but read our bet as weak and has decided to try to test us on the cheap.

Even if he is bluffing, he may have at least one spade in his hand and have outs, or he could have us crushed. If we call here, the pot will be up to $760 and we'd be heading for some sort of river confrontation. What will we do if we call this smallish raise here, and he comes back and makes a pot-sized bet on the river?

If you aren't prepared to handle a normal bet on the river, you have no business calling, no matter how cheap your opponent makes it for you to keep following along. He's either roping you along with suck bets designed to extract maximum value out of the hand, or preparing to bludgeon you out of the pot. If you can't compete, get out of the way and wait for a better spot.

Action: You fold and live to fight another day. With top pair, medium kicker on a flushing, straightening board where your opponent could have literally anything, there are bound to be more profitable opportunities to get your money in. You don't have to force things, or chase risky opportunities when there's another deal of the cards just a few moments away.

A GOOD HAND CAN BE SECOND-BEST

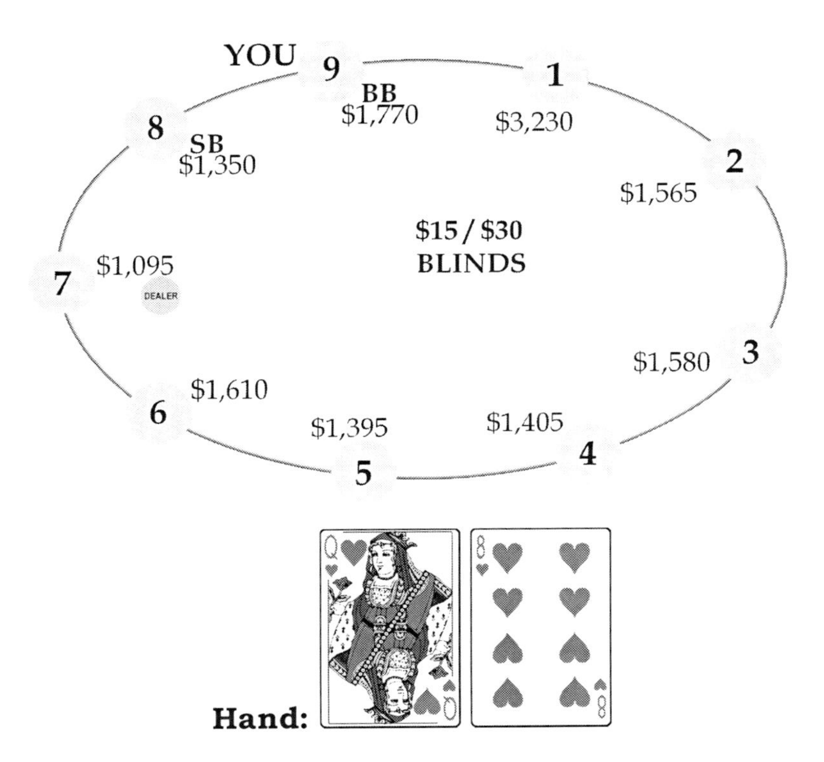

Situation: Early on in a single table online sit and go tournament. One reckless player suffered an early knockout – there's always one of those in every game. You don't have a read on any of the players yet.

Action: Seat 1 folds. Seat 2 calls for $30. Seat 3 folds, but Seats 4 and 5 call. Seat 6 folds. The button and the small blind calls. The pot is now $180, and five other players have limped into your big blind. *What should you do?*

Analysis: These are exactly the types of hands you don't want to get too involved with: large, multi-way pots in the early going when the blinds are low. Raising is absolutely out of the question here: our hand is mediocre, the table is fairly loose thus far, and there's no telling how many more reckless players would eagerly call our raise. We don't want to build a big pot with this average hand out of position.

Action: You check. The pot remains $180, and 6 players see the flop:

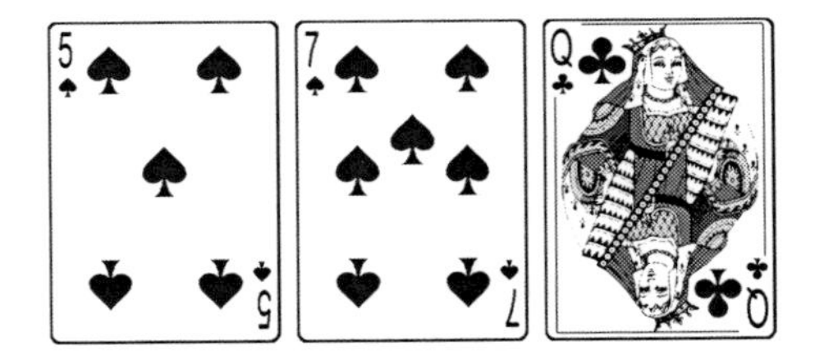

Action: The small blind bets $80. Action is on you.

Analysis: Ugh. These multi-way pots in the early going are treacherous for a very good reason. There's literally no telling what any of the other players might have limped with. And with five other players, there's a nearly 25% chance we're facing a flush draw. There's also a 5% chance someone hit a set, and anyone with a queen has us dominated (we can only beat a Q6, Q4, Q3, or Q2, which aren't very likely even at this loose table).

BEWARE THE SMALL BLIND LEADING OUT WITH A BIG BET

Even worse, the small blind has led right out with a healthy bet into five other players. That's not a great sign. Most experienced players realize how treacherous these multi-way pots can be. By leading out, the small blind is facing the possibility of multiple raises and re-raises. He can't have much hope of taking the pot down right here without a fight.

For all that, we do have top pair. That might be worth something, but it's hard to know where we really stand right now. With a bet in front of us and four players acting behind, a raise here is out of the question. Let's just call and see what develops. We don't want to get too committed to this kind of hand in the early going.

Action: You call the $80. Seats 2 and 4 fold, but Seats 5 and 7 call as well. Four players remain in the pot, now standing at $500. The turn makes things very interesting:

Action: The small blind bets $100. The pot is now $600, and it costs you $100 to call.

Analysis: This is a tough spot. Yes, we now have two pair. If this were originally a heads-up (or even three-way) pot, we'd feel pretty confident about our hand right now. But you must remember that this hand started with six players, and four of them stuck around after the flop with two spades and a queen out there.

WHEN TO FEAR THE FLUSH DRAW

We noted before it's irrational to see a flush draw hiding around every corner. This hand is the exception to that rule: in a low blind environment, with large multi-way action, you should be very afraid of that possibility. Given the action thus far, it's pretty likely one of the other players stuck around with a flush draw.

How could four players call on this flop without someone holding a flush draw? One queen is on board, and one queen is in our hand. That leaves two queens unaccounted for, yet the small blind, Seat 5 and Seat 7 were all interested enough to call a half-pot bet. There aren't enough queens to go around.

Sure, it's possible someone called with second or third pair (5s or 7s), someone else with a pocket pair less than queens, and another player with a better queen that's now second-best to our two-pair. But it's only just possible. And the small blind is once again leading out with a small, but annoying bet.

You probably are obligated to call with your two-pair, and you might throw in a tiny raise to test for a made flush. But we really need to leave ourselves an exit on this hand. Sometimes a good hand just isn't good enough.

Action: You hesitate, then just call the $100 bet. Seat 5 makes a minimum raise to $200. Seat 7 calls. The small blind goes all-in for his remaining $1,140. The action is on you. The pot is now $2,240, and it costs you $1,240 to call.

Analysis: Fold! This hand has become an absolute train wreck. There's clearly at least one flush out against you, if not more. You only have four outs to improve to a full house if that's the case, leaving you a bare 8% chance. Cut your losses now and don't look back.

Action: You fold. Seat 5 goes all-in as well, and Seat 7 folds. We were behind the whole way and crushed on the turn:

It's very surprising that the small blind didn't play his hand more aggressively right on the flop. A pair and a flush draw is an absolute monster hand, one you should never mind taking to war.

But then again, it would have been hard for him to put Seat 5 on a flush draw. When you're holding a four-flush, you tend to discount the possibility of another, bigger flush draw out against you. This is always a possibility; and if you get action in a spot like this, you have to really consider what kinds of hands can call you?

Faced with not one, not two, *but three*, calls on the flop, the small blind should have been somewhat cautious. When you're holding top-pair and get multiple callers, it's extremely unlikely all the other players are also holding top-pair (especially if top-pair is anything other than an ace). If he'd really thought about this hand, the small blind might have feared one of his opponents had a king-high or ace-high flush draw.

In any event, it's a good thing we didn't get too excited about our hand! The problem with playing a hand like Q8 is that it's not always obvious what our clean outs are. Are we rooting for another queen, or an eight? Even if we improve our hand, could that card have helped our opponent more?

Here, it turns out that both of our opponents were drawing, so the eight of spades was not a clean out. You always need to be mindful of whether a card that seems to help you actually gives you a stronger, second-best holding.

Chapter Five

OBSERVE YOUR ENEMIES

Maxim 26: Find out each man's thumbscrew.

'Tis the art of setting their wills in action. It needs more skill than resolve. You must know where to get at any one. Every volition has a special motive which varies according to taste. All men are idolaters, some of fame, others of self-interest, most of pleasure. Skill consists in knowing these idols in order to bring them into play. Knowing any man's mainspring of motive, you have the key to controlling his will.

Have resort to primary motors, which are not always the highest but more often the lowest part of his nature. First guess a man's ruling passion, appeal to it by a word, set it in motion by temptation, and you will infallibly give checkmate to his freedom of will.

Maxim 182: Do not overestimate the other guy.

You must moderate your opinion of others so as not think so highly of them as to fear them. The imagination should never yield to the heart. Many appear great till you know them personally, and then dealing with them does more to lower than to raise esteem. No one oversteps the narrow bounds of humanity: all have their weakness either in heart or mind.

The imagination always jumps too soon, and paints things in brighter colors than the real: it thinks things not as they are but as it wishes them to be. Attentive experience disillusioned in the past soon corrects all that. Yet if wisdom should not be cowardly, neither should folly be rash.

CLASSIFY YOUR OPPONENTS AND THEIR PLAY OF KEY HANDS

You should always pay attention to the action at the table even if not involved in the hand. After seeing the hole cards of one or more players, replay the action at each stage of the hand. Every player, even seasoned professionals, has certain tendencies and predispositions.

Do not overestimate another player and think he is capable of fully "mixing up" his play; your opponents will not be completely random.

Even strong players capable of "mixing things up" will fall back on certain betting patterns and strategies. They will adopt a particular playing style they think most profitable in a given session, and will adapt their play based on how they read their opponent(s). Within any given session, every player will follow certain betting patterns.

If you play each hand in a vacuum without regard to the other players' tendencies and betting patterns, it will be *you* who falls back on mechanical betting patterns that are easy to read.

Do not mix up your play in a purely random fashion (such as employing your watch as a random number generator to help make decisions), but by tailoring your playing style to that of your opponents!

Here's what you need to pay attention to:

1. How many hands is this person playing?

The fewer flops seen per orbit, the tighter our opponent is playing. A player is only dealt a big pair (TTs through AAs), plus AK, AQ, and AJ about 6% of the time. If an opponent will play any pair from any position as well, that would amount to 9.5% of all hands dealt. If our opponent would also play all suited connectors, that would be about 4% more of all starting hands, totaling 13.5% of hands dealt.

If your opponent will play any ace, besides just the big aces previously counted, our (increasingly profitable) opponent is now playing 24.3% of all hands dealt. If he's willing to throw in unsuited connectors as well, he's up to 36.3% of his cards. Finally, if he goes with any two suited cards he's playing nearly 60% of his hands, and I want in on that game.

Of course, few play the same hands from each position; things tend to loosen up as we've seen more people fold and get closer to the button. Some hands not considered here, e.g. one-gappers like QT, J9, etc., are often playable from a very late position. And it's often correct to play a wide variety of hands from the blinds.

But if your opponent is voluntarily entering more than one pot per orbit (i.e. not getting a discount out of the blinds or being folded around to in late position), he's not playing a strictly tight game.

Simply put, the more hands we see our opponent involved in, the lower his starting requirements must be. This is important information, because we can be more aggressive against him/her pre-flop. We should also widen the range of hands we put our opponent on: we will have to use selective aggression to clarify where we stand against a loose player who might be playing any two cards.

2. How often does this player bet or raise?

An unpaired poker hand is better than 2:1 to miss the flop. And you should assume your opponent has an unpaired hand that needs help on the flop, since there's only a 5.9% chance of being dealt any pair. What does all this mean? It means that on average, about 1/3 of your opponent's bets after the flop will be legitimate -- or perhaps 40% if you count all bets with a pocket pair as legitimate (though if you hold a small pair on any board without flopping a set, your "made hand" doesn't look so hot).

If you notice a particular player is betting more often than 35-40%, he's playing an aggressive game and often bluffing. On the other hand, some players are fairly passive by nature and won't even bet the 35-40% of the time they have a hand. You should try to classify your opponents as being "aggressive" (more than 40%), "passive" (rarely betting) or "straight-forward" (pretty much betting the value of their hand) which will help you interpret if their bets and checks are significant.

You should also determine how often your opponent not only bets or calls, but the frequency with which they raise. Raising another player's bet in no limit hold 'em is a big move that's supposed to represent a great deal of strength. But although we can expect to connect with the flop *in some way* 32% of the time and have a pre-flop pair another 5.9% of the time, these are hardly straight-forward raising situations.

A substantial portion of that 32% connection rate with the flop includes second or third-pair. While these are legitimate calling hands, a raise with less than top pair is a fairly aggressive move. And although we're dealt a pocket pair 5.9% of the time, we'll only flop a set 0.7% of all hands dealt (assuming we play all pocket pairs from all positions).

ONE-FIFTH RULE

Taken together, a player is likely to flop a legitimate raising hand about 20% of the time, depending on the texture of the board. If you see a raising frequency much more than one-fifth of all hands, you can assign this player into the "aggressive" category and play back at him appropriately. If you see substantially less than this frequency, you can label your opponent as a "rock", and run for the hills in the face of such aggression.

3. How does this person play a draw versus a made hand?

We should pay close attention to a flop with a draw-heavy board and a lot of action. Loose players will often play very aggressively, including taking a drawing hand to war. But there are loose passive players that are happy to keep calling large bets with a pure draw.

Conversely, tight players will often play a draw conservatively, not wanting to commit many chips without a made hand. But there are also tight players who prefer betting and raising *on the come*, relying on their conservative table image to pressure marginal hands into folding. This is not to say that a particular player will always fall into one of these patterns; but generally you'll see him fall back on the same, comfortable playing habits.

You should determine how your opponent tends to play a straight or flush draw in order to exploit this tendency. Especially if you're playing online with electronic note-taking, jot down some of the key factors you noticed about the hand. How many opponents were in the pot (he may be less aggressive if given good odds to call)? Did he semi-bluff as a continuation bet? Can he fold the hand in the face of a raise or re-raise, or does he commit himself to the hand? If this player does bet a draw aggressively, is it an ordinary bet or raise or a kamikaze all-in move?

When you see a player turn over a drawing hand, record all these important details. There is nothing more important than knowing whether your opponent's betting patterns indicate a made hand, a draw, or a pure bluff.

4. How does he play a monster hand?

If you flop a set, a flush, a straight, a full house, or top two pair (using both your hole cards), you've flopped a monster hand. The odds of having the best hand are quite high. You have a choice to make with your monster hand: play aggressively, hoping your opponents have some lesser hand or draw they can call with (or even better, that they might try to bluff-raise you out of the pot), or slow-play and trap? Obviously, for us this answer will vary based on what we know about our opponent.

If we have a monster hand, we'll often lead out against a tight, aggressive opponent who might have started with a big pre-flop hand, unless we think it's unlikely he has anything (given the texture of the board) and it wouldn't hurt to give a free card. Against a tight, passive opponent, we'll play it the same way except with an additional bias to bet right out, since we won't earn any bets from our passive opponent by checking.

On the other hand, we might give a loose aggressive player some rope to fire one or more bullets at the pot -- he might just bluff off his entire stack with nothing. Against a loose, passive opponent (commonly referred to as a *calling station*, one of the patron saints of poker players) we should bet for value, hoping he can pay us off. Of course, our table image, the particular texture of the board, and the pre-flop betting action will all modify these general guidelines.

Now, many loose, aggressive opponents who flop big will play it just like all their other hands: fast. They're hoping someone will finally stand up to them, and generally also want to disguise their (many) bluffs where they have nothing.

BEWARE AN AGGRESSIVE PLAYER IN SHEEP'S CLOTHING

But many loose players tend towards the other extreme: they will almost always slowplay and trap with their biggest hands, while betting their bluffs most aggressively. These players are easy to counter: if they bet, you can safely raise, and if they check to you on a board perfect for bluffing, simply shut down on the hand. In fact, an aggressive player passively calling along on a hand for no obvious reason should trigger alarms in your mind.

Tight, aggressive players are often fairly straight-forward in their play of hands, representing more or less the true strength of their hole cards. Tight passive players are afraid of committing too much money to any particular hand. When they do play, they have the goods and frequently earn big profits from loose, aggressive players who get out of line against them.

If you ever see a tight, passive opponent (stereotypically a geriatric retiree sipping coffee) raising and re-raising, run! You're badly behind and you'll be walking home if you don't fold.

If you're going to play loose, it's absolutely critical to know when to fold. Much less of your decision-making reflects the value of your own hand. Loose players must be particularly observant of their opponent's betting patterns to avoid big trouble. This is the main mistake inexperienced players make when loosening up: they don't know when to back off.

5. How does he play pairs?

The odds of any player at a nine-handed poker table being dealt a pair and flopping a set is roughly 5%, assuming that all pairs are played from all positions. It's unlikely that all pairs will be played from all positions at an aggressive table, however.

You should pay particular attention to showdowns involving a pocket pair. Note the details of the hand. From what position did the player enter the pot with his pair? Did he limp with the pair, make a min-raise, or make a standard raise? Did he lead out, flat call, or raise when he flopped a set? Was he willing to call a substantial raise with his pocket pair?

Perhaps the biggest landmine in no limit hold 'em is the hidden set. It's pretty much unbeatable by hands like top pair, besting such holdings 92-97% of the time depending on possible straight or flush draws. It's also concealed in a way that other big hands can't be. A single, innocuous card on the board (usually of low rank to boot) can cost you your entire stack.

In contrast, you can, and should, spot all possible straight and flush draws. A pair on board is an obvious warning sign, depending on the card. But there is little warning sign about a set -- which is exactly why the hand is so profitable. The only protection is to recognize something in your opponent's betting pattern. If he's very interested in a ragged board with few good draws, proceed with extreme caution.

Chapter Six

PUT YOUR OPPONENTS TO THE TEST

Maxim 213: Use mild contradiction to ferret out the truth.

Embarrass others to get a reaction. Skepticism acts to purge all secrets. It is the key to a locked-up heart, and with great subtlety makes a double trial of both mind and will. A sly depreciation of another's word fleshes out all secrets.

By letting the other person respond to your doubts, his thoughts appear while otherwise his heart was inscrutable. An expression of doubt is the subtlest picklock that curiosity can use to find what it wants to know.

TEST YOUR OPPONENT WITH A RAISE OR RE-RAISE TO CLARIFY THE HAND

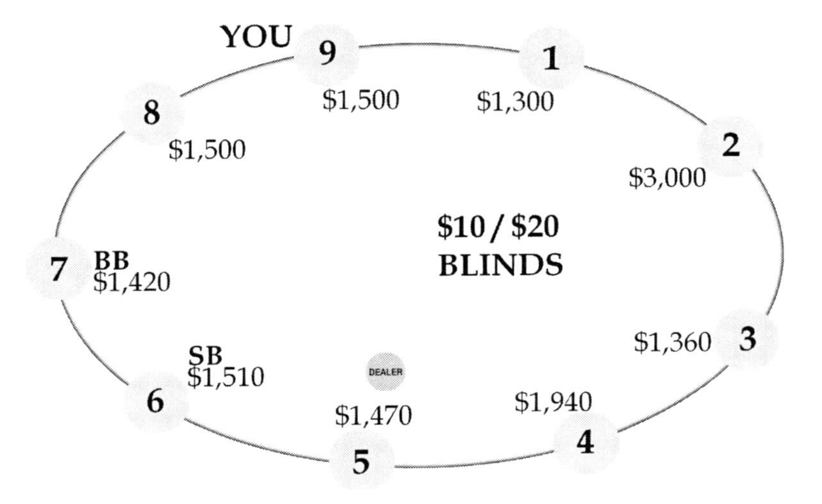

Hand: 

Situation: Early stages of a single table online sit and go tournament. You haven't had much opportunity to observe, although one terribly loose and erratic player has already staged an early exit. You're in second position with your AQ off-suit.

Action: Seat 8 folds under-the-gun. You make a standard raise to $60. Seat 1 folds, but Seats 2 and 3 both call the raise. The 4 and 5 seats and the two blinds all fold. The pot is now $210. Three players are going to the flop, and you're first to act:

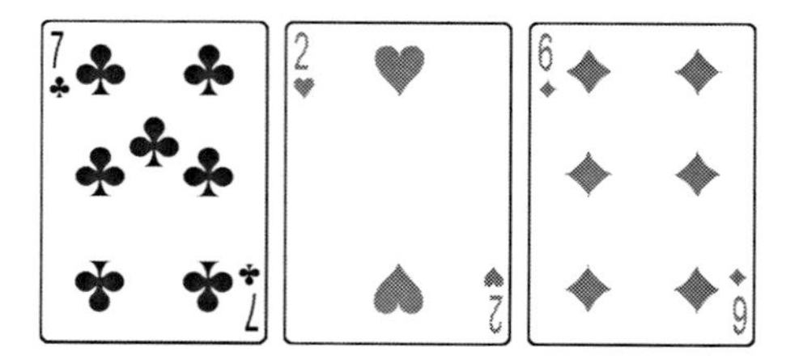

Analysis: You don't need me to tell you those are completely the wrong cards! This hand illustrates our point from Chapter 2: big cards have a lot of potential but are difficult to play when they miss. Here, you may still have the best hand with ace-queen high, but how much do you really want to bet on it?

Since we're first to act, we have to decide whether to check or to bet into our two opponents. Many players make an automatic continuation bet in spots like this, but you should consider being more conservative here. It's early in the tournament, one of our opponents is now a big stack, and there's not much money in the pot. In addition to all of this, how plausible is our bet here going to be?

Raising pre-flop from early position followed by an apparent continuation bet on this ragged 7-high board can easily be read for weakness. If we lead out here, we're hoping to represent a big premium pair like AAs, KKs, or QQs. Our opponents know it's not very likely we have a hand that big, and if we did we might go for a check-raise in this spot.

That said, it's still early in the tournament and the other two players may not want to contest such a small pot, even if a continuation bet looks suspicious. On balance, I'd prefer checking, with the intention of considering a check-raise bluff *if the player in last position takes a stab at the pot.* This is because the player last to act is more likely to be bluffing, since he's seen two checks and would interpret that as weakness.

I wouldn't run that bluff if the middle player leads out, since he's showing real strength by betting out of position into the initial raiser with a player still to act behind him.

Action: You actually lead out and bet two-thirds of the pot, $140. Seat 2 quickly folds, but Seat 3 makes a minimum raise to $280. The pot is now $630, and it costs you $140 to call. *What should you do?*

Analysis: A minimum raise in this spot means one of two things: (1) your opponent doesn't believe you, and is using a cheap bet here to ferret out whether your bet was serious; or (2) it's a *suck bet* designed to extract some extra chips, because your opponent has a big hand and isn't afraid to give you cheap odds to keep playing. Which scenario is more likely?

Consider that you raised pre-flop, and then made a healthy continuation bet: two-thirds of the pot (as opposed to half the pot or less). You've shown strength throughout the hand, but the board is such that your opponent has reason to be skeptical. If he has a real hand, what could he have here?

1. **A flopped set** – This is certainly possible, and when you see a min-raise -- or any serious interest for that matter -- on a ragged board with three low cards you should be particularly afraid of this scenario. He could have easily called your small pre-flop raise with 2s, 6s, or 7s and gotten lucky. You don't want to obsess over this possibility, but this is the exact scenario to worry about: cheap blinds, multi-way action, and strong interest on a ragged board.

2. **A straight draw** – There are a few possibilities here, including the 54 or the 98 for an open-ended low-end or high-end straight draw. A T9 would give him two over-cards and an inside-straight draw, which might be a nice semi-bluffing hand in this spot. A 43 has a gutshot as well, and an 85 is possible if he's a whacko. A straight draw is less likely, because many players would have either called your bet on the flop to see the turn or made a healthy raise to put you to a serious test. If you're going to raise on a draw, you should look like you're committed to the hand.
3. **An overpair** – This is probably the least likely scenario. If your opponent has a pair of 8s or better, he should want to make a healthy raise so you don't spike something on the turn or river. I wouldn't feel comfortable stringing an opponent along with a min-raise unless I had QQs or better (then I'd only have to fear a king or ace on the next street). You're simply inviting disaster if you let your opponent draw cheaply. And if he had a hand as strong as QQs, he probably would have re-raised pre-flop with two other players in the pot, rather than smooth-calling our small initial $60 raise with many players still to act behind him.

Now, the hands we're worried about are a flopped set and the remote possibility he hit two-pair if he had exactly 76. Those are the only hands that would explain his actions here.

On the other hand, if we're beat, we're really beat, and we're not going to catch up. The risk of being wrong here probably outweighs the benefits of aggression; if we wanted to turn the thumbscrew we should have gone for the check-raise bluff.

However, if we still want to test our opponent, we can use his own tactic against him. Delay for a solid period of time to consider his small raise (and to convey an impression of seriousness), and then make a min re-raise to between $420 and $500. If he wants to play then, he'll probably come over the top for all his chips. That would be a huge move if he was bluffing entirely. If he can raise your re-raise, he flopped a set. But generally, let's cut our losses on this hand.

Action: You actually decide to push all-in, reasoning (apparently) that he probably doesn't have a set or two-pair and can't call such a big raise on a draw or semi-bluff. Your aggressive move is ill-timed, however, as Seat 3 turns over a set of deuces and leaves you crippled in the tournament.

Analysis: Aggression is fine, but sometimes mild bets and raises are a lot more effective than all-in moves. They're certainly cheaper. To be a great poker player, you have to be willing to play a pot. You can't hit the all-in button every time you want to apply some pressure. *Use **mild** contradiction to ferret out the truth*: never bet more than you have to; a lesser re-raise would have accomplished our purpose here.

If your opponent is generally aggressive, you'll have a harder time trying to detect a concealed set. This is why the aggressive playing style is so successful: by constantly stealing pots with weak hands, you can provoke a big confrontation when you're actually strong. But if you've noted a particular pattern of play when an opponent flops a set, you have a better shot at avoiding a train wreck.

At the very least, you should upgrade the possibility of a flopped set when you're playing against a set-chaser, but remember that you're still looking at a maximum 5% chance of such a disaster. If you go too far with this fear, you'll end up like a little child afraid of monsters in the closet. You'll lose much more than you'll gain by such irrational caution.

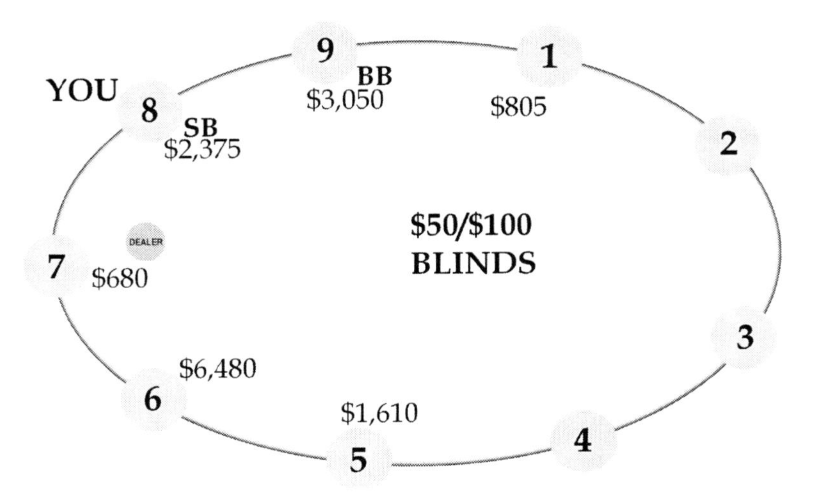

Hand:  

Situation: Late middle stages of a single table online sit and go tournament. This particular structure starts with ten players and pays the top five, so we're on the bubble with six players left. Play has tightened considerably for everyone except the very large stack in Seat 6. He's been wielding his chip lead as a cudgel against the scared short stacks, stealing most pots with small raises pre-flop. Flops are few and far between.

Action: Seat 1 calls. Everyone folds around to you in the small blind. The pot is now $250 and it costs you $50 to call. *What should you do?*

Analysis: Our hand is fairly bad, but we're being offered 5:1 on a call. Generally, I wouldn't play high-low card combinations like this without at least two limpers into the pot (giving us 7:1 odds). We can make an exception here because $50 is a small price to pay if we can eliminate a player on the bubble.

Action: We call, and the big blind checks. The pot is now $300, and three players see the flop:

You and the big blind both check; you should almost always check out of the small blind, especially with a real hand. Seat 1 bets $100.

Analysis: That's a great flop for our hand. When you're playing high card-low card combinations, your best case scenario is usually to pair your lower card on a ragged board like this (with no aces or face cards out against you). The early position limper has bet into us, but that bet looks very suspicious. His limp, followed by a weak lead-off bet, looks like he's trying to represent a big hand. It's not very believable, though.

BEWARE THE EARLY POSITION LIMPER

Experienced poker players have an old saying about avoiding the early position limper. When the blinds are low at an aggressive table, savvy players will frequently limp from early position with big pocket pairs. They're hoping to disguise the strength of their hand and get raised from one of the players in late position. It's a standard move you'll see a lot.

In fact, novice players employ this move too much for their own good, often finding themselves unable to fold their AAs in a multi-way pot with a dangerous board. That's a recipe for ruin.

This move can also be used in the late stages of a tournament. If you're on the short stack, you're looking to get as much action as possible from your big hands, even if you have to let more players into the pot to do so. If you have a healthy stack, but there are short stacks acting behind you, you might limp with a big hand in hopes they'll try to take the pot away from you.

LATE-STAGE, FIRST POSITION LIMPING

In nature, some animals are adapted to mimic the look of fierce predators. Although generally harmless in themselves, their deceptive appearance is enough to protect them from being hunted.

Since the limp-with-a-big-hand-in-early-position move is so well-known, many players will try to mimic this strength. This is particularly noticeable towards the late stages of a tournament.

Rather than risk all their chips by shoving in first position, you'll see some players (especially with small or medium stacks), limp frequently from first position. They're hoping the tight play in the late stages will prevent them being raised from late position. They'll bet at any flop, particularly if they're heads-up against the blinds. It's a low-risk way to steal a pot.

This may or may not be the case here, but consider: why would Seat 1 limp for $100 with only $805 remaining in his stack? With a $300 pot and a $705 stack on the flop, why would he bet a measly \$100? If he really had a big hand, wouldn't he be a little more aggressive in protecting it or trying to extract more value?

Seat 1's actions don't make a lot of sense. Maybe he does have a stronger-than-average hand, like AK, AQ, AJ, KQ, KJ etc., but didn't want to risk an all-in move. If so, he's missed the flop and is now trying to buy the pot. It's hard to put him on much of a hand.

More importantly, we've hit second pair; we only have to fear a big pocket pair, a 9, or a pocket pair between the 9s and our 5s (6s, 7s, or 8s). Those possibilities are all unlikely. There's an off-chance that Seat 1 limped with a really big hand and is sucking us in, but we need to take it. We can afford to be wrong here.

Action: We raise to \$300. The big blind folds, and Seat 1 calls the additional \$200. The pot is now \$900. Seat 1 has \$405 remaining in his stack, while you have \$1,975. The turn is heads-up:

You're first to act.

Analysis: That's a good card for us. It's extremely unlikely that Seat 1 limped from first position with a hand containing a three. Who knows why Seat 1 just called our raise on the turn? Maybe he really somehow has a flush draw (a 5% chance). It's more likely he has overcards (like AK, KQ, KJ, etc.) and was being stubborn about folding the hand.

Whatever his reasoning, we need to set him all-in right here and let the chips fall where they may. There is no other move for us.

Action: We bet Seat 1's remaining $405 in chips. Betting the exact amount the other player has left is more intimidating than going all-in ourselves. After a brief pause, Seat 1 folds.

Analysis: That was unexpected. He seemed committed to the pot after calling our raise on the flop. If he had a flush draw, maybe he got cold feet about the board pairing? Perhaps he did just have overcards? In any event, we won this pot by effectively judging the relative strength of our hand and putting our opponent to the ultimate test.

Chapter Seven

PLAY THE SITUATION, NOT THE HAND

Maxim 140: Find the Good in a thing at once.

There is nothing without good in it, especially in books, as giving food for thought. But many have such a scent that amid a thousand excellences they fix upon a single defect, and single it out for blame as if they were scavengers of men's minds and hearts. So they draw up a balance sheet of defects which does more credit to their bad taste than to their intelligence and discernment. They have the luckier taste who amidst a thousand defects seize upon a single beauty.

Maxim 224: Never take things against the grain.

It matters not how things come. Everything has a smooth and a seamy side, and the best weapon wounds if taken by the blade, while the enemy's spear may be your best protection if taken by the staff. Many things cause pain which would cause pleasure if you regarded their advantages.

There is a favorable and an unfavorable side to everything: the cleverness consists in finding the advantage. Things always look different in another light. Some find joy, others pain, in the very same thing.

CONSIDER ALL YOUR OPPORTUNITIES, WHETHER YOU HAVE A HAND OR NOT

The pre-flop action narrows down the range of your opponent's likely holdings. If there has been a significant investment, you can assume your opponent will generally have stronger cards. If there's been little or no pre-flop betting, you must be careful. If the blinds are still low, don't assume that a standard raise will clear out random hands. This is why you must be cautious in the early stages of a tournament.

After the flop, you begin to analyze the hand. Start by gauging your own potential: do you have a made hand, a drawing hand, overcards, or nothing much?

Some players don't go much further than this stage. They consider the strength of their own hand, and if they're weak, they shut down. This is not effective poker. A computer program could play its own cards. To be effective, you must consider how strong your opponent may be.

Just because you don't have a hand doesn't mean your opponent does. In fact, if you missed the flop completely, it's more likely than not your opponent also missed. He may be playing one or more of the same cards as you, or the board is pretty ragged. In either case, your opponent's weakness is an opportunity you can exploit, regardless of your own hand.

Evaluate the hand as a whole and consider all the potential good before you write the hand off as a loss. If you're playing against competent players that know how to fold, you can often salvage a hand that might otherwise be lost.

Just because you didn't flop quite as big as you hoped doesn't mean you're beaten. This is especially so with small pairs: they're not just drawing hands. Any wired pair is a made hand, and if the flop is ragged, you probably have the best of it.

A PAIRED BOARD IS A PRIME BLUFFING OPPORTUNITY

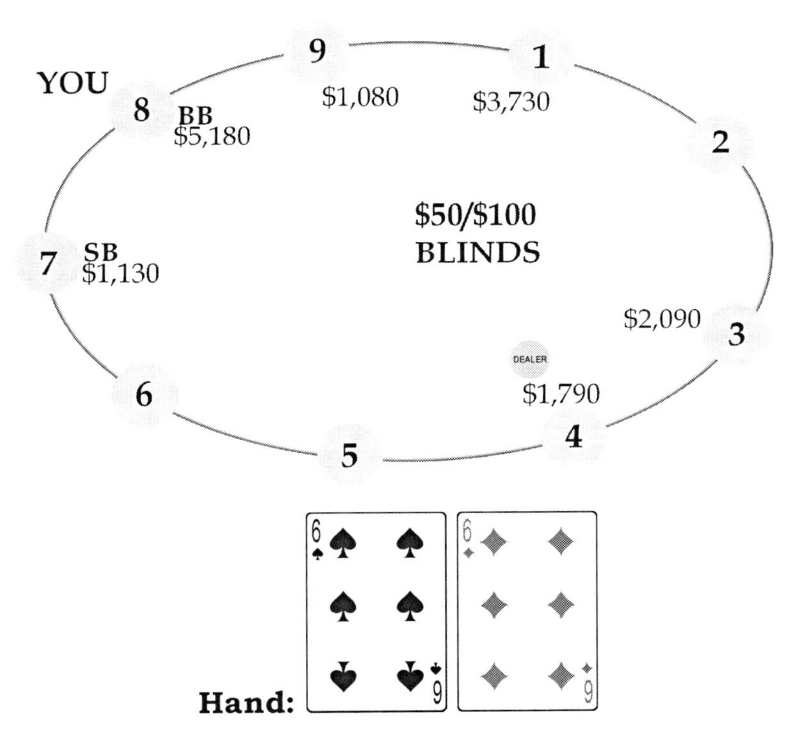

Situation: Middle stages of a single table online sit and go tournament. We've been playing tight, aggressive poker and have run down a few key bluffs to build a big stack. Seat 9 has been playing a loose, aggressive, and fairly erratic game. He'll be increasingly desperate as the blinds for each round of play are now nearly 15% of his stack.

Action: Seat 9 makes a minimum raise to $200 under the gun. Seat 1, the second largest stack, calls right behind him. Seat 3 folds, the button calls, and the small blind folds. We're in the big blind and it costs us $100 to call a $750 pot. *What should you do?*

Analysis: Obviously we're not folding our pair of 6s. There is a strong argument for raising here, to force a heads-up confrontation with Seat 9 and the $400 in dead money from Seats 1 and 4. It is safe to assume both those players would probably fold to a big raise from us rather than risking their tournament life, especially since they haven't shown much strength so far (flat calling a min-raise from a small stack is not signaling strength). This is big stack poker play, and I'd have no objection to anyone making that move.

The alternative play is to take the great odds we're being offered (7.5:1) and just call. This also has advantages: we (1) avoid risking an expensive confrontation with the second-largest stack; (2) can evaluate the board at a cheap price; (3) keep the other two players in the pot to gang up on the small stack, in the hopes one of us can take him out; (4) expect Seat 9 to jam the pot almost regardless of what comes, having invested 20% of his stack pre-flop; and (5) contrary to popular belief, pairs (unlike high cards) actually play very well in multi-way pots – your made hand is either good on the flop or it isn't.

In short, if we had AK or AQ here we should almost always drop the hammer right now and raise Seat 9 all-in. With a small pair like 6s, however, we can consider being patient.

Action: You call the extra $100. The pot is now $850, and four players see the flop:

Analysis: We're first to act. The first thing you look for when you're holding a small pair is whether you made a set. But just because that didn't happen here, doesn't mean we're through. Our small pair is a made hand, while on this type of ragged and paired board, no one else is likely to have much of anything (unless they hit a ten or played some very weird cards with a four).

Could one of the other three players in the hand have flopped a ten? Yes, it's possible they could have T9, JT, QT, KT, or AT. How will we be able to tell? It's simple: we need to check to the pre-flop raiser. The short-stacked Seat 9 invested nearly 20% of his chips before the flop, and we can anticipate at least a continuation bet here.

We won't be worried about Seat 9's bet though. It's unlikely he raised with a hand containing a ten. Did he really min-raise with a big hand, like a pocket pair?

Seat 9 was desperate. If this were an earlier stage of the tournament, and if Seat 9 wasn't one hand away from the big blind, he might be trapping us with a big hand. Here, it's safe to assume he could have any two cards, and will automatically bet if checked to.

Our check is designed to get information from Seats 1 and 4. If Seat 9 bets and one of those players comes over the top, we can possibly get away from the hand. Even if we decide to play, at least we won't risk a raising war by leading out.

Action: You check. Seat 9 bets $350, and both Seats 1 and 4 fold. The pot is now $1,200, and it costs you $350 to call. *What should you do?*

Analysis: We're going all-in against the short stack. He started the hand with $1,080, raised $200, and has now bet just $350 of his remaining chips. That's a very weak bet given the pot and three other opponents, less than half his remaining stack. It looks like he might be trying to save some chips if he decides to fold.

More importantly, this board is a prime bluffing opportunity. You see it all the time: a player raises, then the flop comes something like QQ5. Does he really have a queen? Probably not; when the board is paired, it's likely no one has anything unless there's large multi-way action.

Here, on a board of T44, our opponent either has a ten, a big pair, or nothing at all. But how likely was he to raise pre-flop with a ten in his hand? How about a 4? Even if he hit that ten, why wouldn't he have bet more money into three other players? Why would he lay them good odds to come along, and maybe catch a lucky turn card? This smells like a continuation bet bluff.

A paired board is a prime bluffing opportunity, and it's extraordinarily likely Seat 9 is bluffing given his situation in the tournament and his actions in the hand. Set him all-in and see if he's serious. If he was lucky enough to be dealt a premium pair on the cusp of being slowly blinded off in this tournament, he'll double up this hand.

Action: You raise Seat 9 all-in. He takes a very long time to call all-in, and turns over a KQ of clubs. The turn is a trey of diamonds and the river a deuce of diamonds. Your two-pair (6s and 4s) beat his pair of fours with a king-kicker.

THE FIRST TO BET USUALLY TAKES IT

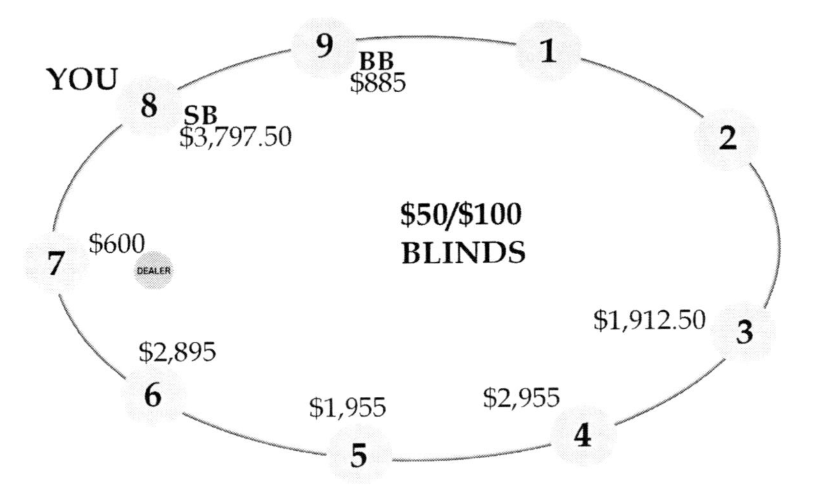

Hand:  

Situation: Mid-stages of a single table online sit and go. You currently have a small chip lead. Seat 6 is aggressive, and he usually raises in position.

Action: Everyone folds to Seat 6, who raises to $320. The pot is $470, and it costs $270 to call.

Analysis: You have a playable hand for this situation. Seat 6 routinely raises when folded around to in position. He may have little or no hand; at most he may have a weak ace. His slightly larger than usual raise is also suspicious. He's trying to discourage action; he's probably just robbing the short-stacked big blind.

Since we suspect larceny, should we re-raise right here? I wouldn't fault any player for making that move. We're out of position with a hand that has solid showdown potential. We can also use our big stack to intimidate our opponent. But if Seat 6 has a good hand and we commit ourselves to this pot, we'll be crippled in the tournament.

If Seat 6 had a somewhat smaller stack I'd favor re-raising right here. Because we're up against another big stack, though, I favor taking the more conservative approach. I wouldn't argue with either play, but I'd lean towards calling.

Action: We call the raise, and the big blind folds. The pot is now $740, and it's heads-up:

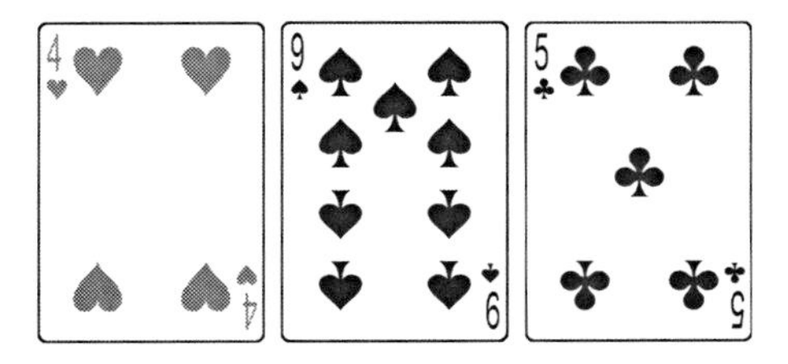

Analysis: That flop shouldn't have done much for any legitimate raising hand Seat 6 could have. If he makes a standard continuation bet, we shouldn't be too quick to give him credit for a hand. We could lead out right here, but that might look suspicious. If we really have a strong hand, why wouldn't we check to the raiser and earn at least one more bet? Let's check and wait.

Action: You check. Seat 6 checks behind you. The pot remains $740, and you're off to the turn:

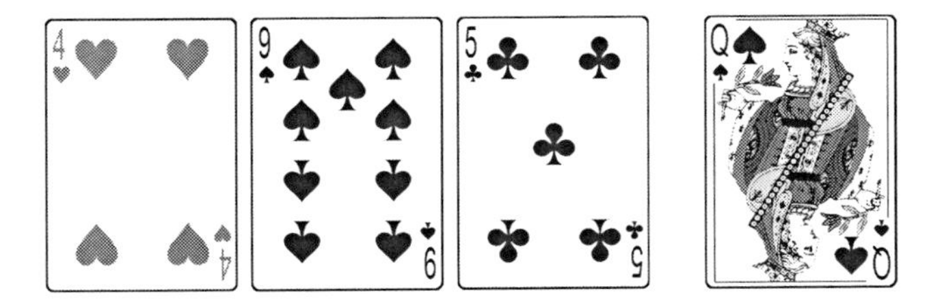

Analysis: No continuation bet? He's either weak or really strong. Either way, we can't check again.

THERE'S NOTHING WEAKER THAN CHECKING TWICE IN A ROW

When a player checks twice in a row, he's basically conceding the pot. Only a monster hand is going to offer two free cards. And even with a big hand, you should be trying to extract some value out of it before the river. Checking twice in a row is the equivalent of waving a white flag.

If you're in position and the pot's been checked to you twice, you must bet. You should probably bet even if there's a strong possibility of a trap, as long as you can afford to fold without much damage. It's simply too good an opportunity not to pounce on this sort of weakness.

Sometimes, your opponent simply wants nothing to do with a pot. He's gauged the situation to be too dangerous, and has simply decided to shut down on the hand. Exploit this.

If we check again here, our opponent will probably bet. His bet could mean anything: he started with a big pair and was trapping on the flop, he really hit that queen, he flopped a set, or he has nothing and sees us as weak. His bet won't mean anything after we've checked twice.

On the other hand, if we bet into our opponent, we force him to make a decision. We're saying we either trapped the flop or turned a queen: and we're done giving free cards. If he really has something, he'll raise here against the chip leader. *That bet will really tell us something.*

Action: You bet $440, and Seat 6 quickly folds. You take the pot with king-high. This hand shows betting to extract information. Checking isn't free; it often costs more than betting right out.

Chapter Eight

BE ABLE TO FOLD

Maxim 19: Manage your expectations.

The real can never equal the imagined, for it is easy to form ideals but very difficult to realize them. Imagination weds Hope and gives birth to unreal imaginings.

However great the excellence, it never reaches the ideal, and instead of appreciation for the good there is disappointment at the lack of perfection. Hope is a great falsifier of truth. If honest efforts yield poor results, you need not commit yourself to the final object.

Maxim 183: Do not hold your views too firmly.

Every fool is fully convinced, and every one fully persuaded is a fool: the more erroneous his judgment the more firmly he holds it. Even in cases of near-certainty, it may be fine to yield: our reasons for holding the view cannot escape notice, and prudence demands flexibility. There are some heads of iron most difficult to turn: add caprice to stubbornness and the sum is a wearisome fool. Steadfastness should be for the will, not the mind.

DON'T GET MARRIED TO A STRONG STARTING HAND

Hand:  

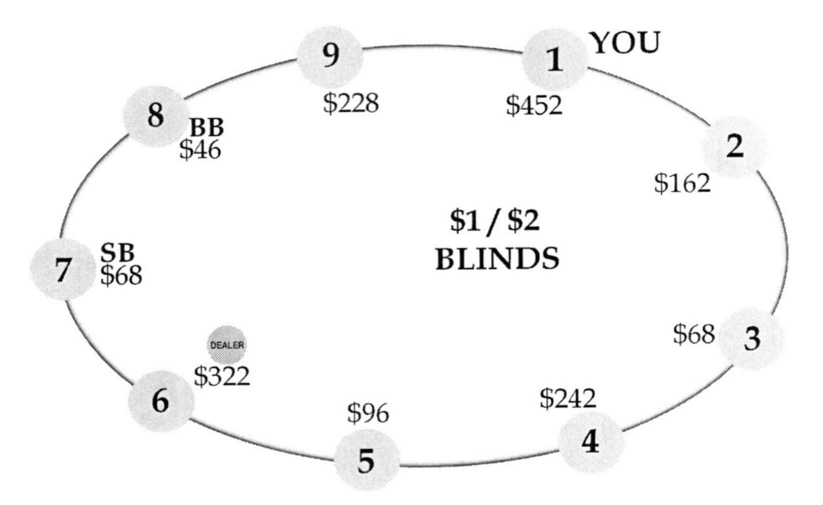

Situation: Low-stakes $1 and $2 no limit hold 'em cash game in Las Vegas. You've been fortunate thus far, picking up a few big hands against (mostly) drunken tourists. The entire table is loose and errs on the side of calling large bets for no reason, so it's hard to classify your opponents. Your tight, straight-forward style of play has been highly profitable at this casino, with drinks on the house and all.

Action: Seat 9 folds and you're second to act with your AK of hearts. *What should you do?*

Analysis: You need to raise here given how loose this game is, and it must be a fairly large raise to attract any notice. A raise to 6 or 7 times the big blind is nothing in a low-stakes, live cash game like this.

Action: You come in for a raise to $12. Seats 2, 4,

and 6 all call. The blinds fold. The pot is now $51 and four players see the flop:

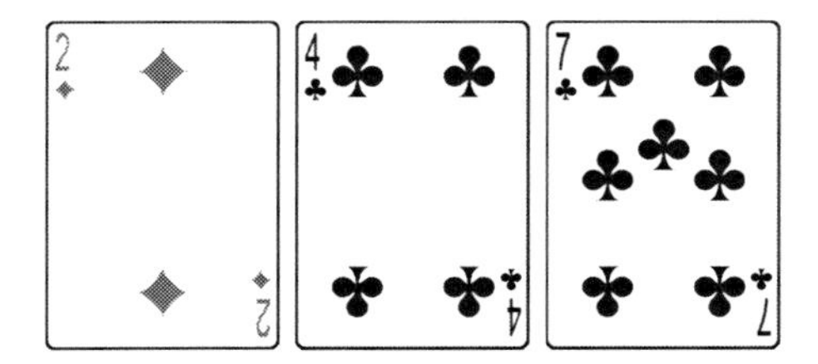

Analysis: Well, you missed the flop completely and you're playing against three other players who all called your pre-flop raise. It's conceivable that your ace-high could still be the best hand here, but it's not very likely. Still, you had a strong hand pre-flop, your programming kicks in here, and tells you to automatically make a continuation bet. What are you hoping to represent here? A big overpair likes aces or kings? Will your loose, erratic (and possibly drunk) opponents believe you? Is it not possible they have at least an overpair to the board as well?

Action: You decide to make a strong lead-off bet here of $40. You're hoping to represent an overpair that wants to shut down any flush or straight draws. And you want to keep the lead in the hand and show that you're serious about this pot. Hopefully this will work. Seats 2 and 4 fold, but the button calls $40. You realize after he makes the call that Seat 6 loves to call in position. He plays a lot of pots when he has the button and often calls on the flop. He could have almost anything here. The pot is now $131 and you and the button see the turn:

Analysis: Well, that card still doesn't help your hand, but the button doesn't know that. Even if he didn't believe your flop bet, you realize you could represent a hand like AQ or KQ here that just made top pair on the turn. If your opponent had second pair or bottom pair on the flop, or even an overpair to the sevens, perhaps he'll be afraid of that queen.

In any event, you feel that checking here would make you look weak, and you think it's still possible the button has some weird straight or flush draw he might now be willing to fold. You decide to fire a second bullet here and see if he goes away.

Action: You bet $60. Player 6 calls quickly. The pot is now $251. You have $340 left in your stack and Player 6 has $210. You both see a complete blank on the river:

Analysis: You still have only ace-high, you've invested $112 into this pot, and Seat 6 has not gone away despite your pre-flop raise, your strong bet on the flop, and your decent bet on the turn. What can you hope to gain by betting here?

Action: You check. Player 6 bets $50. The pot is $301 and it costs you $50 of your remaining $340 to call this bet. *What should you do?*

Analysis: Fold. This smells like a suck bet from a relatively experienced cash game player who senses weakness but is hoping to extract a little more money. It's only barely possible this is a weak, post-oak bluff with a missed drawing hand.

We've represented at least a big pair throughout this hand, so Player 6 shouldn't really expect us to fold to a weak bet here. This is especially true in a loose, live casino cash game. Face it, you're beat.

Action: You actually call, and Player 6 turns over a set of 4s. You quietly muck your hand. You lost $162 in this hand with just ace-high.

Conclusion: This is a classic mistake that tight players make, especially if they have more tournament than cash game experience. They see a strong starting hand, fall in love, and quickly get married to it. This is fine if you're facing rising blinds in a tournament with tight time constraints, but not in a cash game with fixed blinds.

Here, we convinced ourselves that our opponent was calling large bets with just a drawing hand, when there was no real reason to suspect that was the case. We basically built a big pot without a big hand, and we lost over a third of our stack because of this.

Always remember, a "big" starting hand like AK suited is only 70-30% against a 72 offsuit. If you miss the flop, you have nothing but ace-high and you're probably going to lose the hand if the action goes past the flop.

This hand is so treacherous it earned another nickname besides the more-commonly known "Big Slick" or "Anna Kournikova" – "Walking Back to Houston." In the early days when Texas Hold 'em literally grew up in the back streets of Texas, players often lost a LOT of money with this hand and had to "walk back home" (hopefully not literally). Don't play AK like AAs... the winning percentages of the two hands are nowhere near comparable.

Don't get married to a big starting hand if you don't improve. The cost of going to the river with a big pre-flop hand which doesn't improve is too costly if you're wrong. You can even fold aces if the board is truly frightening (excessive straight, flush, and two-pair possibilities). In poker, there is no advantage in stubbornly refusing to fold in the face of danger. Always be prepared to reexamine and reconsider a situation in light of new information. Don't let exaggerated expectations commit you to the hand without a good reason.

Maxim 25: Know how to take a hint.

We must know how to take a hint, especially in confronting our own illusions. He cannot make himself understood who does not himself easily understand. The very truths which concern us most are only half spoken, but with attention we can grasp the whole meaning. When you hear anything favorable keep a tight rein on your credulity; if unfavorable, give it the spur and listen most intently.

Maxim 227: Do not be a slave to first impressions.

Some marry the very first account they hear: all others are thereafter concubines. But a lie often travels much faster than the truth. We should neither satisfy our will with the first object nor our mind with the first proposition. Many are like new casks who keep the scent of the first liquor they hold, be it good or bad.

If this weakness becomes known, it is fatal, for it gives opportunity for cunning mischief; the ill-minded hasten to color the mind of the credulous. Always therefore leave room for a second hearing.

YOU DON'T HAVE TO GO BROKE WITH TOP PAIR

Even experienced players often fail to remember this simple truth: sometimes you simply must lay down top pair. There are scenarios where this hand should never be folded, of course (say, in the late stages of a tournament), and if you have one of the top pairs (aces, kings, or queens) you should hesitate to make this fold.

Unless you can construct a hand that plausibly explains your opponent's betting pattern, it's dangerous to take a single pair all the way to the river. The odds that you're simply beat increase with each opponent and each new betting round you face.

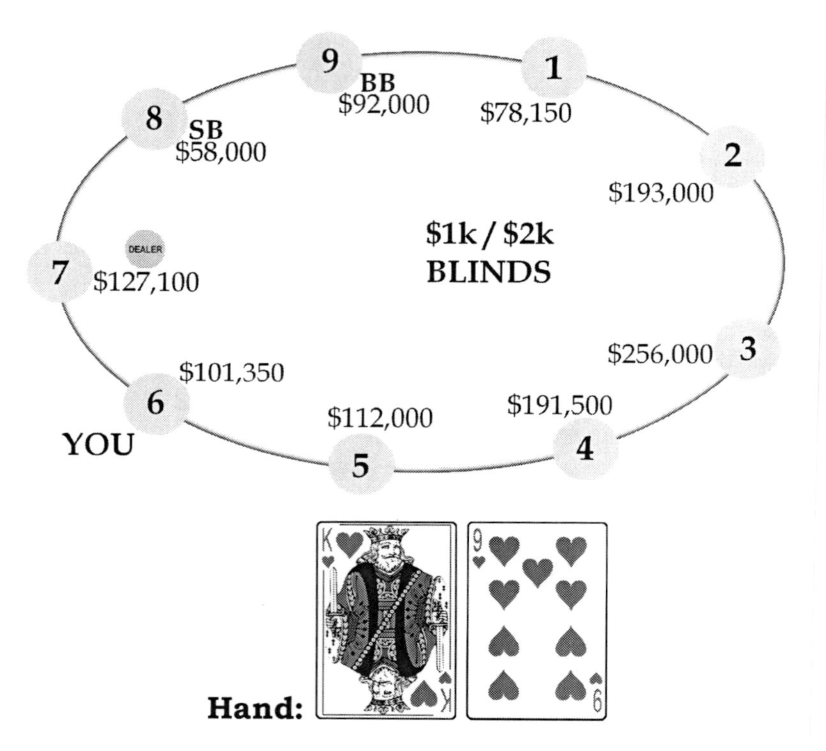

Situation: Fifty players from the bubble at the World Series of Poker. Play is quite tight since few want to risk their tournament lives so close to the money. The small blind is a famous tournament pro with a reputation for looseness. But after early missteps, he's tightened up considerably on the short stack. You've been playing a tight and very aggressive game thus far and have done quite well.

Action: Everyone folds around to you in the cut-off. You raise to take advantage of the tight play with a quick steal of the $3,000 in blinds. You raise to $6,000. The small blind calls the extra $5,000 and the big blind folds. The pot is now $14,000 and the two of you see the flop:

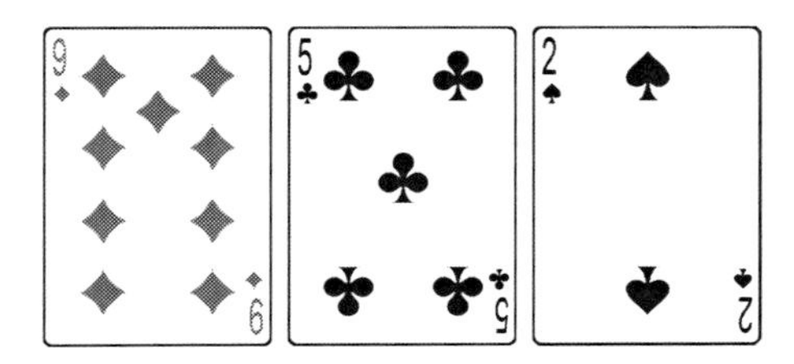

Analysis: You raised with a thoroughly mediocre hand to try to steal the blinds, you got unexpected (and unwelcome) action, but this is one of the best flops you could have hoped for. Your first impression is that top-pair, second-kicker is likely the best hand right now. You should bet your hand and scoop the pot.

Action: You bet $9,000 and the small blind goes into a deep think for several moments. Then he announces raise, and shoves in his remaining chips. Your opponent's huge raise says he's not afraid of an overpair or top pair on this board. The pot is now $77,000 and it costs you $44,000 to call. You have $86,350 left in your stack.

The TV crew has been rolling on the chance that the big poker name could be all-in this hand. Your first impression was that top-pair should be golden on a ragged board like this; now you need some time to think about this one. The more time, the better!

Analysis: That was unfortunate. The problem with a hand like K9 is that if you flop a pair of kings, you could easily be out-kicked by a better king. But if you flop top pair, you only have a pair of 9s. Now, thinking back on the hand, you realize that this loose, aggressive player was on the short stack and had indeed tightened his play, looking for an ideal spot to double up.

There are no obvious draws on this board, except for a 43 which would have been a very ambitious call into what was likely to be a heads-up pot. The professional player is capable of making a move here on the bubble of course, but you have him covered and can call without being eliminated. The presence of the TV crew should also have you thinking: would this pro player really be making a move here with absolutely nothing?

Even if he only had a couple of overcards, that would give him up to six outs twice, which is about a 24% chance he could make a winning hand by the turn and river. He could have flopped a set, or slow-played an overpair before the flop. From his perspective, you've represented strength both pre-flop and on the flop, and can afford to make this call. He may be hoping to capitalize on his loose reputation to get a call on his large overbet here.

If we call here, what are we rooting for our opponent to turn over? Probably our best hope is that our opponent isn't giving us credit for a 9. If that's the case, he might make this move with a pocket pair less than 9s (but not 5s or deuces, which just made a set). The chance of our opponent being dealt any particular pocket pair is 0.45%, and there are five pairs lower than the 9s that didn't just make a set.

What are the odds for our best-case scenario? That would be (0.45% x 5) = 2.25%, or over 43:1 against. That's clearly not a great hope. Our next best scenario - that our opponent just has a couple of overcards - would leave us barely 3:1 favorites, depending on whether one of those overcards is a king. We'd be huge dogs if he started with a big pair, or flopped a set on us.

This is a case where, given the stakes, top-pair is a relatively weak hand. All things considered, it's simply too expensive to play this hand if you're wrong, and you should strongly consider getting away from your 9s here. But this is a tough decision for most of your chips.

Action: You actually call, and your professional opponent turns over a set of 5s. You're drawing mighty thin against that hand, and the turn and river don't help your hand. Interestingly, even at the river you still have top pair, but you've lost over half your stack with the "dog hand" (K9).

As with most things in life, folding is an exercise in supreme judgment. Only good players can get bluffed, because only they can lay down a strong hand that doesn't figure to be best. If you're holding top pair and face strong resistance, you must gauge the situation, the board, your opponent, and whether you can afford to fold. What are you risking if you're wrong? What are the odds your opponent is bluffing?

Before you call large bets with just a single pair, be sure you've put your opponent on a hand you can beat. If the action doesn't seem to square with a plausible hand you can beat, fold and don't look back. There'll be better opportunities to make some money later on.

Know how to take a hint if you're representing top pair and your opponent's actions say he can beat you.

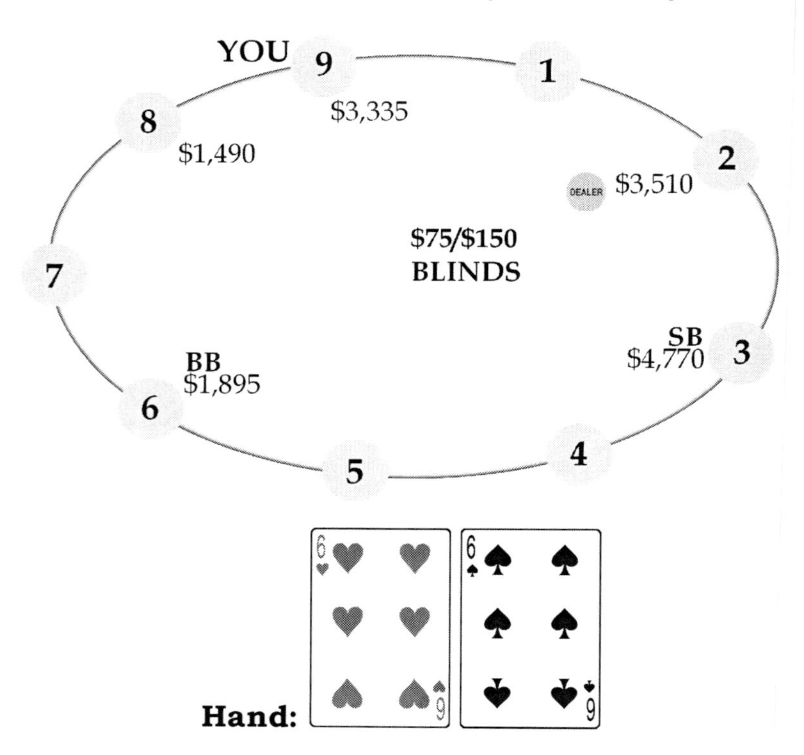

DON'T TAKE UNNECESSARY RISKS

Situation: Mid-late stages of a single table online sit and go. You've played a tight, aggressive game throughout, and have shown down only quality hands. Your table image should be very good. Seat 6 has only one move: all-in before the flop. He seems to be selective in jamming, though unsurprisingly he's shown down few such hands.

Action: Seat 8 folds. Given the higher blinds, you make a smaller than usual raise to $400. Everyone folds to the big blind, who goes all-in for his remaining $1,745. The pot is now $2,370, and it costs you $1,495 to call. *What should you do?*

Analysis: First, let's look at the pot odds. You're getting about 1.6:1 on a call here. That means you need to win 1/2.6 of the time to break even, or a bit less than 40%. If this is a coin-toss situation (i.e. he has overcards), you have the odds to make this call.

What is the chance that we're a solid favorite here? Practically zero. The only way that we're substantially ahead is if our opponent is making a move with a smaller pair (deuces through fives) or a *very* weak ace (A6 or lower). It's possible our opponent isn't giving us much respect here, or that he's just making a move, but our chip lead and tight table image argue strongly against that interpretation. He knows we haven't been raising with trash and have the chips to call him here; he probably has *something*.

What are the chances we're in really bad shape? We're 4:1 dogs if he has a pair greater than ours. There are eight higher pairs. There's a 0.45% chance of each player being dealt one of those pairs, or 3.6% per player. With four opponents, we know there was a 14.4% chance of one of them being dealt a pair higher than our own. Seat 6 is signaling he has a hand, and if it's a pair, we're in a lot of trouble.

To summarize: there's no chance we're a solid favorite, some chance we're an underdog, and the best-case scenario is we're looking at a coin toss for half our remaining stack. If we call and lose here, we'll be the new short stack at the table with just $1,440 in chips. If we fold, we'll still have $2,935 and a strong third chip position.

Calculating the various scenarios, we might have the pot odds to make this call. But we shouldn't. Calling here is an unnecessary risk. If we had better odds, more chips and/or our opponent was particularly loose, we could seriously consider taking a chance. But we need to make the smart play here and fold. Wait for a better spot to earn some chips.

Chapter Nine

SELECTIVE AGGRESSION

Maxim 4: Knowledge and courage are the elements of greatness.

They give immortality, because they are immortal. Each is as much as he knows, and the wise can do anything. A man without knowledge, a world without light. Wisdom and strength, eyes and hands. Knowledge without courage is sterile.

Maxim 54: Know how to show your teeth.

Even hares can pull the mane of a dead lion. There is no joke about courage. Give way to the first and you must yield to the second, and so on, and to gain your point at last is more costly than could have been won with an earlier stand.

Many have had eminent qualities, yet, for want of a stout heart, they passed empty lives and found a tomb in their own sloth. Wise Nature has thoughtfully combined in the bee the sweetness of its honey and the sharpness of its sting.

FIND THE COURAGE TO FIRE THE SECOND BULLET

Perhaps no single betting strategy has been more debased by the rise in poker literacy than the continuation bet. One of the first lessons most poker books teach is the need to follow-through on a pre-flop raise with a bet on the flop, whether you hit your hand or not. It's become a textbook play -- an obvious play.

The problem is that although it's still a necessary strategy, it's far too easy for a savvy player to exploit. Many loose players will now call a tight pre-flop raiser with position and readily call anything that looks like a continuation bet on the flop. These players then look to take the pot away on the turn. What was intended as a show of strength is now frequently read as weakness. The answer? In some (selective) situations, you have to be ready to fire the second bullet.

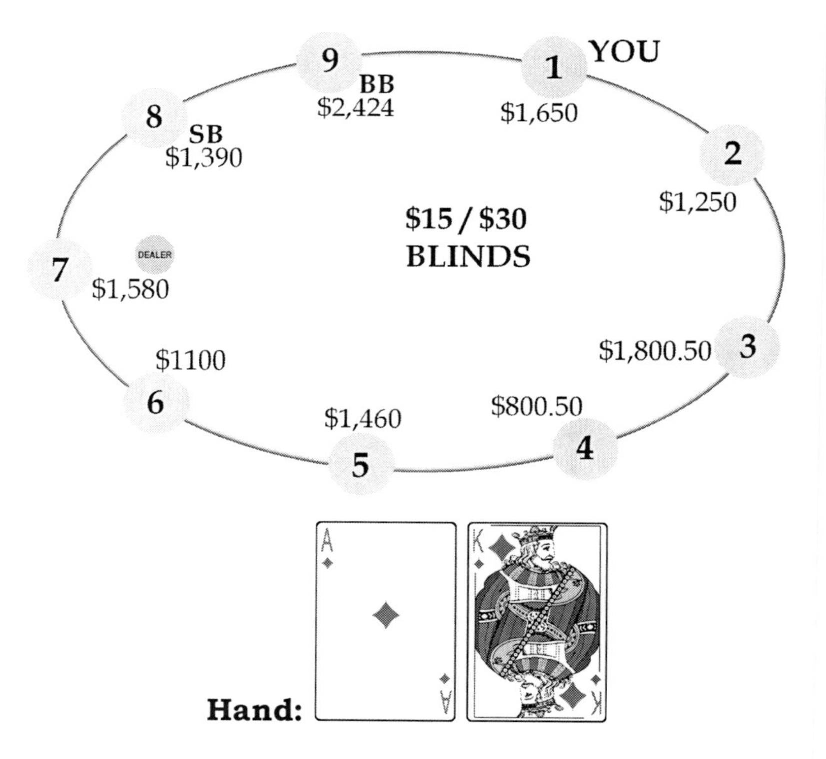

Situation: Early stages of a one-table online sit and go tournament. You're in first position when you pick up your suited AK. You've been playing a tight, patient style which is best-suited to this stage of a sit and go. Player 7 is fairly loose and somewhat aggressive.

Action: You make a standard raise to $90. Everyone folds around to the button, who calls. The blinds fold. The pot is now $225, and you and the button see the flop heads up:

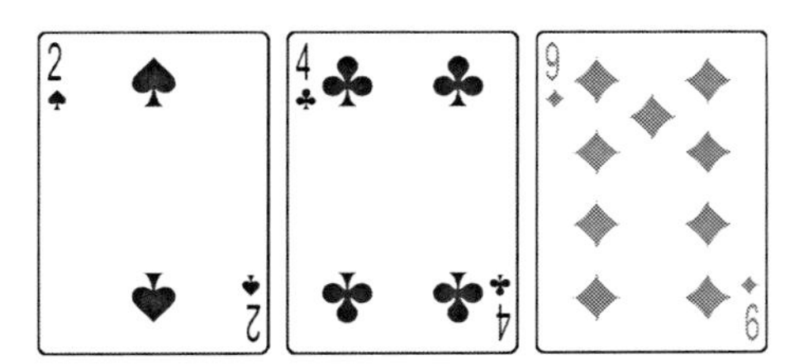

Analysis: Obviously that flop didn't improve your hand, but unless your opponent started with a pocket pair that flop is unlikely to have helped his hand. How many playable hands could he have called with that contain a deuce, a four or a nine?

You probably have the best hand, but an unpaired AK can never feel too confident. Still, we need to represent confidence. The textbook says to make a half-pot bet here as a follow-through on our pre-flop raise, and that's what you do.

Action: You bet $115, and the button quickly calls. The pot is now $455. You and Player 7 see the turn:

Analysis: The "textbook" play on the flop wasn't given any respect at all. In fact, it has been my experience that the half-pot continuation bet no longer represents strength, but rather weakness. Even though the texture of that flop probably didn't help our opponent, he saw our bet and interpreted it as weakness.

Look at the hand from his perspective: he saw a standard raise from first position followed by a predictable half-pot bet on a 9-high flop. He probably puts us on exactly the hand that we have: AK or AQ. He feels he can take the hand away from us on the turn.

What should we have done differently? The first thing to do is to bury the half-pot bet as a continuation bluff, especially if the blinds are still relatively low. Simply remove it from your arsenal. In fact, this type of bet is so widely read as weakness that it's better used when you're really strong.

This is not to say that we're abandoning the continuation bet; it's still a fundamental part of any aggressive playing style. However, we need to bet more to get respect: try throwing out 65-75% of the pot, or the entire pot if the stakes are low. Here, if we're representing an overpair to the board, we should bet $150 or $160.

Dealing with the hand as it stands, however, the turn was a blank. The situation is clear: either you started the hand way ahead with your AK and are still way ahead (vs. some sort of JT or other drawing hand) or the button is trapping you. If he really had a pair on the flop, he would have put us on over-cards and made a decent raise. He could have a set of 2s or 4s, but if you always fear a hidden set you can't play winning poker.

Here, you need to be willing to fire the second bullet. It looks like we might have the best hand. Consider that our pre-flop raise was called by a loose player *in position*; such a player doesn't need much to call on or near the button. His call on the flop also didn't signal any strength. There are no obvious draws unless he has a 53, which seems unlikely. We can't check-fold to a loose, aggressive player who has nothing but position.

We could lead out here and fire another bullet, but an even more aggressive action would be to check-raise. If we check, we'll be announcing our flop bet was a continuation bluff and give the button license to steal the pot. The check-raise should be interpreted as a very aggressive move, and one we wouldn't make without a big hand.

In effect, we'll be saying to the button, "I had a big pair before the flop, and I bet it on the flop, and it's such a big hand I didn't mind giving you a free card here on the turn. But since you're betting, I'm raising!" He should take the hint.

You might minimize your risk by making a min-check-raise, which is doubly aggressive: a check-raise is a sign of real strength, and a min-raise looks like you're just suckering your opponent in. Double the effectiveness of this move!

Action: You check, and your opponent bets $300. You check-raise to $600, raising the pot to $1,355 and leaving you with $845. Your opponent has $1,075 left. Your opponent runs the online clock down to zero and is auto-folded. He was likely saving face on his obvious bluff. You fired the second bullet and scoop a big pot.

Analysis: What a perfect play given this situation! A check-raise is scary, a min-raise is really scary, and appearing pot-committed (determined to play the hand out to the end given the size of the pot relative to your stack) is really, really scary. That's a lot of scariness for the button to stand.

Even if your opponent has top pair in this spot, it looks like he should fold. There aren't many hands he could have that can stand this kind of pressure, unless he has a set. If he does, he'll push all-in instantly and it'll be an heroic fold for us. The odds are he isn't that strong.

We can make this big move because we saw our opponent had just enough chips left to fold. He had committed about 1/3 of his stack, and while that's substantial, he still has over $1,000 in chips. It would be a painful loss for him, but he can fold and still have some chance of winning.

Don't give any credence to the button running out the action clock. In my experience, that is rarely a sign of a real tough decision; it's usually just a bluffer being caught in a wild bluff and trying to save face.

He's just posturing to convince you he really *does* have a hand and is thinking about pushing all his chips to the middle -- so hopefully you won't call him on his next bluff. Your opponent probably had nothing if you come across one of these "running out the clock" folds.

KNOW WHEN TO SEMI-BLUFF

One of the most commonly misused plays is the semi-bluff. Many players fail to consider the strength of possible hands they may be facing. Remember, although a straight or flush draw has the potential to become a powerful hand, you're still bluffing. You don't *want* action when you're drawing! Try and catch your opponents weak.

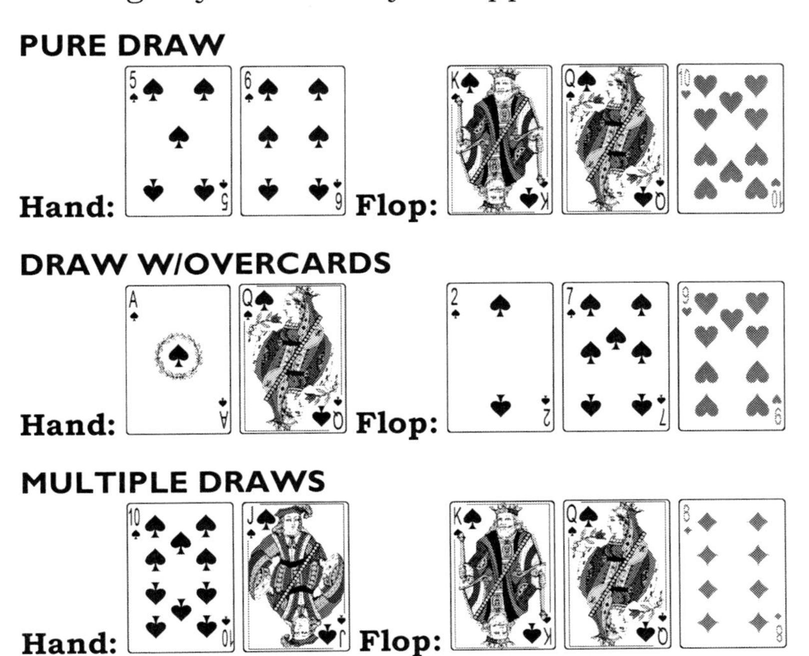

Multiple draws include both a flush draw and some type of straight draw. The ultimate multiple draw is a straight flush draw, which is actually a favorite over any hand your opponent could be holding except a set (a 58-42 matchup).

You rarely want to bluff with a pure draw, unless you're up against few opponents who are unlikely to have connected with the board. Instead, you'd like to draw cheaply. You want to keep as many people in the hand as long as possible, for two reasons: (1) the presence of more than one caller will improve your pot odds to call along on each betting round; and (2) if you make your hand, you want someone to call a healthy bet. For both reasons, it pays to play a pure draw passively, in a multi-way pot.

Conversely, you're happy to push a straight and flush draw aggressively, even if the straight draw isn't open-ended. Your hand has so many outs that you shouldn't mind playing for all the chips. Since you don't have a made hand yet, you'd be happy to take the pot without a fight.

Whether you push a draw with overcards depends on the number of opponents and the action in the hand. The more players you face, the likelier it is that someone will have something they'll feel comfortable sticking around with. And you can never be sure that your overcards are *clean outs* – they may help your hand while also improving your opponent's. This situation calls for balance and judgment.

Chapter Ten

INSPIRE OTHERS TO FEAR

Maxim 5: Create a feeling of dependence.

A man grows great not by adorning others but by having their adoration. The wise man would rather see men needing him than thanking him. To keep them on the threshold of hope is wisdom, to trust in their gratitude foolish; hope has a good memory, gratitude a bad one. More is to be made from dependence than from courtesy. He that has satisfied his thirst turns his back on the well, and the orange once sucked falls from the golden platter into the waste-basket. When dependence disappears, good behavior goes with it as well as respect. Let it be one of the chief lessons of experience to keep hope alive without entirely satisfying it, by preserving it to make oneself always indispensable.

Maxim 95: Keep others in a state of anticipation.

Keep stirring it up. Let much promise more, and great deeds herald greater. Do not rest your whole fortune on a single cast of the die. It requires great skill to moderate your forces so as to keep expectation from being dissipated.

Conservative players will often view a loose, aggressive player as a slot machine they're hoping will eventually pay out a jackpot. They'll maneuver to trap the loose player in a big pot when they have a strong hand. It is well for the loose player to keep this hope alive without ever realizing it. Keep up the aggression, but give up the small pots in the face of strong resistance.

Remember: you know exactly how strong your hand is when you're leading the betting, but it will cost the conservative player a lot more chips to raise and re-raise to find out if you're serious. Keep your losing pots small, keep the pressure up, and you're likely to win more than your fair share.

GIVE UP THE SMALL POTS TO WIN THE BIG POTS

An effective strategy for driving conservative players crazy is to continuously needle them with low-level, aggressive betting. Always remember that most flops miss most hands, and that conservative players want to have a hand before they get into a big confrontation.

By making small bets pre-flop, on the flop and possibly on the turn, regardless of the strength of your hand, you scramble their strategy and force them to either step up their aggression or to crawl back into their shell, giving up too many pots.

The key to making this strategy work is to be able to give up small pots in the face of strong resistance. You're adopting a guerilla strategy. Needle your opponents with small attacks while avoiding a major conflict. When you decide to play a very large pot, you will have a solid hand (and hopefully a decent chip lead).

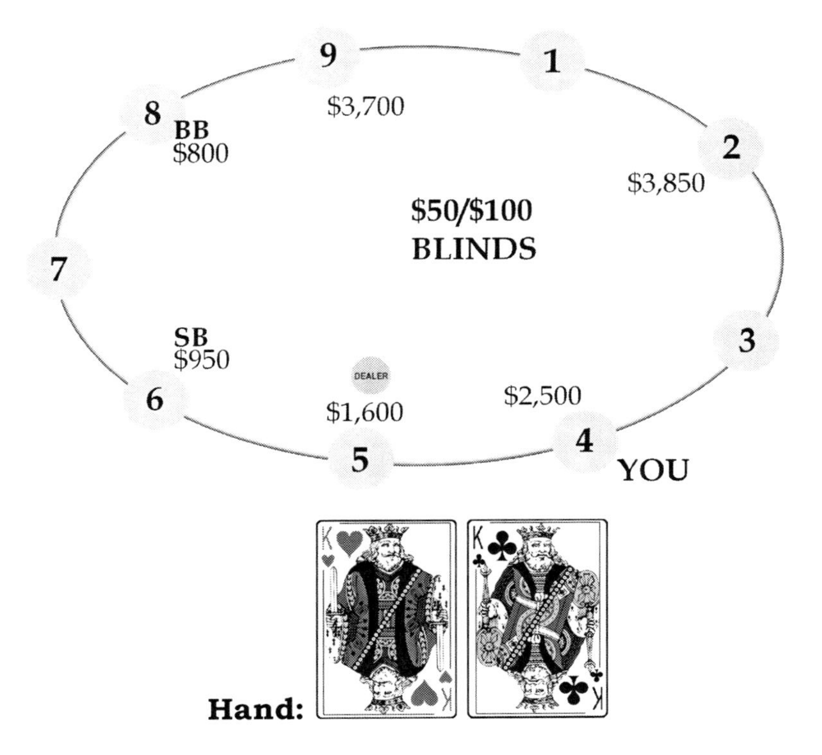

Situation: Mid-level of a one-table online sit and go. You've been loose and aggressive all-game, continuously making small raises pre-flop and usually betting on the flop and turn. This has been especially successful against the sixth and eighth seats, who are playing a tight, conservative game and haven't made much happen so far.

The last couple of hands have seen increasing aggression in response to your bets from the players to your left. You've folded in the face of strong raises (giving up a small pot when you had nothing anyway). You're in the cut-off when you pick up pocket kings.

Action: The ninth and second seats fold to you in the cut-off. *What should you do?*

Analysis: You've obviously got a strong hand here, but that's no reason to change your strategy. Since you've been making small bets and raises with relatively weak (though playable) hands, you should play your strong hands the same way. This has the added virtue of looking like a cheap min-raise steal from the big blind, perhaps prompting an aggressive re-raise from one of the players to your left.

Action: You make the minimum raise to $200. The button thinks for a few moments and then folds. The small blind goes all-in, raising us his last $800. The big blind folds and it costs us $800 to a call a $1200 pot. We instantly call with glee, and the small blind turns over JT offsuit. Our hand holds up and we scoop a big pot.

Conclusion: Nothing drives a player crazy quite like getting run over. By constantly needling an opponent with small bets and raises, we can get inside their heads and get them off their game. In the face of such constant attacks, many otherwise tight, conservative players will start to loosen up and will respond to such bets with increasing aggression.

The key is to be able to back-off when this happens, giving up small pots to win a really big pot when our opponent chooses a bad time to "match fire with fire." In this hand, the small blind assumed you were making a small raise with nothing again and decided his resilient drawing hand was a decent match-up to any junk you might be raising with.

Conservative players who've seen an aggressive player run over the table will never give him credit for a hand; however, everyone gets the same cards over time and it's important to remember even an aggressive player can have a hand sometimes. Constant, low-level aggression will keep your opponents guessing as to what you have and can lead them to make really big mistakes in your favor.

You always want the other players to fear what you might do. Repeated aggression will keep them off-balance while you wait for a good spot to catch them. Remember there's no shame in walking away from bluffs gone bad. That's the advantage of being the aggressor: you know how strong you are and how far you're willing to carry things.

You can't be afraid to commit chips. When you're sitting at the poker table, you must never think of the chips as money, or the things that money can buy. They are tools in a game, and you can't get too attached to them. If you fear losing, that fear will cripple your effectiveness.

Don't be scared to splash some chips around. Just be sure that when *all* the chips go in the middle, you've either got the best of it or a darned good reason to gamble.

SQUEEZE PLAY: ISOLATE & DESTROY

While there are times when it pays to cooperate in eliminating an opponent, it's often more profitable to squeeze players out of a juicy pot with a short stack. Using the threat of elimination, you can push other players out of the pot, accomplishing two objectives: (1) you raise your overall chances of winning; and (2) you increase your equity in the pot with the other players' *dead money* (i.e. the money they've put in, which, having folded, they cannot win back).

The choice between allowing a multi-way pot and pulling a squeeze play depends on the stage of the tournament, the strength and resilience of your hand, and the tightness/looseness of the short stack and the players to be squeezed. The textbook squeeze play involves coming over the top of a short-stacked all-in and medium-stacked caller with a hand like AK or AQ.

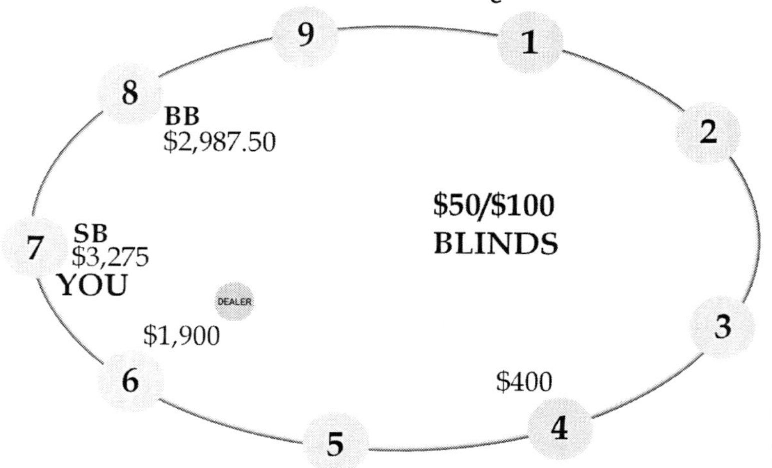

Hand:  

Situation: Mid-stage of a single table online tournament. There are six players remaining. Seat 4 is two deals away from the big blind with an extreme short stack.

Action: Seats 1 and 2 fold. Seat 4 goes all-in for his remaining $400. Seat 6 hesitates several seconds before calling. Action is on you.

Analysis: The conservative play would be to call and see a flop here. There's a chance that Seat 6 may be willing to check the hand down if nothing materializes. But there are several problems with that play.

If we merely call here, the big blind has to call $300 to see a $1,350 pot. In other words he's getting 4.5:1 on a call, almost irresistible odds with any kind of hand and an above average stack. Our AK will not hold up well in a four-way pot. Remember, big cards have the most value if they get to the showdown.

We're also out of position: we'll have to act first on every round of betting. If no one's holding a pocket pair, we may have the best hand right now. After the flop, we'll have no idea where we're at. But if we limit our competition and guarantee that we get to see all five cards, we won't have any difficult decisions to make after the flop.

The quicker, easier play is to move all-in right here. Seat 6 may or may not call. It would be a tough laydown, but he can make it and still have an M of 10. Even if he calls, our AK has a better than average chance of winning.

The beauty of the squeeze play is that we're not really plunging ourselves into three way action. Either Seat 6 gets out of the way or he sticks around, and then we only have to beat *him* to come out well ahead on this hand. We can afford to lose Seat 4's $400 raise if we can win Seat 6's remaining stack ($1,500).

We profit if Seat 6 folds by having a good shot at a $1,200 pot we only invested $400 into. We also profit if he calls, because Seat 4 has padded the pot with $400 in what is now effectively a heads-up pot between us and Seat 6. Meanwhile, the squeezed player is forced to choose between gambling for all his chips and retreating with a badly damaged stack.

Action: Seat 6 takes up almost all his time before folding what he says were a pair of tens. Your AK holds up against Seat 4's A9, and you scoop the pot. Note that the board ultimately came down 238J7, so you would have lost if Seat 6 stuck around. The beauty of the squeeze play is that the squeezed player rarely sticks around if your timing is right.

Chapter Eleven

PEOPLE JUDGE A BOOK BY ITS COVER

Maxim 99: Appearance is generally mistaken for reality.

Things pass for what they seem, not for what they are. Few see inside; many take to the outside. Even the pure truth will appear a lie if it is shown in a false light.

Maxim 130: For most, reality is only what is seen.

Things do not pass for what they are but for what they seem. What is not seen is as if it was not. Even what's right receives no credit if it does not seem right. The observant are far fewer in number than those who are deceived by appearances. Deceit rules the roost, and things are judged by their jackets, and many things are other than they seem.

ALWAYS CONSIDER WHAT HAND YOU'RE REPRESENTING TO YOUR OPPONENTS

There are three essential factors to the play of any poker hand. The first step is to consider the strength of your own hand and what potential it may have. This is simply a matter of reading the board and gauging if you have a made hand, a draw, or absolutely nothing. Always remember that the strength of any hand is relative to the cards on the board.

The second step is to put your opponent on a range of possible hands and gradually narrow down his likeliest holding, based on his betting patterns. The third step is to think about the hand you're representing to your opponent.

Poker is not a game of chance, because over time everyone receives the same number of good hands and bad hands. Poker is a game of information, a conversation between players, and to win such a contest you must pay very careful attention both to what your opponent is telling you and what you are revealing to your opponent.

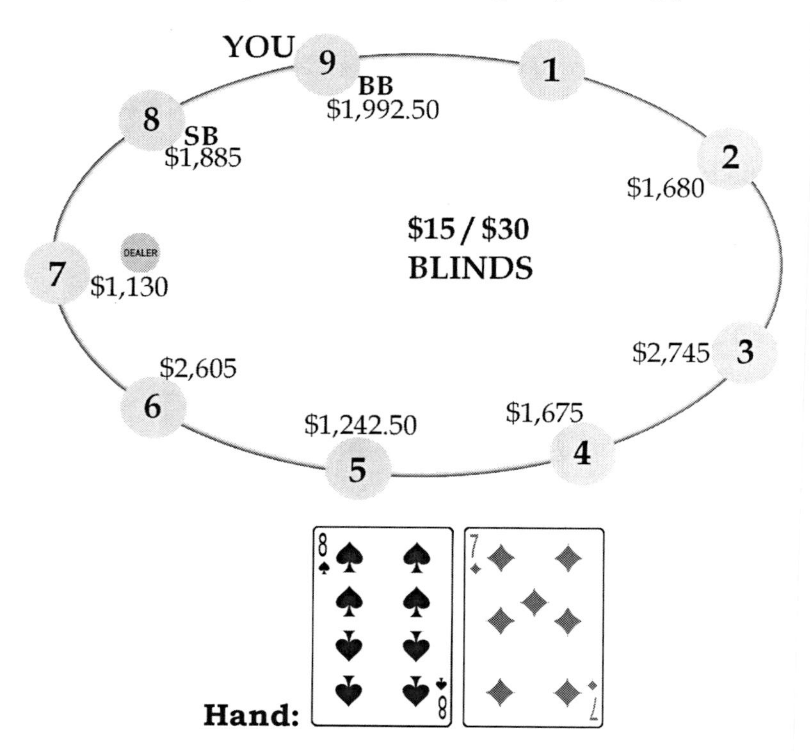

Situation: Early stage of a one-table online sit and go tournament. The top five players get paid. Realizing that this format rewards patience, you've been playing a very tight, conservative game in the early stages. Player 3 seems to play nearly every hand and has gotten lucky thus far, so you can safely assume he's a fool. You're in the big blind with your unsuited connector.

Action: Player 2 folds. Player 3 limps in for $30. Everyone folds around to you in the big blind. You gladly check to see a free flop with your hand, which has excellent potential to earn some money if it hits. The pot is now $75, and you and Seat 3 see the flop:

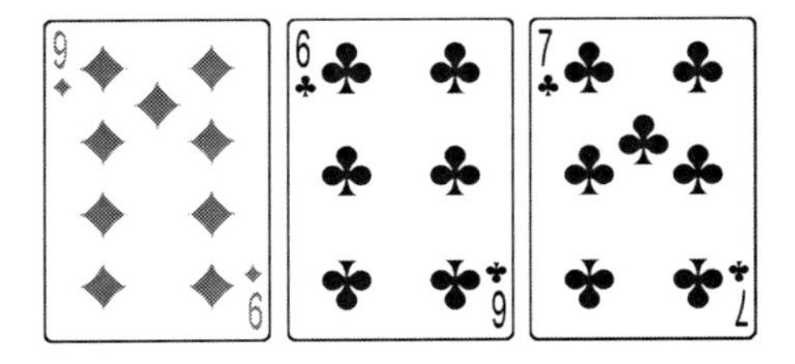

Analysis: This is exactly the flop that a small drawing hand wants to see! With these types of hands, you're looking to get in cheap and flop a big draw. With two suited cards, you'll flop a flush 0.84% of the time but have an 11% chance at seeing a flush draw; with two connected cards you'll flop a straight 1.3% of the time and have a 10.45% chance of a straight draw. Flopping a draw is 8-13 times likelier than flopping a made hand here, and even when you flop a draw you're 2:1 against making it.

The conclusion is simple: don't invest too much with these speculative hands! To make these hands profitable, you need to get in cheap and ensure you'll get decent odds to draw; this means waiting for a multi-way, unraised pot before getting involved, or taking a free look from the blinds.

With mid-pair and an open-ended straight draw, we probably have the best hand right now, and even if we don't, we have eight outs twice to improve to a straight (which will happen nearly 1/3 of the time). It's also possible that another seven or eight could give us the best hand if we are behind (though we'd fear the eight putting a four-card straight on board). That's a total of up to five more outs, if we're not already ahead. This is a hand we shouldn't mind taking to battle right now.

We should bet, and bet aggressively. We gain little by checking here, because this doesn't look like the sort of flop that would have helped an early position limper, unless he flopped a set. If he limped with a weak ace or a hand like JT, why give him a chance to take a free card here?

Action: You bet about the size of the pot, $70. Seat 3 calls within a second. The pot is now $215, and both players see the turn:

Analysis: When you're first to act on the flop, all you have to go on is the pre-flop action. A player who limps from early position can have just about anything: a big pair he's hoping to trap with, a small pair hoping to flop a set, some sort of suited connector, or maybe just a suited ace hoping for that magic flush. The range of hands is simply immense. But a pre-flop limp followed by a quick call on that flop, given the board, gives us more information to narrow down our opponent's hand.

Think about the action from our opponent's perspective: he knows that we're in the big blind and were given a chance to see a free flop. That means we could literally have almost any hand, though probably not a premium hand, since we might have raised pre-flop. When we made a pot-sized bet on the flop, however, we were representing a made hand that wanted to shut down any possible draws (little could he realize that we had both a made hand and a strong draw).

Given the action thus far, we effectively said to our opponent: "Hey, you let me see a cheap flop, and I flopped a good pair here, either the 9 or the 7 with a decent kicker. I think you have nothing, but given the flush and straight-draws on board, I want you to go away. Now! Step away from my pot and no one gets hurt."

What would he make a lightning-fast call with here? If he had a pair, wouldn't he want to raise? That's a dangerous board, and if he had a hand like A9 or K9 or J9 there aren't many cards on the turn that could help him, and plenty that would make him afraid he no longer had the best hand.

In fact, even with a set of 6s, 7s, or 9s, he might well want to raise here. There are just too many scare cards that can come on the turn (a 5, an 8, a 10, or any club). With any made hand on a board like this, most players would raise to find out where they stand.

So we can start narrowing down our opponent's hand: the likeliest explanation of his action is that he has some kind of draw. An open-ended straight draw is unlikely, both because of the 8 in our hand and because playable hands with an 8 (98, 87, or 86) are unlikely given the board and the action thus far. An A8 is somewhat possible, as loose players will frequently limp with weaker aces.

He could also have a gutshot draw with something like a JT, and be making an ambitious call with two overcards and the inside draw. If he had exactly a 54, he made a sucker call drawing at the sucker end of the straight, and got there. Even very loose players likely wouldn't limp from an early position with 54 or make such a bad call, but stranger things have happened.

A more likely scenario is that he's drawing at the flush. Very loose players like Seat 3 love almost any two suited cards, and they'll pay a high price to chase any draws if they flop big. Given that a draw is the likeliest possibility and the 3 of hearts shouldn't have connected with any of the straight or flush draws, we should charge him for the privilege of continuing to draw: a lot. A loose player will likely pay us off, but we probably won't pay him if the flush card hits.

Action: You bet $120 and Player 3 instantly calls. The pot is now $455. You both see the river:

Analysis: We might have bet a bit more on the turn and gotten paid off from this loose player who's now pretty obviously chasing some kind of draw. That's not a bad card for us, though we didn't improve our own hand. If he was calling all the way down with bottom pair on a board with straight and flush possibilities, he's very brave, very foolish, and he just got very lucky.

Such things happen on occasion. Of course, the fact that the board has paired 6s means our opponent probably doesn't have a 6 in his hand. The instant call on the turn, without any thought of raising on a board full of draws, means he's probably drawing. The 6 of diamonds missed any straight or flush draw he had. So what do we do here? Bet our hand for value?

Definitely not! While you should never do anything all the time, a bet on the river here is generally a mistake. Yes, we're almost certain that he missed his draws, and we have the best hand.

But we don't always bet just because we have the best hand. If we're right, and he has nothing but a busted flush or straight draw, he's not going to call our river bet. Think of the hand we've been representing all along: we made strong bets on the flop, on the turn, and now we're making another decent bet on the river! We've represented strength from start to finish, and unless he's been slowplaying some kind of monster hand he won't pay off one more nickel.

No, we need to check here. This gives us a chance to make some more money off the hand, whereas a bet almost certainly does not. If we check here, it will be a sign of weakness. He'll look down at his nothing hand, and he might just decide that perhaps *we* had some type of busted draw as well, and after his calls on the flop and turn have decided to give up the hand. Perhaps he'll think we're afraid of that 6 for some reason.

Always remember what hand you're representing and the range of hands you put your opponent on. A bet on the flop at a draw-heavy board, on the turn after a blank, and then a quick check on the river could look like we were semi-bluffing all along with an eight or two clubs. This is the story your opponent will *want* to believe, since we're pretty sure he has nothing.

Many players with no hand by the river will pounce on a check from their opponent as an invitation to steal. They let greed cloud their better judgment. ***Appearance is generally mistaken for reality***, and this display of weakness at the end disguises our earlier show of strength.

If you think your opponent has no hand and no chance to improve to the best hand, you can't bet for value. Instead, feign weakness, especially on the river. An aggressive opponent will grasp at any sign of weakness to try to steal the pot. Profit from your opponent's greed.

Action: Instead, you follow the old maxim of "if you have the best hand, bet it" and put in another $200. Your opponent instantly folds and you earn nothing from your bet. Had you stopped to think about the hand, the strength you represented by firing out at each street, and your opponent's likeliest holding (some type of busted draw), you could have earned hundreds of dollars in chips by giving him enough rope to hang himself.

YOU CAN'T BLUFF BY CALLING

Even experienced players sometimes find themselves tempted to get attached to a drawing hand. Remember though, you ***never want to call all-in on a draw***. You want to push the action, not react. But if your opponent beats you to the punch, pull back and wait for another opening.

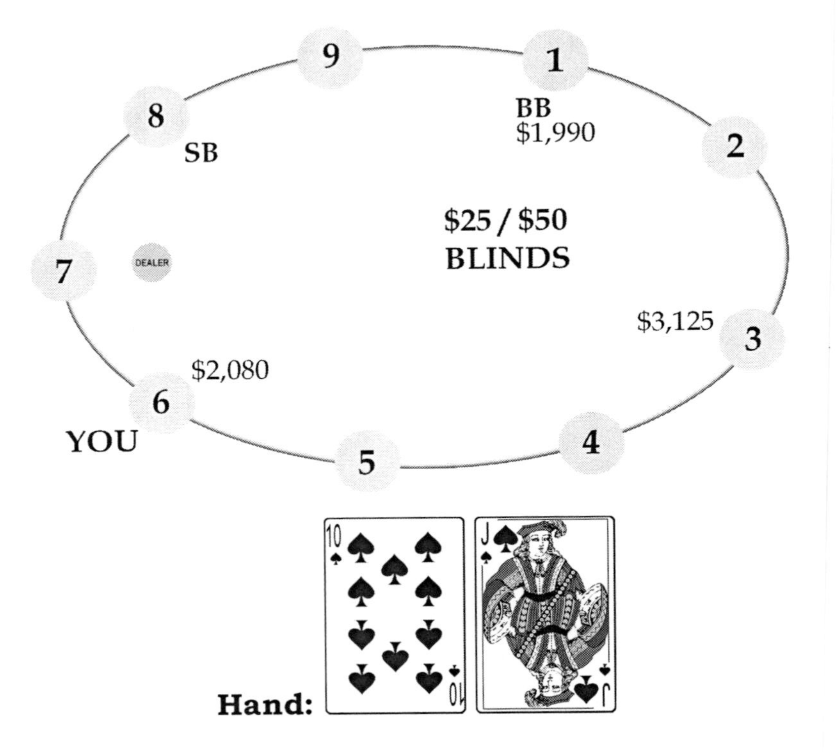

Situation: Mid-stage of a single table sit and go. Seat 3 has been tight, and the few hands he's played he's bet very aggressively.

Action: Seat 3 raises to $150. You and the big blind both call. The pot is now $475. Three players see the flop, and you have position:

Action: The big blind checks, and Seat 3 immediately bets the pot, $475. The pot is now $950. We have $1,930 remaining in our stack.

Analysis: Our pre-flop call was speculative and aggressive, and we've been rewarded with a good flop. Unfortunately, Seat 3 won't let us draw cheaply. Some players come out swinging, betting at least the pot on each and every street. Seat 3 fits this mold. He's not going away easily now that he's committed chips to the pot.

Our options aren't great here. Although this is exactly the sort of flop we're looking for when we speculate with a hand like JT, it could quickly get too expensive to keep playing. In fact, it already may be too costly to make this call.

We have a pure draw; we must spike a 9 or an ace to have any kind of hand at all. We're about 32% to make our straight *by the river*, but we face another round of betting on the turn. It seems very unlikely, given the king-queen high flop here, that our opponent will check the turn to us.

If we just call here, we'll have $1,455 left in chips. If we then are forced to fold the turn, we'll have a below-average stack heading into the late-mid stages of the tournament.

On the other hand, it would be foolish to push all-in: our opponent is too likely to call us if he has AK, KQ, AAs, KKs, or QQs. We might be able to bully AQ or a pair of JJs into folding. But Seat 3 is a stubborn player who's already invested a lot of chips. Such opponents are not easily semi-bluffed in an obvious drawing situation.

Action: You call, and the big blind folds. The pot is now $1,425. You have $1,455 left in your stack, and its heads-up to the turn:

Action: Seat 3 bets $1,425, almost all our stack.

Analysis: You fold. Obviously any hope that Seat 3 would dial back the aggression after your call on the flop has evaporated. He's not bluffing, but even if he *thought* he was bluffing our opponent can certainly beat jack-high!

It may be painful to throw away a perfectly good drawing hand that connected so well with the flop, but you have to do it. Remember, even after a good flop, *drawing hands still come to nothing two-thirds of the time.* If you don't have a good opportunity to semi-bluff with your draw (and you often won't), then you throw the hand away and move on. You don't get stubborn about it.

You have no hand. A bet here would be a bluff. But your opponent has bet ahead of you, and you can't do anything about it. A call is out of the question. You can't bluff by calling!

Chapter Twelve

EXPERIENCE IS THE BEST EDUCATOR

Maxim 6: A man must strive toward his highest point.

We are not born perfect: every day we develop in our personality and in our calling till we reach the highest point of our completed being, to the full round of our accomplishments, of our excellence. This is shown by the purity of our taste, the clearness of our thought, the maturity of our judgment, and the firmness of our will. Some never arrive at being complete, always somewhat wanting: others ripen late. The complete man, wise in speech, prudent in act, will seek and find the company of other wise souls.

Maxim 18: Both action and ability are required to attain.

Where action and ability unite there is the greatest eminence. Mediocrity obtains more with application than superiority without it. Work is the price which is paid for reputation. What costs little is little worth. Even for the highest posts it is only in some cases application that is wanting, rarely the talent.

This may seem strange advice to read in a book, but poker wisdom is not exclusively book knowledge. Poker is a game of judgment, psychology, observation, information and mathematics. With the exception of the math (which is more than mere hand match-ups, extending also to things like bet-sizing, counting pots and stack sizes, and analysis of tournament structure), these are all matters that cannot be taught exclusively from a book. These things take time and experience to develop. What is the quickest and most profitable way to develop such experience?

EXPERIENCE IS BEST GAINED IN A LOW-RISK ENVIRONMENT

1. Online single-table sit and gos, particularly with more generous pay-off structures.

This is easily the single best place to start when learning the game. Single-table sit and gos combine the excitement and fixed buy-in of a tournament structure while providing a decent chance of actually winning. Whereas multi-table tournaments typically pay the top 10% of all players and skew the pay-out towards the top few of that 10%, sit and gos will pay at least 30% of the players at the table a decent return.

While the big prize payouts for the top three players at a 500-person multi-table tournament can be enticing, they really are a bit like buying a lottery ticket. The only way to be successful is to aim for the very top of that prize structure and hope that your bankroll can support the inevitable losses until you hit a big win.

Sit and go tournaments are also easier to beat than ring games. There's no doubt about it: the slow pace and fixed blinds of cash games take a great deal of patience and discipline to maximize wins and minimize losses on each hand. The rising blinds and the fact that tournament chips don't represent anything like real money creates faster, more exciting action and allows you to employ far more aggressive tactics than you'd see in a ring game.

Also see if the poker site you play at has a sit and go format that pays more than the top 3; Bodog, for example, offers a "Beginner Tournament" format that pays the top 5 players. If you finish in the top half of such a tournament, you at least get your money back. That's a very attainable goal and should minimize losses while learning the game.

What strategy should you employ in these tournaments? You need to play tight early on when the blinds are very low, playing only strong aces and pocket pairs. As the blinds increase, you can (slightly) lower your starting-hand requirements. Be patient, especially if more than the top 3 get paid. The greater the percentage of players that are paid, the more conservative you can afford to be.

BUBBLE AGGRESSION PRINCIPLE

You should be most aggressive when you're on the bubble (i.e. one player off from the pay-out), since your opponents will be loathe to take a big gamble when they're so close to winning. This is where most players make their biggest mistake: they tighten up on the bubble when there's easy money to be made. You should profit on their weakness through aggressive play, but be sure you're the one making the big bets. Do not make foolish all-in calls without some kind of hand.

Never let yourself get below 5x the big blind, even if you have to push all-in with a 72. If the blinds rise to something like $200/$400 or higher, just push all-in pre-flop relentlessly. There's no time to play poker when the blinds reach absurd levels, just push in and hope to steal a few easy pots before your opponents make a stand. At that point it's better to risk a coin-flip situation for all your chips than to risk getting blinded out.

2. Buying in for the minimum in a low-stakes online ring game.

It's possible to buy-in to a ring game online for $5 or less with nickel blinds. The fact that online sites do not pay for infrastructure and labor allows them to spread ultra low-stakes games. But playing in a low-stakes game with 100x the big blind probably just means you're going to lose money *very* slowly while you learn the game. There is an alternative.

Instead of buying in for the standard 100x the big blind, you can buy in for the minimum (perhaps 20x or even 10x the big blind) in a higher-stakes game. There, you employ a strategy that's basically impossible for the big stacks to defend against: you lie in wait for a big hand and either get your money in pre-flop or on the flop, preferably while two big stacks are maneuvering in a big hand.

If a big stack raises to 5x the big blind and receives a call from another big stack, you can just shove your little stack in and try to triple up. You've put your chips in there with what figures to be the best hand, and you may get odds handed to you if one of the players folds, leaving dead money in the pot. It's infuriating to the players with normal stacks, since they can't really defend against your strategy: they can only hope you have bad timing or bad luck when you make your move.

You will have "bad luck" on occasion, but you're risking very little money and can simply re-buy when you do. Over time, this is a winning -- albeit a somewhat boring -- strategy. You're guaranteed to get your money in with favorable odds, a long term recipe for success. And you observe the play of various hands and learn from more experienced players.

Maxim 11: Cultivate those who can teach you.

Let friendly intercourse be a school of knowledge, and culture be taught through conversation: thus you make your friends your teachers and mingle the pleasures of conversation with the advantages of instruction. Sensible persons thus enjoy alternating pleasures: they reap applause for what they say, and gain instruction from what they hear.

Maxim 43: Think with the few while speaking with the many.

To dissent from others' views is regarded as an insult, because it is interpreted as a personal offense. Truth is for the few, error is both common and vulgar. The wise man is not known by what he says on the house-tops, for there he speaks not with his own voice but with that of common folly, aware all the time of his own truth.

The prudent avoid being contradicted as much as contradicting: though they have their censure ready they are not ready to publish it. Thought is free, force cannot and should not be used to it. The wise man therefore retires into silence, and if he allows himself to come out of it, he does so within a small circle of fellow-thinkers.

Maxim 44: Model yourself after great men.

It is an heroic quality to agree with heroes. 'Tis like a miracle of nature for mystery and for use. Esteem towards an heroic figure leads to a sympathy of hearts and minds, and gradually transforms us into our heroes. It persuades without words and obtains without earning. Do not allow your heart to be tainted with jealousy towards their achievements. As sympathy with great men ennobles us, so dislike for them degrades us.

Maxim 81: Renew your brilliance.

Talent is wont to grow old, and with it fame. The staleness of custom weakens admiration, and a mediocrity that's new often eclipses the highest excellence grown old. Try therefore to be born again in valor, in genius, in fortune, in all. Display startling novelties, rise afresh like the sun every day. Change too the scene on which you shine, so that your loss may be felt in the old scenes of your triumph, while the novelty of your powers wins you applause in the new.

EXCELLENCE REQUIRES EXPERIENCE, PATIENCE AND GOOD EXAMPLES

Wall Street financiers like Sherman McCoy (of *Bonfire of the Vanities* fame) may call themselves "Masters of the Universe", but there have been few such individuals in history. Alexander the Great may be considered one "Master", a man who conquered the entire known world by the age of thirty and changed the course of history. How did he do this?

Although he possessed military genius and his armies employed the best cavalry of their age, Alexander's most important asset was his exceptional boldness. A lesser man in the exact same circumstances as Alexander would never have embarked on an adventure to the edge of the known world, squaring off with ancient empires and armies several times the size of his own. Where does such boldness spring from?

Alexander believed himself the son of the King of the Gods, Zeus. The ancient Greeks of his age believed in the literal truth of the Homeric tales of heroes borne of the gods. The most famous of these heroes is still well known in our day, by the Latinized name of Hercules.

Alexander's mother told him from a young age that he was the son of the King of Gods, with a divine destiny to fulfill. He studied the example of Hercules and his superhuman feats and set out to achieve the same (and more) on the world stage.

There are many brilliant people in the world who know enough to doubt their own ability, and there are many more fools who have the certainty to never suspect their own ignorance. When genius marries unflinching confidence, true greatness is born.

All those conquerors who followed Alexander (Julius Caesar, Napoleon Bonaparte, et. al.) imitated his real-life example just as Alexander modeled himself after the gods. The quickest path to success is to follow in the footsteps of one who has gone before.

For our purpose, we don't need to be god-like to achieve success at the poker table, but modesty isn't a virtue either. A deep conviction in your own talent, ability, and boldness, if tempered with the wisdom to avoid recklessness, will give you an edge. Picture yourself as a future Daniel Negreanu or Phil Hellmuth.

These people weren't always top-notch professional poker players. At one point, they were just young kids playing their friends in local home games. But they learned how to be excellent. And *if one person can learn how to do something, anyone can.* When you realize an "impossible" goal is entirely possible – because it's all been done before – you have a distinct advantage over everyone else.

When you're modeling Negreanu, Hellmuth, or Ivey, always remember to keep a rounded perspective; don't picture only their rabidly aggressive moments and most outrageous bluffs. In a tournament, they spent many hours playing small pots, making less exciting moves to build a solid chip stack. They made hundreds of routine folds to set up that big play you saw on television.

The select few hands you see broadcast on the World Series of Poker or the World Poker Tour are the most unusual, unrepresentative, exciting hands. You can't judge someone's playing style by a few big hands. Often, the professional players are able to make such bluffs because they've set that play up on previous (unshown) hands, or they have a good read based on hours of prior play (also unshown). Experienced poker players do not swing for the fences on each and every pot they play.

IT'S NOT WHO WINS THE MOST POTS... IT'S WHO WINS THE MOST IMPORTANT POTS

To profit in a cash game or to win a tournament, you need to win the *important* pots. You can lose three or four small pots if you're able to win one big, key pot *at the right time*. Often, what separates the great, from the merely good, is a well-timed, difficult fold that prevents disaster.

If you should find yourself playing against a professional or semi-professional player, don't be intimidated. Their advantage lies in their superior experience. They've literally seen most everything that can happen at a poker table. But every hand is a new deal, and just because they can draw from a vast reserve of experience doesn't mean they can run over you. Remember the following advice about celebrity:

Maxim 28: Be common in nothing.

O great and wise, be ill at ease when your deeds please the mob! The excesses of popular applause never satisfy the sensible. Some there are such chameleons of popularity that they find enjoyment not in the sweet savours of Apollo but in the breath of the mob. Take no pleasure in the wonder of the mob, for ignorance never gets beyond wonder. While vulgar folly wonders, wisdom watches for the trick.

You should be common in nothing. Don't stare and wonder how another player could be so great (hint: he's just been at it a lot longer than you). He may be a celebrity, he may be experienced and talented, but that doesn't mean he's any wiser than you. Our celebrity-obsessed culture may believe that popularity is a virtue – it's not.

Don't wonder with your mouth open; keep your eyes open for their tricks.

Besides modeling great players in your thoughts and actions (a tall order to be sure, but an important one), here are some other ideas to improve your play:

1. Visit online message boards. It is truly surprising the amount of useful information that can be obtained on such sites. If you can wade through piles of useless "bad beat" stories, a chorus of whining complaints about "cheaters" and the poker industry generally, a lot of shockingly poor mathematicians (which makes one truly wonder about the state of the Western educational system), and a fair bit of vapid parroting of the truisms of televised poker, there are some real pearls of wisdom here.

It's true this wisdom is often cast before swine (who love to criticize), but the discerning reader who is capable of thinking with the few while speaking with the many will separate the wheat from the chaff. Three of the best such discussion forums are found at: **www.cardschat.com** **pokerforums.fulltiltpoker.com** **forumserver.twoplustwo.com**.

2. Review selected books. The true value of a book is often found in one or two bits of wisdom that stand out from what others have written in the field. It is often these few key ideas that make the greatest impression on the reader, long after the specifics have faded from consciousness. Every fair-minded poker author has to give deference to the three-volume tournament hold 'em series by Dan Harrington as truly exceptional on this subject.

Beyond that, I would recommend books that teach specific principles by applying them to sample hands, as I have attempted to do. By walking through the play of real-life hands, the reader learns *how to think like a poker player*. Poker is not a particularly knowledge-intensive game, but it is a game that requires clear thinking and processing of information. Any book that teaches this thought-process has my whole-hearted recommendation.

3. Occasionally play outside your comfort zone. No matter the endeavor, to make progress you must challenge yourself. This usually means breaking out of your comfort zone and pushing yourself to new levels. Athletes perform better when playing against superior athletes. Intellectuals push the boundaries of thought by reviewing and critiquing the established literature in the field.

At the poker table, you challenge yourself by moving up in stakes. As you do, you'll play against more competent, aggressive players that will keep you on your toes. Just as a weight lifter will stop making progress unless he lifts heavier weights, your progress will stall if you don't challenge yourself. Don't get caught in PARTY POKER[1] purgatory.

PARTY POKER PURGATORY

At the height of the site's popularity, Party Poker featured hordes of the absolute worst poker players to ever grace a card room. While this was a profitable situation for experienced players, it also presented a problem: many new players were so random they were impossible to read. They could go all-in at any time, for any reason, with any hand.

---

[1] Party Poker is a trademark of the PartyGaming corporation. It is used here for identification purposes only. No endorsement or affiliation with Party Poker or PartyGaming is suggested or implied.

The only way to adapt is to sit back, wait for the cards to come to you, and trap one of these broncos. And you also need a healthy sense of humor to deal with the occasional suck-outs.

At the lowest stakes, you'll still find new and inexperienced players. They're rarely Party Poker bad these days, but they are predictable and easy to exploit. Fancy moves are useless against these players, because they spend most of their energy reading their own hand and give little if any thought to the cards you're representing.

Instead, you fall back on ABC poker, sticking to solid card values and straight-forward value betting. You bluff occasionally, and make some moves, but there's not much room for imagination. In fact, if you're not very careful, these loose players can completely confound you by playing any two cards from any position. Madmen do have certain advantages in a fight.

This is Party Poker purgatory. Frustration with illogical, random play can harm your own game. Worse, adapting to bad poker play involves stooping down to their own level --to understand what the heck they're thinking.

Many poker authorities say you're giving up some edge when you move up. This may be true in some cases, but if you feel trapped in Party Poker purgatory you may find the higher stakes more lucrative. There, you'll find players operating at your own level. It's easier to read (and to counter) someone who thinks like you.

RISK OF RUIN

Whenever you move up in stakes, there is a serious risk of burning through your bankroll. Fluctuations happen, and even winning players can have severe losing streaks. Manage your bankroll careful to limit the risk of ruin.

If you're a cash game player, you should buy in for less than the maximum at higher stakes to guard against this possibility. If you favor sit and go or multi-table tournaments, be sure you can afford a run of 10 losses.

This is conservative, but ten losses in a row can happen -- especially if you play multi-table tournaments that only pay the top 10%. In that case, you may want to bank for 20 losses or more. With multi-table tournaments, you're hoping one big win can cancel out a lot of bust-outs.

If you feel like you're outclassed by your opponents and find yourself doubting your own instincts, step back down, analyze your missteps, and regroup. Remember the most important factor in poker success is enjoying an edge over inferior opponents; if that doesn't exist, you're hoping that luck will save you.

In that case, you might as well be playing lottery or feeding a slot machine.

Chapter Thirteen

FOCUS ON THE WIN, NOT THE PAYOUT

Maxim 10: Fortune is fickle, but fame endures.

Wealth may last an entire lifetime, but fame survives death; fortune is desired by others and creates envy, while true fame is earned by respect. The desire for fame springs from man's best part. It was and is the sister of the giants; it always goes to extremes -- producing both horrible monsters and brilliant prodigies. Do not rely on Fortune and Her blessings to see you through, but the true fame that is born of accomplishment.

Maxim 66: Look past the moment and focus on the end goal.

Some regard more the challenge of the game than the winning of it, but to the world the discredit of the final failure is all that matters. The victor need not explain. The world does not notice the details of the measures employed; but only the good or ill result. You lose nothing if you gain your end. A good end gilds everything, however unfortunate the means. Thus at times it is part of the art of life to break the rules, if you cannot end well otherwise.

No matter the game, a purely defensive strategy is rarely a winner. In war, formations deployed defensively can be outmaneuvered and cut off from supplies. In chess, you must sacrifice some pieces to force your opponent to make mistakes. A purely defensive investor will underperform the market over the long term. And in poker, you must take some gambles to win an advantage. If you're focusing on your money, and not the end goal of victory, you won't perform at your best.

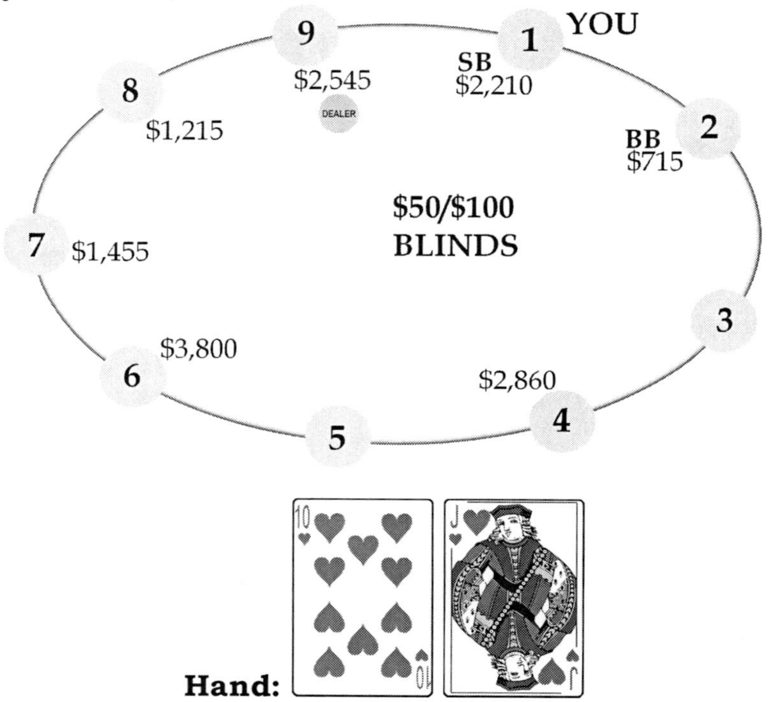

Situation: Mid-stages of a single table online sit and go tournament. There are seven players remaining, and the top 5 players get paid. Seat 9 has been playing a tight, somewhat aggressive game. Seat 2 is a bit short-stacked but has played a very weak, tight, conservative game.

Action: Everyone folds around to the button, who makes a standard raise to $300. The pot is $450, and it costs you $250 to call. *What should you do?*

Analysis: Given our decent chip position and the pot odds we're getting, this is a playable hand. We might be concerned about calling this raise with a short-stacked big blind, but with $715 in chips after posting he's not automatically committed to the hand. This is especially so since Seat 2 is playing a weak tight game and trying to hang on until the money. I wouldn't fault anyone who took the conservative approach and just called here.

However, what happens if we raise? The great thing about a suited connector like JT is its resilience; it will hold up well against almost any hand our opponent might have. Consider, even if the button has a hand as strong as AK, he'd only have a 59%-41% advantage over us.

The very, very worst-case scenario is our opponent has a big pair (AAs, KKs, QQs, or JJs... and believe it or not our hand would hold up best against the aces and progressively worse against the lesser big pairs), but we'd still win over 20% of the time against that range.

What are the odds he is that strong? He's 1.8% to have a big pair and 1.2% to hold AK... for a total of 3%. That's 32:1 against, meaning the much likelier scenario is that Seat 9 is raising with anything on the button (or a weak ace at most), trying to pick on the short stacked big blind. If he's actually weak, or has a weak ace, will he want to risk almost all his chips on this hand?

By raising here, what message do we send the button? We're saying, "Yes, I saw you raise enough to commit yourself to the hand if the big blind went all-in. And despite that, I'm re-raising you here, knowing that the short-stacked big blind is still to act." That's a power play, and any strong opponent in Seat 9's position will have to respect this move.

Will he really want to risk busting out on this hand, with Seats 2, 7, and 8 all below-average in chips? He can fold here and still have $2,245 in chips -- more than enough to be competitive. If you're trying to push someone out of a pot, be sure they have an escape route. If they're *pot committed,* you've just trapped yourself into playing a big pot with the worst hand.

Here are the factors that make this a valuable opportunity for a pre-flop re-raise:

1. Our opponent is raising from the button and may be making a move at the pot with nothing but position (relying on the fact that anyone calling his raise will have to act before him on the flop). Many players will almost always raise on the button if first to act.

2. We're edging towards the bubble of an online tournament, when players will tend to tighten up, not wanting to risk their tournament lives on marginal situations. As with most things in life, you should do the exact *opposite* of what others tend to do.

3. Our opponent has not raised enough to commit himself to the hand... he has not put

1/3 of his chips or more at stake and can afford to fold and still remain competitive.

4. We have enough chips so that if our opponent calls and loses, he'll be crippled.

5. We have a resilient drawing hand that even if called stands a decent chance of winning against our opponent's likely range of holdings.

6. Our opponent is a fairly tight, strong player who is actually capable of folding. Remember, you can't make a move against someone who simply won't fold. Don't even try it.

All those factors are present here; I would not advocate making this move if the majority of those statements -- especially the last one -- were not true. But how much should we raise? We need to raise a larger than ordinary amount, because the last thing we want is for Seat 9 to actually call our raise in position.

While our hand has great potential to win against most hands *if it gets to the showdown*, we're going to miss the flop about 68% of the time. Keep that figure in mind: with unpaired cards you will only make a pair or better roughly 32% of the time. In short, you're more than a 2:1 dog to hit the flop, and then having to act first with absolutely nothing is a very bad position to be in.

I would raise about half our stack here, $1,100 to $1,200. This is enough to let our opponent know that we are going with this hand no matter what: he can't raise us out of the pot, and if called, we're throwing all our remaining chips into the pot regardless of the flop.

Why not just raise all-in here? I wouldn't fault anyone who made that play, but in my mind a less than all-in raise often appears stronger. From your opponents' perspective, they'll be wondering why you'd make a giant raise with a very strong hand.

The key with a pot-committing raise is to choose an amount so large that no one thinks he can call and take the pot away from us on the flop. Usually a raise to 50-60% of our stack is enough to accomplish this purpose, but if this gives other players good pot odds, don't mess around with a less than all-in play.

Action: You raise to $1,200, the big blind folds, and the button lets the online play clock run down before folding his A8. Note that I can't fault Seat 9 for folding here -- it was the right play given the situation, a coin toss for most of his chips. His A8 was only a very slight 52-48 favorite to our JT suited, illustrating both the resilience of suited connectors and the weakness of ace-high. After showing his cards, he says with some annoyance that he'll call us down next time.

Analysis: Perhaps he is more likely to call us next time, but our move (with the worst hand) has earned us another $450 and put us in a decent third chip position. We can now afford to sit tight for a while and wait for the short stacks to get whittled down before making another move.

Focus on the goal of doing whatever it takes to win this tournament: don't wait for blind Fortune to deal you a perfect hand in a perfect situation. If you see a solid opportunity to make a bold move, make it! You can turn a losing hand into a winner.

DON'T NURSE YOUR CHIPS LIKE A MOTHER HEN

If you're playing a ring game and constantly separate your winnings from your starting chips (with the intention of preserving what you've won), you should just cash out and move to a new table. The other players will notice your careful arrangement of your "surplus" chips. They'll also soon pick up on your tepid play.

If you're playing in an online tournament and passing on valuable opportunities to earn chips because you want to assure a pay-out, you'll lose more over the long-term than you'll make by avoiding risk. Ask yourself, "Does it really matter if I limp into the payout and get my entry fee back?" You didn't sit through hours of poker play to break even. You entered with the hope and expectation of winning the thing; you won't be able to limp your way to the top!

Nothing is less successful than passive, scared, tentative poker. Ironically, by "protecting" your chips you're all but guaranteeing that they'll slowly be taken from you.

There are certainly cases where you don't need to make a big gamble with a slight advantage (e.g. calling a big all-in on a pre-flop coin toss). But don't evaluate risk only in terms of what you could stand to lose if a move doesn't work out. Focus on doing what it takes to win the game as a whole. Sometimes your best chance of winning is to take a big chance, knowing you have the worst of it.

Always look past the probabilities of any particular hand to see if you have an opportunity to further your overall chances of winning. Choose these spots wisely.

Chapter Fourteen

MIXING UP YOUR PLAY

Maxim 13: Be unpredictable, acting sometimes on second thoughts, sometimes on first impulse.

Man's life is a warfare against the malice of men. Sagacity fights with strategic changes of intention: it never does what it threatens, it aims only at escaping notice. It aims in the air with dexterity and strikes home in an unexpected direction, always seeking to conceal its game. It lets a purpose appear in order to attract the opponent's attention, but then turns round and conquers by the unexpected.

It always understands the opposite of what the opponent wishes it to understand, and recognizes every feint of guile. It lets the first impulse pass by and waits for the second, or even the third. Sagacity now rises to higher flights on seeing its artifice foreseen, and tries to deceive by truth itself; changes its game in order to change its deceit, and cheats by not cheating, and founds deception on the greatest candor.

Maxim 17: Vary the Mode of Action.

Not always the same way, so as to distract attention, especially if there be a rival. Not always from first impulse; they will soon recognize the uniformity, and by anticipating, frustrate your designs. It is easy to kill a bird that flies straight: not so one that twists and turns. Nor always act on second thoughts: they can discern the plan the second time.

The enemy is on the watch, great skill is required to circumvent him. The gamester never plays the card his opponent expects, still less the one he wants.

Maxim 98: Make your intentions indecipherable.

The passions are the gates of the soul. The most practical knowledge consists in disguising them. He that plays with his cards exposed risks losing the stakes. The reserve of caution should combat the curiosity of inquirers: play possum. Do not even let your tastes be known, lest others make use of them either by running counter to them or by flattering them.

WINNING POKER INVOLVES SOME COMPETITIVE ADVANTAGE

In any endeavor, long-term success or failure is based on the existence of a ***competitive advantage*** over your opponents. If you enjoy such an advantage, you can weather the turbulence of temporary setbacks -- what statisticians refer to as variance, or noise, from an expected result.

There are several unique competitive advantages you can employ in poker:

(1) Play ***stronger cards*** than your opponents, relying on superior discipline to avoid investing in hands with lower (or negative) average profit potential;

(2) apply pressure on your opponents where possible, relying on ***aggression*** to force a fold when you are unlikely to win the showdown;

(3) employ superior ***hand-reading*** skills to avoid investing where you're behind and helping to build pots where you're ahead;

(4) use ***selective bet-sizing*** to maximize gains on winning hands and minimize losses on failed bluffs, based on what your opponents can call given the play of the hand -- professional players spend a great deal of time trying to figure out how they could have "gotten that extra bet" out of a fellow, and analyzing if they could have "bet a smaller amount [on a bluff] and gotten the same information"; and

(5) ***select games*** with weaker opponents that make more mistakes in your favor. These are the five basic principles to profit at poker.

ALWAYS MIX UP YOUR PLAY (SOMETIMES)

As a poker player, mixing up your play is essential to prevent your opponents from reading your hand. This is necessary because poker is a game of information, not a math problem.

Of course, if you could actually see your opponent's hand, poker would reduce to a straight-forward mathematical exercise: betting or raising when you're ahead, folding when you're behind, and calling if you're being offered the right pot odds to draw. There would be no need for deception, unless you thought it could entice your opponent to make or call another bet when he's behind in the hand.

Since the rules unfortunately do not allow us to see our opponent's cards, we do the next best thing: use our analytical skills to deduce our opponent's likeliest holding. And we sometimes mix up our own play: checking when we're ahead, and betting or raising when we're behind.

Remember: we're doing this to confuse our opponent, *even though the optimal play for any particular hand is generally to play it straight.* In other words, we're willing to play a select few hands somewhat backwards just so we're not easy to decipher. We want the other players at the table to think, "*Not that guy, again; there's no telling what he's up to*!" If you want to be respected at the tables, remember:

Maxim 289: Nothing lessens a man more than to show himself like other men.

The day he is seen to be very human he ceases to be thought exceptional. Silliness is the exact opposite of reputation. As the reserved are held to be more than men, so the frivolous are held to be less. No failing causes such failure of respect. A clown can never be a man of weight.

You don't want to be just "one of the guys" at the table. You want to be unpredictable. You want to be a contrarian. You want to play loose when the table is tight, and tight when everyone else is loose. You want to be respected; you want your bets to be taken seriously. You want everyone to know that you're willing to pull the trigger – and more often than not it's fully loaded, cocked, and ready to go.

Mix up your play, and if the other players are adjusting to your style, reverse course completely. The other players should respect you at all costs; you'd rather be feared than be a loveable clown.

While you can't always be straight-forward, it's a much bigger mistake to play every hand deceptively. If in doubt, err on the side of playing the hand "correctly."

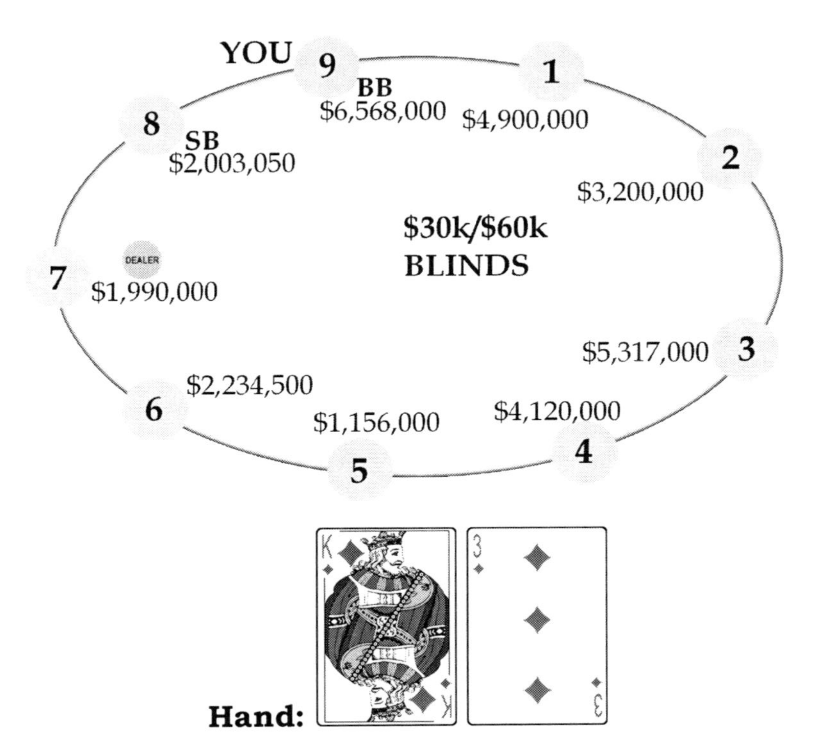

Situation: One of the final four tables at the World Series of Poker. Blinds are at $30,000 and $60,000, with $5,000 antes. Things have tightened up a bit with the higher blinds. You've been fairly tight and aggressive throughout the tournament, and you're currently the chip leader here.

Seat 1 has been fairly loose and frequently mixes up his play. When he comes into a pot you have no clear idea what he's up to. This style has been successful for him and he's in strong third chip position at this table.

Action: Seat 1 limps under the gun for $60,000. Everyone folds around to you in the big blind. With the blinds and antes, the pot is $195,000 and you're free to check or raise. *What should you do?*

Analysis: Well, we should be glad we're getting a free look at the flop here. However, it's getting down to the final few players and you have to be willing to make some moves if you expect to win the World Series of Poker. There's at least a case to be made for raising: we're heads-up against a loose player that hasn't shown any real strength, the pot is not inconsiderable, and with our chip lead, Seat 1 may not want to risk a big confrontation at this stage of the tournament.

We're one of two players at this table that could bust him, and we've been playing fairly tight. He might respect a raise here. If we do raise, we should make it clear to him we're not fooling around.

If we do end up playing a pot, our deceptive play means he could never put us on K3 of diamonds. But we won't feel too comfortable with our hand unless we flop a flush (0.84% chance), two pair (2%), or three of a kind (1.3%). Essentially, we'll have a 4% chance of making a well-disguised monster, and another 10.9% chance of flopping a flush draw.

If we flop merely one pair (26.9%), either the king or the trey, we'll have no idea where we're at in the hand. This is why king-rag, queen-rag, jack-rag, etc. are complete trash - even if you make a hand you can't like it too much.

We can also hope the flop doesn't help him (which will happen 68% of the time) and take the pot with a continuation bet; this is probably a high-percentage play for us given the strength we're showing in raising an early position limper, rather than taking a free check.

Make no mistake, the straight-forward, mathematically-sound, textbook "correct" play is to check here and see the free flop the vast majority of the time. If you raise now, you do so to mix up your game, disguise the weakness of your hand and hopefully take the pot down without a fight.

Action: You actually raise to $250,000, and Seat 1 calls the extra $190,000 without hesitation. The pot is now $575,000, and the two of you see the flop heads-up:

Analysis: Well you obviously don't need me to tell you what a fantastic flop that is: the absolute nuts at this point. Not only do we have the best possible hand right now, but it's unlikely our opponent can catch us even if we give him a free card. There's a slight possibility that he could have flopped a set or two pair and have a draw to a full house, but that's not something we can worry about at this point. How should we play to extract maximum value from the hand?

First we should note that we have absolutely no idea what our opponent could have. Usually a limp from early position indicates either a small pair or some sort of drawing hand. He was willing to call our pre-flop raise, but didn't re-raise us. If he was trapping with a pair of aces, he just got very unlucky, although he has a decent chance to catch up to us.

Still, if he had that hand, he might have sprung the trap pre-flop. If he had a decent ace, we might have expected him to raise, not limp, from early position. But since our opponent is very tricky, we can't really narrow down his holding too much based on what most players do.

But there are several factors that show this is a good spot for a deceptive check:

1. **We have a very strong hand and it's unlikely a free card will help our opponent.**

2. **There are many cards that can come on the turn that give our opponent a strong, but**

second-best hand: (any face card or ten for a straight or two pair, another diamond for a lower flush, or a card that pairs the board and gives our opponent a set).

3. **Our opponent is in position and may bluff at the pot for this reason alone, betting we probably missed the flop.**

4. **The board is particularly frightening (with straight and flush draw possibilities), so it's believable that we might check-fold here.**

5. **Our opponent can plausibly represent a big hand (aces or better).**

6. **Our slowplay of this hand can be interpreted as a flush and/or straight draw.**

On balance, I generally like a continuation bet after a pre-flop raise whether I hit my hand or not. With a very big, well-disguised hand, my opponent might get really out of line and raise with anything. But given the factors outlined above, a bet here doesn't make much sense for our hand. We've represented strength before the flop, and the board could have plausibly given us a very big hand.

If we lead out, we're representing at least a pair of aces and our opponent will fold if he doesn't have a strong hand or a big diamond. But a big diamond is unlikely given our own hand, and if he has a strong hand he'll bet it aggressively for us anyway. Passive play is not generally winning poker, but too many good things can happen if we give our opponent some rope to hang himself. I greatly favor checking this flop over leading out.

Action: You check, and Seat 1 bets what he calls “the speed limit” (the poker nickname for a pair of fives), $550,000. You decide maybe he has a little something, and maybe by just calling here you can represent a flush draw and/or a pair of aces that doesn’t want to build a big pot with this dangerous board. You call, and the pot is now $1,675,000. You both see the turn:

Analysis: That is exactly the type of action card we wanted to see when we slowplayed the flop. Our opponent may now have two-pair if he’s holding AK, AQ or KQ, or possibly a straight if he has exactly JT. Perhaps he has a king or an ace with something like the jack or ten of diamonds, giving him a pair, a flush draw, and an inside straight draw.

Our opponent now has a lot of hands and a lot of possible draws that can call a small bet. Since he showed some interest on the flop, you have to decide the best way to extract some extra value here.

I'd favor a smallish "defensive" bet here, something in the $500,000 to $700,000 range. We want this to look like a probe bet to cover either a flush draw or perhaps a hand like top pair that's now a little scared of this board. But continuing the slowplay is also an option, of course.

Action: You actually check again, and Seat 1 bets another $550,000. The pot is now $2,225,000 and it costs you $550,000 to call. *What should you do?*

Analysis: This is a very strange bet into such a large pot. An undersized bet is usually one of two things: (1) either a probe designed to block a larger bet your opponent might otherwise make, or (2) a suck bet designed to extract just a little bit more from your opponent when you think he can't call a normal bet.

Since the most obvious interpretation of our check on the flop and turn is that we are drawing to the flush, why would our opponent bet so little? If we called $550,000 on the flop, he must know we're almost certain to call $550,000 on the turn with a bigger pot and even bigger pot odds. This can't be a probe bet because he's in position and we gave him a free card; furthermore we know he can't be drawing to the nut flush because that's our own hand.

It's very peculiar, and somehow this looks for all the world like our opponent is trying to suck us in. This indicates some type of very strong, made hand: two-pair, a set, a straight, or maybe a lesser flush. He doesn't seem too afraid of the possibility of a fourth diamond on the river, though, so two-pair is probably out. A set might be willing to give us a cheap river card, but that would certainly be playing with fire. A straight with a diamond in his hand seems more likely, and would explain why he's not too afraid of a possible fourth diamond. A made flush is statistically very unlikely, but seems the likeliest explanation for our opponent's play.

We know he's such a tricky player he could really be messing with us. Maybe he really has nothing and he's hoping this second, smallish bet on the turn will be interpreted as a suck bet with a monster hand. This is very fishy; but we still have the absolute nuts so we don't mind playing along with what our opponent thinks is a "suck bet." Let's give him some more rope and see where this goes.

Action: You actually check-raise to $1,250,000. Your opponent ponders the action for about four seconds before announcing "call" in a fairly determined-sounding voice. The pot is now $4,175,000. You see a blank on the river:

Analysis: That nine of clubs couldn't have helped anything, and your opponent will know that. Any flush or straight draw has missed, and with the board unpaired, your nut flush is the best possible hand. Obviously your goal is to get the most money possible in the middle.

At this point in the hand, the pot has $4,175,000 in it and you've each invested $2,050,000. You have $4,518,000 left in your stack and Seat 1 has $2,850,000 left in his. Should you lead out with a bet, or just check?

The arguments for betting are slightly more compelling here:

(1) To charge a ***guaranteed showdown price*** - many players are (correctly) loathe to bet the river with a medium-strength hand for fear of being raised out of the pot, but willing to call a normal bet since they can see the showdown for a definite price: there are many medium-strength hands, like one or two-pair, our opponent can have here he won't bet but may call us with;

(2) to entice the ***Big River Raise*** - if our opponent has shown strength throughout the hand and we suddenly lead into him with a defensive-looking bet, we may entice him to make a huge, over-the-top raise, with or without a big hand. Here, there are many very strong hands (a set, a straight, a lower flush) and many busted draws that might draw a crazy all-in play, either as an aggressive value bet or a kamikaze bluff;

(3) to ***represent a river bluff*** - if you've been playing the hand passively all along, a sudden bet

on the river when a complete blank comes looks fishy, and may earn a call from very weak hands. Although we showed strength on the turn, leading out on the river could be seen as continuing a possible bluff on the turn.

The counter-argument to leading out right here is that our opponent has shown strength throughout the hand and made what seemed like a suck bet on the turn; he may believe he has a very strong hand and would bet it, and call a big check-raise, even if we don't lead out.

The risk of him checking behind on this scary board, and the reward if he decides to raise us all-in, argue for making a straight-forward value bet the majority of the time. Bet just under half his stack and hope he goes kamikaze.

Action: You actually bet $1,000,000, and Seat 1 quickly jumps out of his chair. "Did you have it all along?! The whole way!" he shouts. "But what would you bet here?" You had put him on some kind of set: maybe aces or kings that ran into trouble.

"Could you have a set?" he asks.

Well, that sounds like he can beat a set – players generally call out hands they can beat when thinking out loud. A straight? That's all that's left, since he seems scared of the flush.

He thinks for half a minute and then just flat calls the $1,000,000. He turns over his cards first and shows a JT offsuit (with no diamond), for the nut straight. You sheepishly turn over your K3 of diamonds for the nut flush, and take down a $6,175,000 pot. You should know the table will re-evaluate your "button tight" image.

Analysis: Well, our opponent had no real business limping in early position with an unsuited connector. He definitely shouldn't have called a large pre-flop raise from the chip leader with that hand.

Leading out on the flop with a gutshot straight draw -- and no diamond -- on an ace-high board was ambitious. He hoped to represent an ace, but if he had a solid ace why would he limp from early position, flat call a raise, and then make a very small bet into the pre-flop raiser on a very threatening board? After these mistakes, he was unlucky enough to turn a big hand -- he did a commendable job in losing the absolute minimum.

He had an automatic call on the river, and he clearly respects our play by taking that long to call with the nut straight. We were both being deceptive, but our hand was clearly much more surprising.

What kind of made flush could he put us on after our pre-flop raise? With both the ace and queen of diamonds on the flop, there weren't many diamonds of high rank remaining. Would we really raise him with the KJ or KT of diamonds? In fact, we raised him with much less!

At the end, he was probably hoping we had something like a pair of kings (maybe with the king of diamonds), and called the flop with our flush draw, the turn with our set, and were (incorrectly) value betting the river. Now it's clear why he didn't fear the flush draw: in his mind, there simply weren't that many hands with the king of diamonds in them that we could be playing.

By mixing up our game, our opponent had no real chance of reading our hand until the last possible moment. By then, it was simply too late.

This all turned out well, but if we hadn't hit our flush hopefully we'd have been as intelligent as our opponent here, and kept our losses to a minimum.

Chapter Fifteen

BE THE NICE GUY AT THE TABLE

Maxim 14: The way a thing is done is more important than the thing itself.

A bad manner spoils everything, even reason and justice; a good one supplies everything, gilds a "No", sweetens truth, and adds a touch of beauty. The how plays a large part in affairs, a good manner steals into the affections. Fine behaviour is a joy in life, and a pleasant expression helps out a difficulty in a remarkable way.

Maxim 52: Never be put out.

It is a great aim of prudence to never be embarrassed. It is the sign of a real man, of a noble heart: for high-mindedness is not easily put out. The passions are the tempests of the soul, and every excess in them weakens prudence; if they overflow through the mouth, the reputation will be in danger.

Let a man therefore be so great a master over himself that neither in the most fortunate nor in the most adverse circumstances can anything cause his reputation injury.

Maxim 83: Allow yourself some minor weakness.

Some apparent carelessness is often the greatest recommendation of talent. Blame is like the lightning; it hits the highest. Let Homer nod now and then and affect some negligence in courage or in intellect--not in prudence--so as to disarm one's enemies, or at least to prevent a worse result. You thus leave your cloak on the horns of envy in order to further your long-term objectives.

Maxim 129: Never complain (especially over bad beats!)

To complain always brings discredit. Better be a model of self-reliance opposed to the passion of others than an object of their compassion. For it opens the way for the hearer to what we are complaining of, and to disclose one insult forms an excuse for another. By complaining of past offenses we give occasion for future ones.

IN POKER, NICE GUYS FINISH FIRST

Poker has a lot in common with high school politics. Just as with adolescent electioneering, it's usually not the most intelligent candidate who does best. It's often not the most physically attractive, though handsomeness is always an advantage. It's rarely the strongest that will capture first, since athletes tend to have other time-consuming interests.

Instead, the winner is invariably the most popular, and that popularity is derived from being able to relate with and understand all of the above groups: a true leader is bright, moderately attractive (but not so attractive as to inspire jealousy), confident, and has a huge social circle to draw from. He or she is comfortable in many settings, and can form relationships with wildly diverse individuals and cliques. If you asked people to describe this junior politician, the most commonly heard adjective would be "nice."

In short it pays to be the nice guy, in poker as with all things in life. It's fine to be sociable, to talk with others at the table as much as possible -

- so long as you're exchanging pleasantries and nothing that discloses your predispositions on the play of various hands. Very few professional players at the highest level are stone-faced and unsociable while playing.

There are two key advantages to being -- or at least appearing -- nice: (1) you may lull your opponents into sympathy with you so that they are somewhat less likely to play back at you aggressively; and (2) you can glean information about your opponents' background, perspective, worldview, and thought process so you can more accurately gauge their style of play.

I especially like to maintain a very sociable relationship with the player to my left. Why? If I should play a pot with him/her, that person is almost always in position against me. This is an inherent disadvantage, so all things considered I don't want to play a big pot with this person. I don't want to be picked on if I should limp from the small blind, and in a ring game I'd prefer to chop the pot if it's heads-up in the blinds.

This effort at likeability is also helped if you avoid gloating over a big win. If you take down a big pot, express sympathy towards your opponent... it raises your likeability factor and can come in handy down the line. The universe is more generous towards a benevolent winner.

It's profitable to be seen as the nice guy at the table. I can't recall the number of occasions when I thought I had the best hand (say top pair), and another player turned a flush or hit some other, unexpected draw and gave me a free check on the river (often with a comment along the lines of, "I don't want to take any more of your money"). I'd have paid that person off, had they bet, but because I'm a nice fellow and made a show earlier of giving them or another player some (usually lesser) advantage, I got that free check that saved me a lot of money.

They were happy to scoop the pot on their unexpected suck-out, and I'm happy to have lost the minimum in the hand. Remember that profit can be earned both by maximizing wins and minimizing losses, and it's often the case that losing the least amount possible in a big hand can turn a losing session into a winner.

Now, some players make a big show of being angry, aggressive types. They hope to needle their opponents into making mistakes with their disrespectful attitude. If you adopt this approach, you should expect to get played back at more often, and you're hoping to have a big hand then. The problem with this is that big hands are rare. Encouraging other players to target you might actually improve their play.

Aggressive poker is winning poker, and even with strong reading skills I find it's better to discourage aggression. At the very least, being a jerk is forcing you to make a lot of big decisions in marginal situations. There are many ways to win, and it's possible to craft a mean, winning strategy, but I think these players win in *spite* of their attitude, not because of it. If you could inspire fear with your mean approach that would be helpful, but inspiring hatred and anger is very unhelpful.

While we want to draw on the advantage of being the nice guy at the table, it's important that we don't take this too far. The people you're playing against are not your friends (unless they are), they're not people you should be trying to impress, and you shouldn't be distracted by their charm. Keep the following principle in mind:

Maxim 191: Do not take payment in politeness.

It is a kind of fraud. Some do not need magic herbs, for they can enchant fools by the grace of their salute. Theirs is the Bank of Elegance, and they pay with the wind of fine words. To promise everything is to promise nothing: promises are the pitfalls of fools. The true courtesy is performance of duty. Compliments are offered not to the qualities that are recognized in a man but to the advantages sought.

Don't let another player's table chatter cause you to go easy on them. Don't be distracted by a pretty face. Don't react to any questions about the strength of your hand, or whether you'll show if the other player folds. Instead, sit there and breathe at a normal pace and clear your mind of any distractions. Chatty poker players are gauging your body language and reactions; nothing can be gained from engaging them. Keep your ego in check and your chips safe.

Be particularly careful not to complain about "bad beats" you've suffered in the past. Experienced players may listen to such stories, but they'll be interested in them as far as they reveal your predisposition in playing various hands. You lost a big pot when your open-ended straight flush draw was called down by bottom pair? Really! They'll say. What a shame!

Then they'll want to know what position you entered the pot from. Did you play the hand aggressively, or merely call your opponent's bets? Did you raise on the turn? Did you bluff the river?

They're looking to see if you have certain starting hand requirements from various positions, how aggressively you play a draw vs. a made hand, if you're conservative or aggressive generally, how you interpret your opponent's bets and raises, if you'll make a big bluff on the river after being called down twice, etc.

Keep your counsel to yourself, and never complain about "bad beats" at the table. You can discuss these things later, with buddies who are legitimately interested in helping you analyze your play. At the table, you have no bad beats to report.

This advice also applies to showing your hands; there is very little to be gained from displaying your hole cards. Perhaps if you're a very aggressive player you might show a big hand that wasn't called pre-flop, but ***never show a hand that went to the flop***. Whether you realize it or not, you have certain predispositions that govern your play of various hands, and nothing is gained by revealing them.

Chapter Sixteen

USE SCARE CARDS TO BLUFF

Maxim 45: Use, but do not abuse, deception.

One should not delight in it, still less boast of it. Everything artificial should be concealed, most of all cunning, which is hated. Deceit is much in use; therefore our caution has to be redoubled, but without alerting others to our skepticism. Remember that deception arouses distrust, awakens revenge, and gives rise to future confrontations.

Maxim 288: Act according to the moment.

Our acts and thoughts must be determined by circumstances. Will when you may, for time and tide wait for no man. Do not live by certain fixed rules. Nor become fixed in your habits, for you may have to drink the water tomorrow which you cast away today. There are some that expect all the circumstances of an action should bend to their whims and not vice versa. The wise man knows that prudence lies in steering by the wind.

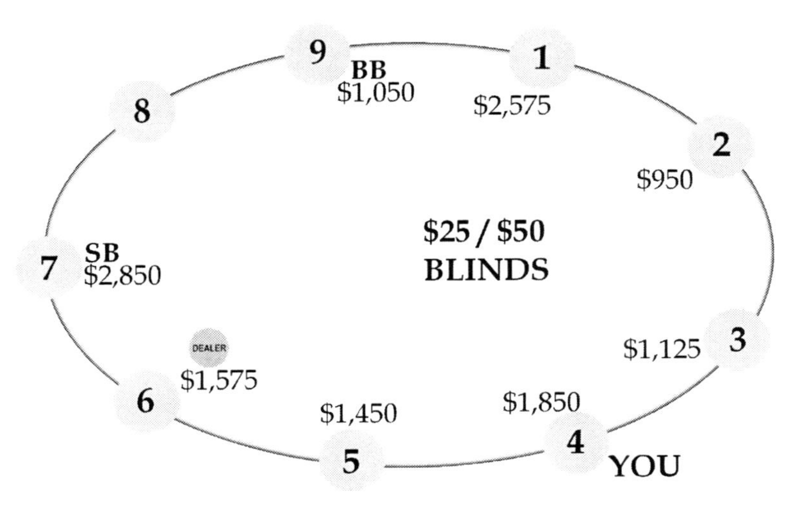

Hand: 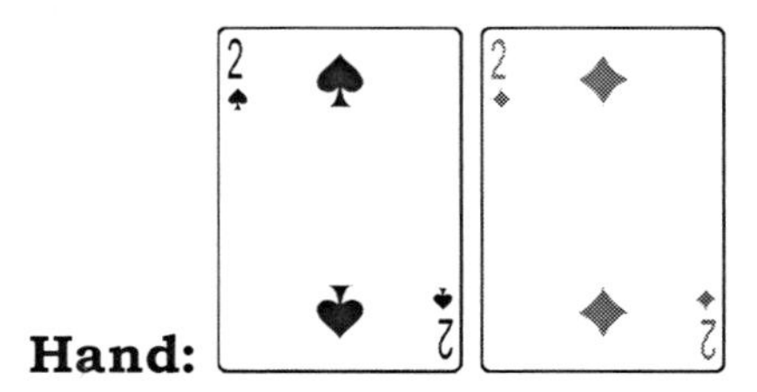

Situation: Early middle-stage of a single table sit and go tournament. The top three players will finish in the money. The button is a tight, somewhat conservative player. The big blind is loose and fairly passive, calling to see a lot of flops and quickly folding when he misses.

Action: The table folds around to you in middle position. You decide to play your small pair somewhat aggressively, and enter the pot with a standard raise to $150. You're hoping to get heads up with the loose, passive big blind.

WEAK LINK PRINCIPLE

Most of your profit at the poker table comes from isolating and exploiting the one or two weak links at the table. As soon as you sit down, you should start searching for the weakest player to pick on. Who's playing too many hands, too passively? Who looks drunk? Who's indifferent to winning or losing?

Perhaps it's a bit bloodthirsty, but think like a predator stalking a herd of gazelles. You'll have better luck chasing the lame than the lithe.

You've seen enough from Seat 9 to realize he is the weakest link. Seat 5 folds but Seat 6 calls your raise on the button. The small blind folds, and the big blind calls the extra $100. The pot is now $475 and the three of you go to the flop:

Analysis: That's a pretty unexciting flop for most hands that might have called our pre-flop raise. With two opponents, each of them has at most a 32.4% chance of improving on the flop (with two unpaired hole cards, and a mere 11.8% chance of improving if they started with a pocket pair). Taken together, that's about a 65% chance one of the two flopped at least a pair. But the generic odds aside, *not all flops are equally likely to hit all hands.*

Here, unless we're up against one of the playable hands with a queen (AQ, KQ, QJ or possibly QT), Seats 6 and 9 probably aren't too happy with that board. Of course, there are some other, more remote possibilities to worry about: a player could have flopped second or third pair, a flush draw, an open-ended straight draw with a 76, or an inside straight draw with a JT. But having a 76 out against you isn't very likely, and JT won't stick around long. And there are a lot of cards that can come on the turn and river to scare away second or third pair.

How about that flush draw? Well, before the flop each of our opponents had about a 5.9%

chance of being dealt two hole cards of a particular suit, whether of clubs, hearts, diamonds or spades. The odds either of them was dealt two clubs has gone down somewhat, since the board has been dealt two of the possible clubs (out of thirteen total). In other words, instead of drawing from a pool of thirteen clubs before the flop, our opponents were only drawing from eleven possible clubs.

Two out of thirteen represents a reduction of over 15% in the number of available clubs from which they had to draw (and the odds are further reduced because it's a double selection from the smaller pool – drawing two hole cards). This means the chance of a flush draw is *less than 5% each* (actually 4.68%), or 9.4% between the two of them. This concept is so important I want to repeat and restate the "don't fear the flush draw" principle:

DON'T FEAR THE FLUSH DRAW

While we need to keep a flush draw in mind as a distinct possibility (especially in a large multi-way pot), ***a flush draw is unlikely with few players and only two of a suit on board! Many amateur players are irrationally terrified of flush draws – again, don't be that guy***!

As in the case of the dreaded set it's less than a 5% risk, although it's less than 5% per opponent while the threat of the flopped set is even more remote, 5% versus the entire table!

So while a pessimist might say, "Well, those are three overcards to my deuces" and "there's a face card out there that might have hit somebody", this is actually a pretty good flop for our hand.

DON'T FEAR THE KING OR QUEEN

When you have a small pair or ace-high and haven't been helped by the flop, you shouldn't mind a king or queen out there. An ace or jack, however, is more likely to have connected with your opponents' hole cards. More playable hands from more positions are likely to contain an ace or jack than a king or queen.

Why? Many players will call with hands like J8, J9, JT, JQ, KJ, AJ and a variety of aces in position. But how many routinely play Q8, Q9, QT, or K8, K9, KT?

Note this principle applies to a *single* face card; if both a king and queen arrive on the flop, tread much more carefully. Then it's much more likely someone hit some kind of hand or draw.

If the flop were either A85 or J85 here, I would actually check this flop against two opponents a strong percentage of the time. In this situation, we either have the best hand, or our opponents are simply too weak to strongly contest this pot. We should usually lead right out with a bet.

Action: The big blind checks, and you bet $300. The button hesitates before calling, and the big blind folds. The pot is now $1,075. You have $1,400 remaining and the button has $1,125. The two of you see the turn heads up:

Analysis: Well, that's a perfect scare card! The most feared possible overcard to the board has arrived on the turn, and it completed the possible flush draw to boot. But consider, who's really more afraid of that ace of clubs?

That ace wouldn't have helped our opponent unless he actually had the flush draw, which we previously determined was only a 5% chance (or 10% combined with the other player in the hand). But the very arrival of a third club on board makes it *even less likely* that Seat 6 started with two clubs. And exactly what two clubs would he have been playing, with the ace, the queen and the eight of clubs all accounted for?

The board rules out a lot of the suited hands Seat 6 may have played: the Ax, KQ, QJ, 98, 87 or 86 of clubs. What's left? Did he really call a raise on the button with a KJ of clubs? A JT of clubs is a distinct possibility, and would fit the action thus far, but you should never bank on your opponent having one exact hand. A T9 or 76 of clubs are also remote possibilities, but either hand (and indeed the JT of clubs) might have not only called, but raised on the flop with that many potential draws.

Consider also that our opponent made a hesitant call on the flop, which often (though not always) indicates some type of relatively weak made hand. Someone with a drawing hand will often call quickly, since there's no real thought given to either folding or raising if the price is right. Perhaps he had a weak queen, like a QT or Q9, or a pair of eights or fives and thought we were just taking a stab at the pot. There's a distant possibility he might have called with just ace-high because he didn't believe us, in which case he just made his hand.

But he invested a lot of his dwindling stack to call with just ace-high, which is an unlikely move for a tight player. A strong made hand -- like an AQ or KQ on the flop -- is even more unlikely, since Seat 6 flat-called on a board with several draws, giving the loose big blind great odds to come along. All these considerations should tell us that Seat 6 likely flopped a weak made hand, and that ace of clubs probably didn't help him.

In fact, that card is a lot more scary to Seat 6 than it should be to us. We raised pre-flop and bet into two opponents, which is an indication of some kind of strength. We could have been semi-bluffing with a flush draw, we could have flopped a strong queen, we could have flopped a set, we could have started with a premium pair.

The button called us, which indicates he has something and also that he doesn't necessarily believe us. But if we were bluffing with nothing, our likeliest hand would be an ace-high, and now even if we were just making a continuation bet we got there.

Consider how hard this call is for Seat 6 even if he actually flopped top pair (queens). He probably isn't that strong, but even if he is, he's now kicking himself for not raising before that ace came on the turn. If we make a big bet here, he'll have to go all-in to see the hand through. He'll feel like an absolute fool if he gets busted with a pair of queens and an ace on board.

Strong, tight players don't want to feel like fools, and he'll rightfully err on the side of folding rather than risk his tournament in this marginal situation. If he has something like third or fourth pair, he'll happily fold, even though he's actually a huge favorite!

KEEP A RESERVE TO FALL BACK UPON

But when you do make a bet here on the turn, keep in mind the following maxim:

Maxim 170: Always keep a reserve to fall back upon.

A man should not employ all his capacity and power at once and on every occasion. Even in knowledge there should be a rearguard, so that your resources are doubled. One must always have something to resort to when there is fear of defeat. The reserve is of more importance than the attacking force: for it may yet snatch victory from the jaws of defeat. Prudence always sets to work with assurance of safety: a part may be greater than the whole.

It would be easy to simply apply maximum force and go all-in on the turn, but there are two problems with this. The first is that a huge, all-in bet is sometimes interpreted as weakness, whereas a more targeted, strategic amount often shows real strength. The second problem is the (unlikely) possibility we're up against a hand strong enough to call us, and any hand that will call this all-in bet can certainly beat our lonesome pair of deuces.

We don't even have the lowly deuce of clubs in our hand to provide a fail-safe, assuming we're not drawing dead against a made flush. While we've determined this is unlikely, it couldn't hurt to keep some chips in reserve if all else should fail.

Action: You bet $600, or slightly more than half of what the button has left in his stack. This is an important psychological threshold to cross, because betting more than half your opponent's stack will make it quite plain that if he wants to proceed with the hand, it's going to cost him all his chips. In the meantime, you've left yourself with $800 if he unexpectedly goes all in, so you can eject from the hand with a decent shot at coming back (with one strategic double up).

Saving this money for your stack gives you a decent reserve to fall back on should the need arise. When you make this bet, the button thinks a long time before folding, saying his eights must not be any good. They were, of course, but you still scoop a big pot!

When analyzing the texture of the board, it's easy to notice when a scare card arrives and immediately assume the worst. But step back, go through the play of the hand, and ask yourself just how likely it is that scare card actually helped your opponent. Would your opponent believe the scare card helped *you*, given the play thus far?

Since this takes a lot of analysis, you should anticipate scare cards that may come on the turn and river and how you should play them. What if an overcard arrives? A flush card? What if there are three or four to a straight on board?

In short, scare cards aren't scary just for you. They present opportunities to scare your opponent off of the best hand. You should plan to exploit a frightening turn or river. That way, you can profit both from cards that: (a) actually improve your hand; and (b) those you can plausibly represent as improving your hand. Act according to the moment, not just according to the strength of your hand.

TAKE ADVANTAGE OF A SCARY BOARD

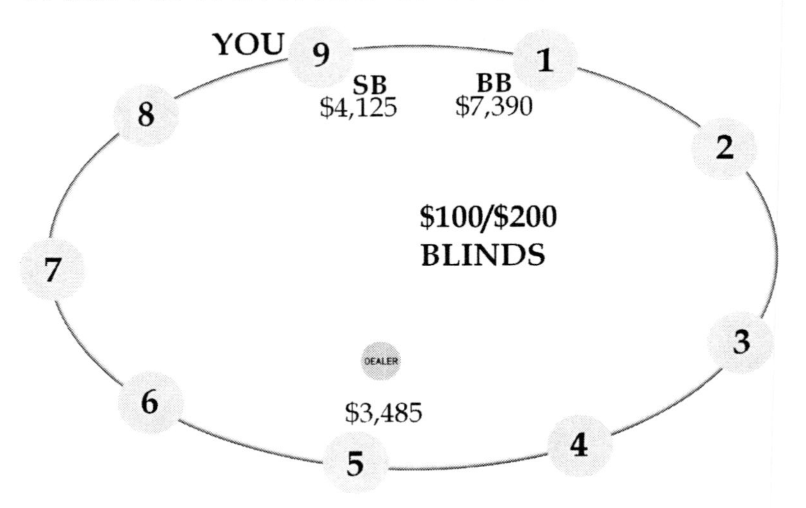

Hand: 

Situation: Late-stages of a single table online sit and go tournament. The table has tightened up the last few hands now that it's down to the final three players.

Action: The button folds.

Analysis: It costs us a half bet to call with a suited two-gapper. We have plenty of chips to spare, and our hand is perfectly playable in this spot. Of course we should call here. We shouldn't seriously consider raising, though, not against the big stack, with the blinds still relatively low. There's too little profit and too much risk in that move.

Action: We call, and the big blind checks. The pot is now $400, and it's a heads-up flop:

Analysis: That's a very scary board if you don't have a king or a diamond! We have no hand and no draw. Our cards are worthless: we'd need something like running jacks or running eights to make a legitimate hand in this spot. Since that's probably not going to happen, we should give up trying to play *our* hand. But that doesn't mean we should give up on playing *our opponent's* hand!

Remember to play the situation and not the cards. If we check here, we're signaling weakness and inviting the big blind to throw out a bet and try to steal the pot from us – with or without a hand. If we beat him into the pot, he'll have to think long and hard about making a move.

THE BIG BLIND WILL BE LESS AGGRESSIVE AFTER A FREE LOOK

Consider the hand from the big blind's perspective: he got a free look, and probably missed entirely. This is an opportunity to steal. Many players are protective of their blind, and will push back if they feel we're trying to rob them before the flop. But if they get a free look and see they've missed, they'll dial back the aggression.

Unless our opponent has a diamond or a king, he can't like his hand. Although he's sitting on the big stack, does he really want to invest a lot of money here, against the second largest stack? For all he knows, we could have a flush and he's pouring his money away!

We have nothing to lose by throwing out a bet here, representing either a pair or a diamond draw. If the blind can call, we know he has *something* and can safely check the turn.

IF A SCARE CARD DOESN'T MATERIALIZE, BLUFF AGAINST BUSTED DRAWING HANDS

If a fourth diamond doesn't come by the time the river rolls around, and the turn was checked, we can assume our opponent likely had a decent flush draw. We should strongly consider making a bluff at that point.

Bluffing the river after an earlier show of strength, when all obvious draws have missed, is one of the few times that a last minute bluff on the end is generally profitable. Usually an opponent that sticks around for the river is fairly committed to seeing the hand through. But if he has a busted draw, he obviously can't call.

Just because an opponent with a busted draw doesn't have a hand to call with, doesn't mean he still doesn't have us beat! Nothing is worse than checking the river in a busted draw situation and losing to your opponent's ace-high! You've effectively handed him a pot that he fully expected to lose. This is a case where you definitely *want to meet your opponent's expectations.*

Note that if we didn't show strength on any of the other streets *and* the river is an obvious blank, it might not be a good idea to bluff the river unless we're convinced our opponent must have nothing at all. The risk of getting called by any made hand (even bottom pair) is simply too great.

Action: You bet $260, and your opponent folds. You scoop an easy pot.

Little pots like this often make the difference between winning and losing. Don't underestimate the cumulative effect of scooping uncontested pots. Just because your opponent has given up on the hand is no reason to ignore those chips out there!

Chapter Seventeen

POKER IS NOT A RACE TO THE FINISH

Maxim 35: Think over things, and think most about the most important decisions.

All fools come to grief from want of thought. They never see even the half of things, and as they do not observe their own loss or gain, still less do they apply any diligence to them. Some make much of what imports little and little of much, always weighing with the wrong scale. Many never lose their common sense, because they have none to lose.

The wise man thinks over everything, but distinguishes where there is some profound difficulty. He asks whether there is more than meets the eye. Thus his comprehension extends as far as his apprehension.

Maxim 132: Do not judge hastily.

Especially when the course of action is unclear, you gain time either to confirm or improve your decision. It affords new grounds for strengthening or corroborating your judgment. If it's an acceptance, the affirmative is the more valued from being well considered than for being promptly bestowed: long expected is highest prized. And if you refuse, you gain time to decide how and when to mature the 'No' that it should be palatable.

Besides, after the first heat of desire is passed the repulse of refusal is felt less keenly in cold blood. But especially when men press for an answer it is best to defer it, for as often as not they are seeking to disarm your attention.

Many poker players behave like there's a race to see who can act on their hand the fastest. This is especially the case with online poker. There's a video game quality to the poker software which encourages hurried action. There's something about graphic avatars, animated action clocks and colorful buttons that encourages fast and loose play.

But if there is a race to act quickly, this is not a race you want to win. As you've seen in the hand examples in this book, there are many factors to be considered at each step of a poker hand.

While some decisions may seem fairly routine and obvious, there are always arguments for another course of action. If you don't take the time to carefully consider your options, you'll fall into predictable patterns of behavior. Your opponents will exploit your predictability.

Just as important as giving yourself time to think is *giving your opponent time to think about what you're up to.* At any moment, your opponent will have one of three hands: (1) a great hand (two pair or better); (2) a decent hand (one pair or draw); or (3) no hand at all.

Consider some numbers: On the flop your opponent is 73:1 against hitting trips with unpaired hole cards, 49:1 against hitting two pair and 7.5:1 against hitting a set with a pocket pair (these numbers do not include any *community hands* appearing on board). If your opponent makes it to the river, he's still 13:1 against having two-pair or trips. In other words, it's likely your opponent has just a decent hand or nothing at all.

Since your opponent is seldom very strong, you want him to think you're always considering an aggressive move. Even if you are fairly sure you're going to play it straight, let him sit there and ponder about what you're up to. He'll start to thinking, "Is this guy trapping me? Did he hit a set? Does he know I'm bluffing? Do I want to take a chance here? Why is he taking so long?! What is he thinking about?!!" All of this is to your benefit.

Players that act slowly and deliberately get more respect than fast-firing players. Those that act almost instantly probably aren't thinking very much. These players are just playing their own cards. They may have multiple tables open. Many are still good enough to beat novice opponents, but they generally aren't competitive at the higher stakes.

So take your time at the tables. You should never feel rushed into taking action. Online, I'd generally wait at least five seconds in a contested hand (except for automatic pre-flop folds, though I'd still avoid "auto-folding"). In person, you can take much more time, often as much as you need.

Just be consistent in your deliberations. You don't want to reveal anything about the strength of your hand by how long you take -- as for example acting quickly with a draw or taking an excessively long time with a monster.

Sometimes tough decisions may require extra thought, but this added delay isn't a problem if your move caps off the action.

To keep your actions evenly timed online, select a particular point on the play clock around which you'll make a decision. If you always take half your available time, for example, the other players can't read what you're up to. In person, play is more slow-paced, so exact consistency is less important. Simply develop a feel for how long on average it takes you to announce your move. Stick within that range.

Take your time, make thoughtful decisions, be consistent in your deliberations, and you'll give yourself an advantage over the fast-firing chip jockeys.

Chapter Eighteen

"PEOPLE ARE JUST LIKE ME" FALLACY

Maxim 58: Adapt yourself to your company.

There is no need to show your ability before every one. Employ no more force than is necessary. Let there be no unnecessary expenditure either of knowledge or of power. The skillful falconer only flies enough birds to serve for the chase. If there is too much display now there will be nothing to show later. Always have some novelty wherewith to dazzle. To show something fresh keeps expectation alive and conceals the limits of capacity.

Human nature is self-centered by design. It's not our fault: we are fashioned such that our entire experience is centered on ourselves. The sights, sounds, and other realities of the world are filtered through our own individual senses; our experience is limited by what we ourselves perceive.

There is a corollary to this self-centered principle: we cannot really understand other people except by relating them to ourselves. Since we literally don't think like they think, see what they see, hear what they hear, etc., we fill in the gaps with our own interpretations and assumptions. And these assumptions are colored by our perception of our favorite subject: ourselves. We imagine other people are pretty much just like us.

Perhaps we can never really know another person. This existential dilemma can be pondered over in a college philosophy class. For our purposes, the "people are just like me" assumption can be exploited at the poker table.

Adapt yourself to your company. If a player is tight and conservative, raise him more often. If another player is loose and aggressive, tighten up and wait for a good hand to play back. Often, the table as a whole will tend to one extreme or the other. You should play the exact opposite of whichever way the table is leaning.

Consider things from your opponent's perspective. If the tight player doesn't adapt, he mistakenly give your raises the same respect he gives his own (reasoning to himself, "*I wouldn't raise in that spot without a hand, so I guess the fellow has something.*")

Conversely, a loose player may assume you're also playing loose, and run into trouble if you manage to trap him. He'll reason to himself, "*I'd call a raise with a variety of cards, so his interest in this pot doesn't mean I'm in trouble.*" You can profit from this self-deception.

This is why it's critically important to keep tabs on your opponents. If you only pay attention to the hands you're involved in, you'll default to the "people are just like me" fallacy in reading your opponents' hands. The question is not how *you* would play a particular pot in *his* shoes: it's how *he* chose to. Try to understand the other fellow's reasoning process – in his mind, his play is perfectly rational.

Maxim 294: Most people's reason is tainted by inclination.

Every one holds views according to his interest, and imagines he has abundant grounds for them. For with most men judgment has to give way to inclination. Two may meet with exactly opposite views and yet each thinks to have reason on his side. Do not dismiss an opposing view out of hand. Place yourself in the other man's shoes and investigate the reasons for his opinion. Understanding the reasoning behind an unreasonable view may yield great advantage.

JUDO POKER: USE YOUR OPPONENT'S PLAYBOOK AGAINST HIM

Even the most observant player at the table pays by far the most attention to his favorite topic: himself. He may remember some of the key hands played around the table in a given session, but he'll certainly remember *every* detail of *every* hand *he* happens to play.

Since his own hands are at the forefront of his mind, your opponent's reasoning will be colored by his own experiences this session. With that in mind, keep a lookout for any betting patterns in shown hands.

Some key examples to look for:

(1) Any ***smaller than average bets*** (less than half the pot) – was he bluffing / semi-bluffing, or just extracting maximum value

from the hand? This is particularly important to notice on the river.

(2) Any ***larger than average bets*** (the whole pot or larger) – is he betting big with a huge hand or trying to blow the other player out of the water on a bluff? Again, pay particular attention to larger than average bets on the river if the hand ends up getting shown down. Did he have it, or not?

(3) Any ***check-raises*** at any point in the hand – tight players will almost never check-raise with nothing, but it's a powerful bluff in the hands of a loose player.

BECOME A REVERSE CHAMELEON

Once you've seen a player make one of these big moves in a session, note it. The next opportunity we have to play a heads-up pot against that fellow, we're looking for a chance to run his own play against him – in reverse.

Let's say the player in Seat 3 over-bet the pot on the river. He turned over an absurd bluff after his opponent folded. Trust me, he feels good about his audacious move. It will be right at the front of his mind for the rest of this session. It might even be one of the standard plays he *always* employs. He's now *looking for* that move.

The first thing to enter his mind when he sees an over-bet on the river will be the association he's now formed with his own prior bluff. Consciously or not, he assumes that other players are generally just like him. And in his mind, if he's fully capable of that play, everyone else is too.

Since this player's first thought will be along the lines of over-bet on river = bluff, we're going to over-bet the river with a very strong hand. You'll be surprised how often you'll be called down. Even when a player would mostly fold to an over-bet on the river, his reasoning process is tainted by the earlier play.

Over-bet on river = bluff = won a big pot = felt good about myself. It will take a great deal of evidence to the contrary to convince him otherwise. He may still be able to get away from a nothing hand, but he'll open up his calling range substantially. This is a great opportunity for profit.

It's important to keep adapting your play like this. If a particular opponent bets at least the pot when he hits the flop hard, you do the same (when you miss the flop completely). Don't make the mistake of always betting x amount whether you have it or not. This may be a good way to ensure you can't be read, but fails to exploit the psychology of the other players at the table.

In short, we pay attention to the other players' betting patterns *not only to read them*, but also to *bluff them*. One of the easiest ways to do this is to give them exactly what they expect (their own moves), but to reverse their meaning entirely. We know how they think – and we're thinking differently.

If this player is new to you, he usually won't adapt within a single session. Over several sessions though, a competent opponent will realize what you're up to.

Then we'll run our own moves against him, and let *him* try to figure *us* out all over again.

HOW DOES AN OPPONENT BET THE NUTS (OR NEAR-NUTS)?

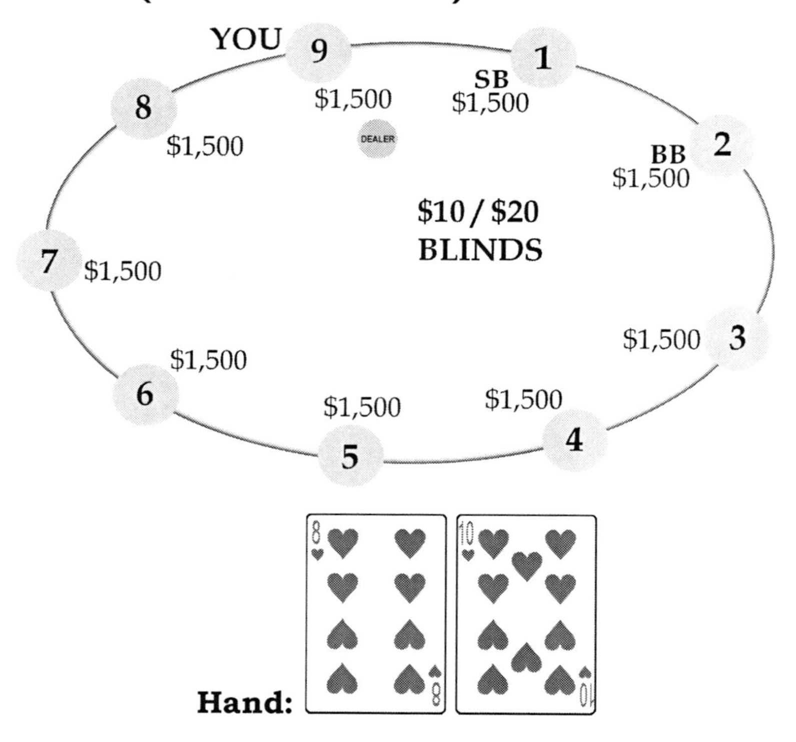

Situation: First hand of a single table sit and go.

Action: Seat 3 folds. Seat 4 raises to $70. Everyone folds around to the cut-off, who calls the $70. Action is on you on the button.

Analysis: The standard play is to fold here. Our suited one-gapper is not quite as robust as a suited connector, and we could be dominated by a lot of playable hands (T9, JT, QT, KT, or AT).

Nevertheless, there are some good reasons for calling here. Seat 4 raised from second position, so we have some idea about the range of hands he may be holding. Generally, players have a better than average hand when raising in early position at a full table (AK, AQ, KQ, AAs, KKs, QQs, or JJs). Meanwhile, Seat 8 had a hand strong enough to call, but not re-raise with. So we can tentatively assume he has either a small pair or a drawing hand. By narrowing down our opponents' likely holdings right from the start, we can adapt to whatever develops later on.

Another reason to call here is that it costs us very little to speculate, and we're in position. Against two deep-stacked opponents with the blinds so low, we may be able to earn a huge profit if we hit our hand. And if we miss entirely, we can easily fold later on.

So usually we should fold here. But if we're feeling aggressive and want to speculate a bit, a call isn't out of line in this spot. Just be sure that you don't routinely make calls like this.

Action: You call the $70. The blinds fold. The pot is now $240, and it's a three way pot. You're last to act in position. The flop comes:

Action: Both players check. Action is on you.

Analysis: That's very strange. Two face cards and a suited board with two other players and no one takes a stab at it? Why didn't the early position raiser make a continuation bet? He could easily represent AK.

In fact, what did he raise with that he doesn't want to bet now? The only hand that makes sense is something like AQ, with no spades. Any of his other likely hands are now worth a continuation bet (AK, AAs, KKs, QQs, JJs, or KQ).

Seat 8's check is not too mysterious. If he has a drawing hand, he may have paired that jack, with or without a spade to go along with it. If he has a small pair, he missed unless he had exactly a pair of sixes. He may or may not have a spade then, but if he does it's a low ranked spade. So he doesn't want to take the lead in the hand.

We of course have no hand and no draw. We also have no good reason to bet here, not until we know more about Seat 4's hand. He passed up an obvious bluffing opportunity. When a player checks in an obvious betting situation, you should proceed with extreme caution. He may have a monster and just be trying to string us along for a little bit.

Action: You check. The pot remains $240, and the three of you see the turn:

Both players check. Action is on you.

Analysis: Very strange. Maybe Seat 4 really doesn't have a hand? Even if he flopped a big hand (e.g. a pair of kings with the ace of spades) or a set of kings or jacks, would he really check twice on a board this dangerous? The flush, straight, and two-pair possibilities are beginning to mount.

And he's missing the opportunity to extract value from his cards. If he really had a big hand, why wouldn't he be trying to earn some money from one of us calling with second pair or a lone spade? Once the river comes, he won't get any action from some of the draws he could be facing.

The standard play when faced with two checks in a row is to *always bet*. There is nothing weaker than an opponent who checks twice. And two players checking twice are practically inviting a steal. It's possible our opponents are playing passive poker in the early-going. Let's exploit this. If we face resistance, we'll eject.

The argument for checking here isn't very good, but would go something like this: we now have a real hand (a pair of eights). Our opponents are acting suspiciously by checking twice in an obvious betting situation. The board is heavy on draws, so if we bet here we may get action we don't really want. The pot is big enough for our weak hand, and if we bet and get raised, we could be folding a hand that could win a showdown.

Action: You actually check. The pot remains $240, and the three of you see the river:

Seat 4 bets $100, and Seat 8 calls. The pot is now $440, and it costs you $100 to call.

Analysis: You now have two-pair (Ts and 8s), and probably have to call getting better than 4:1 odds. The hand has been played so passively that it's hard to put your opponents on much of anything.

Still, Seat 4's tiny little bet here on the river doesn't look like a bluff. Instead, it looks like a suck bet to extract a bit of value.

The odds are really good that our opponent backed into a big hand on the river, and our small two-pair probably isn't good enough to win. We still have to (reluctantly) call. This is what poker players refer to as a *crying call.* We're pretty sure we're throwing our money away, but at least in theory our hand might be good. We'll call, see the unlikely hand that beat us, and "cry" about it.

When you see a suck bet on the river, immediately consider what hands make the nuts or near-nuts. Here, those include a flush or an AQ, which just made a straight. The flush is unlikely, since the king and jack of spades are accounted for. The only way the early position raiser has a flush is if he raised with a suited ace-x of spades, but not AK or AJ. That leaves the AQ of spades or a trashy ace. It's not very likely that Seat 4 has one of those hands *and* that he decided to trap for two consecutive betting rounds only to throw out a very tiny bet on the river.

An AQ and a made straight are much more likely. That hand fits the action perfectly: a pre-flop raise with a strong hand, followed by two checks on a dangerous board. He's betting the river only because he's finally made his hand.

Nevertheless, we should still probably call. It's a long shot, but this could be a post-oak bluff, and Seat 8 could be calling with just a single pair.

Action: You call, and Seat 4 wins with AQ and the nut straight. You've lost a bit of money, but learned a valuable lesson. *Seat 4 makes tiny suck bets on the river with the nuts (or near-nuts).* The next time we play a hand against him, we should consider a post-oak bluff on the river! He won't automatically dismiss such a bet, since he uses it himself when he has a big hand.

Chapter Nineteen

FIRST-MOVER ADVANTAGE

Maxim 63: To be the first of a kind is a long step towards greatness.

To be the first mover is a great advantage when the players are equal. Many a man would have been a veritable giant if he had been the first of the sort. Those who come first are the heirs of Fame; the others receive only hand-me-downs: whatever they do, they cannot persuade the world they are anything more than parrots.

By the novelty of their enterprises sages write their names in the golden book of heroes. Some prefer to be first in things of minor import than second in greater exploits.

Business theory has long recognized the advantages of being the first-mover into a new market. Competitors are forced to react to the first-mover's initiative. They must choose between matching the first-mover's investment (with an uncertain profit outlook) or else ceding that ground to the established first-mover.

In the middle and late stages of a poker tournament, the blinds and antes become relatively expensive. Naturally this increases the competition for each and every pot – the high blinds present a lucrative market opportunity. Whichever player secures more than his fair share of these late stage pots has a definite advantage in the tournament.

Ideally, you would like to secure these expensive pots without a fight. But if your fellow players are going to resist, put the pressure on them. Don't wait for them to start pushing you around. Force them to respond to your initiative.

SKLANSKY'S GAP PRINCIPLE

David Sklansky, in his *Tournament Poker for Advanced Players*, states the Gap Principle:

"[Y]ou need a better hand to play against someone who has already opened the betting than you would need to open yourself."

Why is this so? If everyone has folded before you, you have two advantages: (1) some players are out of the hand, thus reducing your competition; (2) you can limp into the pot cheaply; and (3) if you raise, there's a chance everyone else might fold.

However, if the pot has been raised in front of you, none of these advantages exist. You have at least one serious competitor, you can't limp, and if you want to steal this pot you must make an expensive re-raise. Perhaps the initial raiser will fold to a re-raise, and perhaps not. It will cost you more to find out than it did for him to toss in the initial raise, however.

Perhaps worse, if you just call, there's always the chance someone can come over the top of you. You'll then be sandwiched between the initial raiser and the late re-raiser. Clearly, this is not a spot where you want to have a below-average hand, especially at an aggressive table. For all these reasons, your calling standards must be tighter than your raising standards.

HARRINGTON'S FIRST-IN VIGORISH

Dan Harrington, in his *Harrington on Hold 'em Vol. II*, adapts the Gap Principle to the late stages of a poker tournament. He points out there is an inherent advantage in being the first player to push all-in before the flop. When you're the first mover, there is always a significant chance that all the players acting after you will fold. You'll win valuable chips without a showdown.

On the other hand, by committing yourself before the flop, there's no chance of getting bluffed and folding the best hand. Players acting behind you are forced to gamble in the dark. Unless they hold AAs, you're often no worse than a 70-30 dog to their strongest hands, and you might be 60-40 or better.

Of course if we expect to be called as a 60-40 dog then this move rarely makes sense. But if we combine our winning percentage with the *vigorish* we gain by moving first at the pot (and causing everyone else to fold), this becomes a winning play. The *first-in vigorish*, in other words, represents the amount of money in the pot multiplied by the probability of everyone folding behind us.

First-in Vigorish = Pot x P(everyone folding)

To estimate the probability of everyone folding, we need to know something about their expected *calling ranges.* This means how strong they must be to call us down.

For example, if we're at a particularly tight table, perhaps the players acting behind us would only call our bet with a pair of jacks or better or AK. The chance of being dealt a pair of jacks or better is (0.45% x 4) = 1.8%; the odds of being dealt AK is 1.2%. Therefore, there is only a 3% chance of each player behind us having a hand within their expected *calling range.*

At an average table, players may call our pre-flop shove with a pair of nines or better, AK or AQ. The chance of being dealt a pair of nines or better is (0.45% x 6) = 2.7%; the odds of being dealt either AK or AQ is 2.4%. Therefore, there is roughly a 5% chance of each player behind us having a hand they will call with.

At a loose table, players may call our pre-flop all-in with a pair of sixes or better, AK, AQ, AJ or KQ. The chance of being dealt a pair of sixes or better is (0.45% x 9) = 4.05%; the odds of being dealt AK, AQ, AJ or KQ is (1.2% x 4) = 5.8%. Therefore, there is a roughly 10% chance of each player behind us calling our all-in. Let's illustrate these numbers with examples.

If there are 3 players to act behind us at a tight table, then there is a 3 x (3%) = 9% chance of being called down if we push. That means there's a 91% chance of everyone folding. If there were 7 players to act behind us at a loose table, then there'd be a 7 x (10%) = 70% of someone calling us, and only a 30% chance of escaping without a showdown.

As we can see from these figures, whether or not we should push any given hand is a function of three variables:

(1) Our opponents' expected *calling range*; the looser they are, the higher the probability we will be called – this reduces our first-in vigorish and means we need a higher win rate on our hand to make this play profitable.

(2) How many players are left to act– the odds of being called increases proportionally to the number of remaining players; this also reduces our first-in vigorish and increases the strength of the hand we need to move with.

(3) The size of the pot – the larger the pot, the greater the first-in vigorish will be, since we stand to win more if everyone should fold behind us.

A fourth variable to be considered are the relative stack sizes. The stack sizes of the players at the table are important because they affect our first variable, their expected *calling ranges*. If your stack is substantially below average, your opponents will widen their calling range, since it's less costly to gamble with you.

If you have less than three times the starting pot, then you have practically no *vigorish* at all. It is extremely likely someone will call you down. You simply wait for the best possible hand to get your money in.

It's a mistake to let things get to that point: attack relentlessly if your stack falls below average. Move while you can still do some damage.

WATCH OUT FOR THE EXTREME STACKS

The presence of either big stacks or critically small-stacked players behind you dramatically increases your chances of being called. The big stacks may want to gamble while they can afford to, and the small stacks are looking for any good spot to get their chips in.

You ideally want to push against medium stacks that can afford to fold. On the bubble, these medium-stacked players will have the tightest calling ranges.

Considering all these factors, you have the greatest first-in vigorish (and therefore profit potential), in a large pot with only one tight, medium-stacked player acting behind you. This scenario is actually quite common: if everyone folds around to you in the small blind, take the opportunity to steal from the big blind. If he can call, good luck to him.

Conversely, you have the least vigorish in a small pot with several loose, big-stacked players behind you. That's why we don't raise in early position at a loose table without a solid hand.

PUTTING IT ALL TOGETHER: "SHOULD I PUSH OR SHOULD I FOLD NOW?"

While the discussion above puts forth the general theory behind first-in vigorish, players want to know whether they should push or fold in particular situations. What hands do you need from what positions, at what stakes, to push at a pot in the late game?

The strength of your own cards is basically irrelevant. You can push with any non-trash hands, including ace-high, king-high, suited or unsuited connectors, one-gappers, two-gappers, and any pair. You can fold the weakest 50% of your hands in all but the most desperate (or favorable) of circumstances. Of course, you should also push with your legitimate hands.

Unless you're unlucky enough to run into a premium pair, the top half of your hands should give you the odds to push in the high blind stages (you have an M of 5 or less). Your *M factor* is the number of orbits you can afford to play at the current blinds if you do nothing but fold.

The main factors to consider in making a push are the blinds and your opponents' expected calling ranges. We saw before that a tight player will call with about 3% of all hands, an average player with 5%, and a loose player about 10%.

Fortunately, as our opponents loosen up (i.e. call with weaker holdings), our expected win rate will also increase. We can expect to win about

30% of the time against the tight player (20% if he has an overpair, 30% with one live card, and 40% if two live cards), 35% against the average player, and 40% against the loose player's calling range.

We get the following expected value formulas:

Tight Player: (.97)(Pot) + (.03)(.3)(M+1)(Pot) - (.03)(.7)(M+1)(Pot)

Average Player: (.95)(Pot) + (.05)(.35)(M+1)(Pot) - (.05)(.65)(M+1)(Pot)

Loose Player: (.9)(Pot) + (.1)(.4)(M+1)(Pot) - (.1)(.6)(M+1)(Pot)

The left side of the equation is the probability of our opponent folding (we win the pot); to this we add the probability of getting called and winning the starting pot *plus our whole stack* (i.e. we double up, which amounts to winning M+1 times the initial pot); finally, we subtract the probability of getting called and losing our whole stack. When these equations yield a positive result, we can push with an expected net positive value on the play per opponent. Simplifying:

Tight Player: (.97)(Pot) – (.012)(M+1)(Pot)

Average Player: (.95)(Pot) – (.015)(M+1)(Pot)

Loose Player: (.9)(Pot) – (.02)(M+1)(Pot)

I'll spare my readers the binomial mathematics used in solving these equations for multiple players. (For those that enjoy math, set the equation to zero and solve for M+1; multiple players involve reducing the uncontested win rate and increasing the expected loss rate if we're called proportionally to the number of players).

The handy little chart below will show you the maximum M you can push with and still turn a profit from an all-in move against the remaining players at your table under three scenarios: if your table is playing tight, average, or generally loose.

NOTE: Maximum M means you can push profitably if your M factor is less than or equal to the value listed in the chart.

Players to Act	**Maximum M - Tight**	**Maximum M - Avg.**	**Maximum M - Loose**
1 (small blind)	79	62	44
2 (button)	38	29	19
3 (cut-off)	24	18	10.666
4 (cut-off+1)	17	12	6.5
5	13	9	4
6	10.4	6.8	2.333
7	8.4	5	1.14
8	7	4	0.25
9	5.7	3	**Never**

NOTE: These figures assume you are the first-mover at the pot. If someone has limped or raised in front of you, play your hand according to its relative strength.

This chart doesn't have to be applied mechanically. For example, if your M is close to the maximum value for pushing from your position, the play will just barely be profitable. You may wait for a better spot with your tournament life hanging in the balance.

Further, if your M is above 10, you can play normal poker. You don't need to take the risk of shoving and running into a big hand, even if on average the play is expected to be profitable. Remember, your goal in a tournament is survival for the longest possible time, not necessarily maximizing expected value from each hand (as it would be in a ring game). You can avoid marginal situations if doing so furthers your objectives in the tournament.

Nevertheless, notice the broad take-away points from the chart. It rarely makes sense to push from early position at a loose table without a very strong hand. It always makes sense to jam the big blind if everyone else folds. A tight table can be exploited mercilessly (this is the basis for the bubble aggression principle). You can also see why it makes sense to raise from the cut-off and one off from the cut-off, except at the loosest of tables.

Let's go through a series of hands from an actual sit and go tournament to illustrate the first-mover advantage. As we start the sit and go, our hero is short-stacked in a six-handed game. In fact, with a stack of $1300, he's actually down from his initial $1500 in chips.

With blinds at $100/$200, he has an M of just 4.5 (i.e. he can survive for only four and a half more orbits at the current blinds levels). This is below what Harrington refers to as "*the red zone*" – our only move is to push. Things are certainly looking bleak for our hero.

Twenty-six minutes (and eighty hands) later, he finishes in first place. Never give up on the short stack, but don't force things to happen. You're not going to win the tournament in a single hand. Keep chipping away at the other players until you claw your way into the hunt. Let's ride into the red zone with our hero.

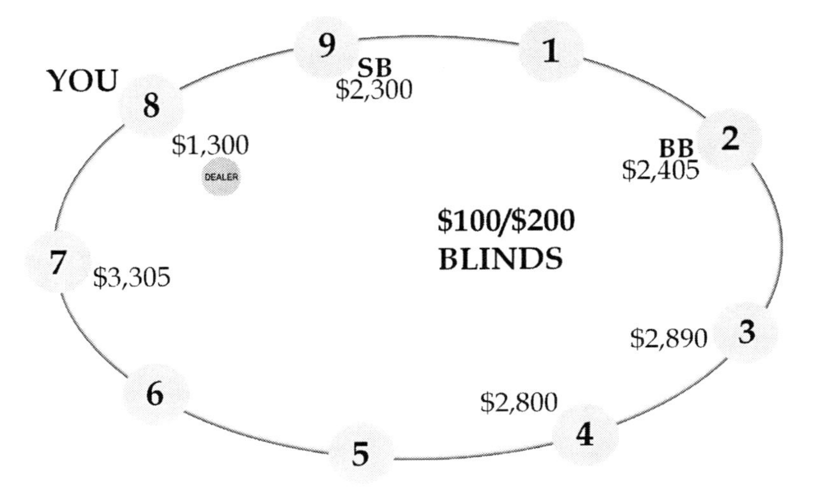

Hand: 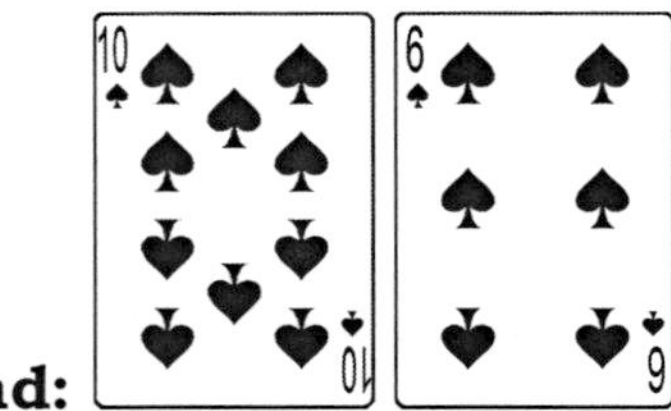

Situation: Late stages of a single table sit and go. Despite the fact that the blinds have risen to $100/$200, six players remain! With an M of just over 4, we need to make some moves in a hurry. Our only moves are all-in or fold. The table has been fairly tight all game.

Analysis: We're on the button with an M just above 4. From the table above, we can see that we're shoving with any hand if the table folds around to us. Even if the table were particularly loose (which it isn't), we'd still be right to shove with an M of 19 or less. We're well below that level and we need chips in a hurry.

Action: Seats 3 and 4 fold, but Seat 7 raises to $500 in the cut-off. The pot is now $800, and it costs us $500 to call from the button. *What should you do?*

Analysis: Fold. We don't have first-in vigorish since the pot was raised in front of us. He probably doesn't have much, but we don't have the chips to force him to fold. If we raise all-in here, it will cost him only another $800 to call a $2,100 pot. He'd be getting more than 2.5:1 on a call. Unless he knew we had aces, he could call with a variety of hands at that price. And he has the chips to do so.

Action: You fold, and both blinds fold. Seat 7 scoops the pot.

Note the dilemma of the first-mover advantage: it's best to push in late position (with fewer players to call), but by the time it gets to late position it's usually been raised in front of you. Sometimes you'll have the chips to consider coming over the top of the early position raiser, but usually it's not worth the risk.

In the late stages of a tournament, it's often a race to be first in the pot. This is a balancing act, though, because you don't want to take unnecessary risks by raising from a very early position and running into a legitimate hand. Try to be patient, but under no circumstances allow your M to fall below 3.

Let's hope we get a clear shot next hand.

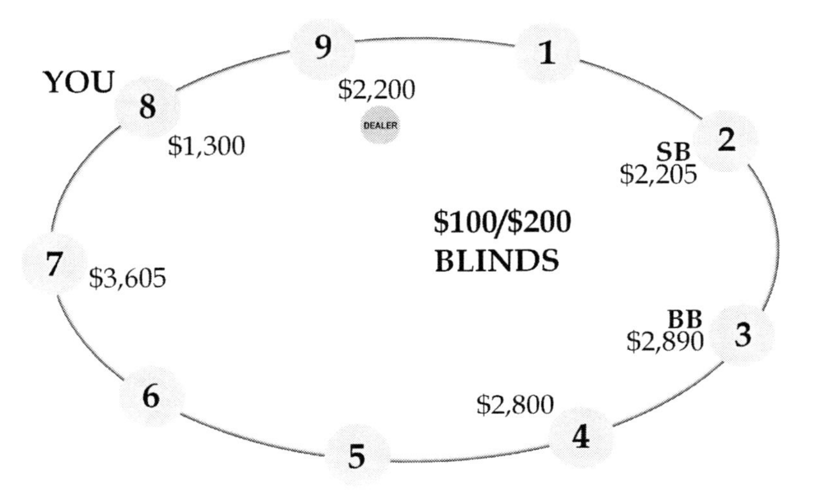

Hand: 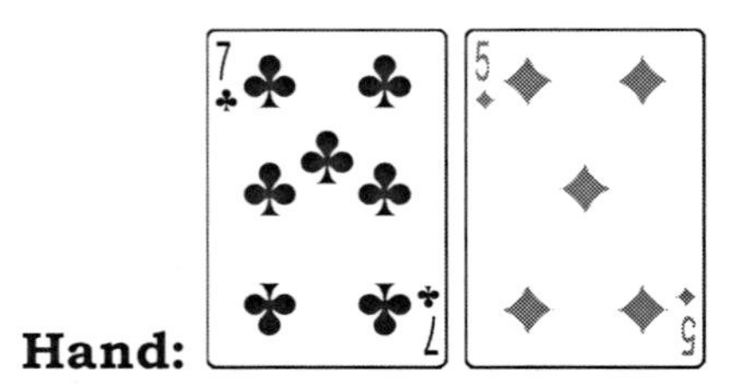

Situation: One hand later. We're in the cut-off with a fairly mediocre hand. If we fold here, we'll only have two hands to go before the big blind arrives.

Action: Seat 4 limps under the gun. Seat 7 folds. The pot is now $500, and it costs us $200 to call. *What should you do?*

Analysis: Fold. Calling is out of the question with an M just above 4. Our hand is fairly worthless anyway – at high blinds we're not looking to play drawing hands after the flop. It's all-in or fold. Unfortunately for us, a player has limped ahead of us.

Strong players rarely limp into pots with blinds this high, especially under the gun. It could be a trap, or our opponent could just be unskilled at poker tournament strategy. Either way, if we push all-in here and it's folded back to Seat 4, the pot will be $1,800 and it will cost him $1,100 to call.

He'd be getting 1.6:1 on a call. Those odds might be tempting, especially since he can lose this pot and remain in contention. When you're looking to shove, you don't want to make it easy for your opponent to call.

Shoving here would be a bold play, it just might work, and if our hand wasn't so weak it would be worth seriously considering. But the odds are that we'll get a better hand and a clear shot if we wait for the next deal before making our move.

High-blind limpers can be annoying when you find yourself in these must-move situations. If we had more chips to threaten our opponents with, we could ignore the limpers and push in regardless. Here, the early limper has killed our first-in vigorish, and we need to wait for a better spot to move. It's likely that we'll get our shot when we're second to act next hand. With only one player acting before us, it's likely we'll get our opening to be first-in the pot.

Action: You fold. The button calls, the small blind folds, and the big blind checks. The button ends up winning a $2,300 pot with his KJ vs. the big blind's K4, after the turn brings a king.

SHOVING ALL-IN RIGHT BEFORE THE BIG BLIND LOOKS DESPERATE

Almost without thinking about it we're making our move next hand. Nothing looks weaker than shoving all-in on the short stack right before the big blind comes around. Everyone recognizes that as a surefire sign of desperation. If we shove next hand, we won't look quite as pathetic.

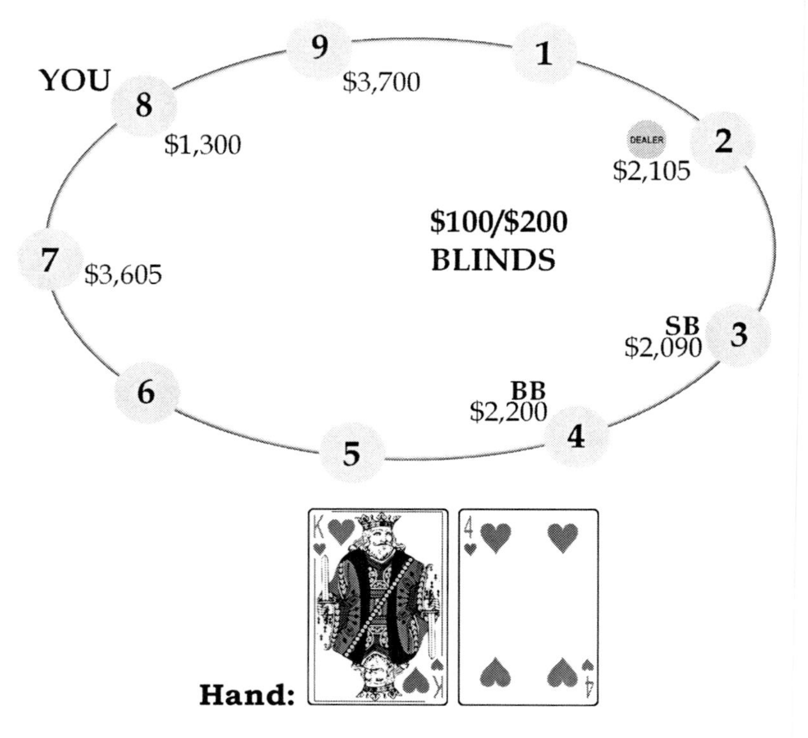

Situation: We're second to act before the flop, with an M of 4. Lucky for us, Seats 3 and 4 in the blinds just lost several hundred dollars the previous hand. This has leveled the distribution of chips somewhat, and we now have a big enough stack to thoroughly cripple either blind if they call and lose.

Action: Seat 7 folds. The action is on you.

Analysis: This is a no-brainer. One of the two larger stacks has exited ahead of us. The blinds were both weakened in the previous pot. And our suited king-high is the best we could hope for in this spot. Any king or ace-high is golden.

Don't fool around with a small raise. We don't want a call; we can't play king-high, no kicker after the flop. Our hand is not worthless: it has some *showdown* value. But we can't raise and fold, and we don't want action. Just push all-in.

Note that if we fold here, we'll have to shove the next hand or else put 15% of our stack into the big blind the hand after that. We don't want to look desperate by shoving right before the big blind; we don't want to push under the gun. This is the best spot we're likely to see.

Action: You push all-in. The rest of the table folds, and you pick up $300 in blinds. You increase your stack nearly 25% without a fight.

With $1,600, our M is over 5. We're still on the short stack. Our work isn't done by any means. But we're facing the blinds soon and we may have to surrender the gains we made here. Keep up the aggression without panicking.

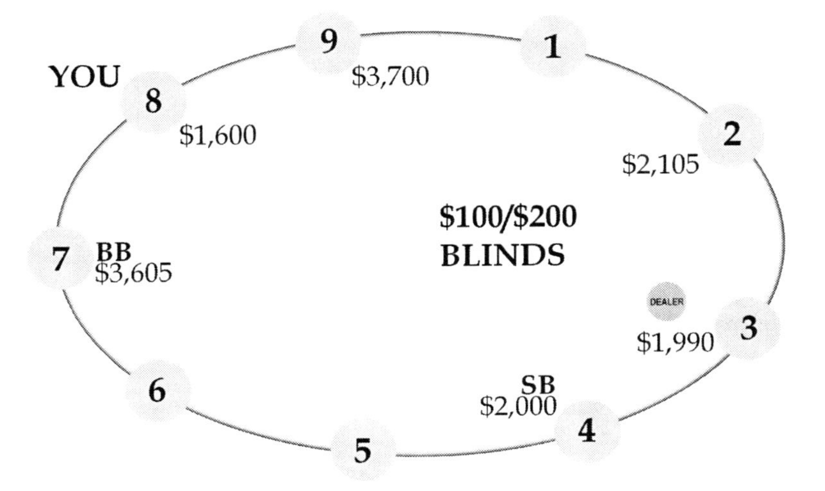

Hand: 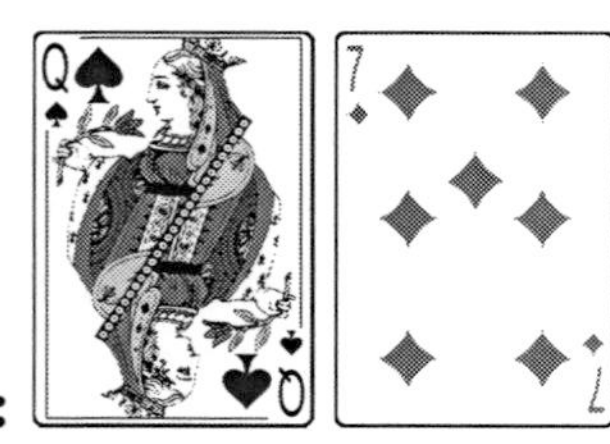

Situation: One hand later and we're under the gun with our Q7 off-suit. The action is on us.

Analysis: If we look at our chart, with our M of 5, a push is justified at a tight or average table, but would be unprofitable at a loose table. This is a pretty marginal situation, though. There are a lot of competing considerations about moving in here.

THE SECOND RAISE IN A ROW IS USUALLY FOR REAL

Players rarely raise twice in a row with nothing. They may or may not have a strong hand the first pot. If they raise the very next hand, however, they often show down a premium hand. It takes a tricky, deceptive, and bold personality to bluff twice in a row. Certainly there are players capable of raising back-to-back with nothing, but they're the exception. An all-in move could exploit this "second raise is for real" perception.

On the other hand, we don't want the rest of the table to think we're just pushing them around. We're not looking for action, and if we keep jamming they'll loosen their calling requirements.

Back-to-back all-ins, especially right before the big blind comes around, may look awfully suspicious. If they're willing to lower their expected calling range to "loose" standards, a push would be a mistake here.

In addition, our hand is pretty average, and there's a big stack in the big blind (and one to act directly behind us). The big-stacked big blind will have some odds to call us.

On balance, folding is probably more prudent. Facing the blinds again without picking off another pot may feel like treading water. This is fine. No one's running away with the game right now. If we can hold our own until we get a chance to double up, we can still win this thing.

YOU'RE NOT GOING TO WIN A TOURNAMENT BY STEALING BLINDS

A lot of players, especially on the short stack, impulsively try to steal their way back to the top. That's not how it works, though. The point of stealing pots is to keep ourselves in contention, with enough chips, so that when we finally double up we're back in the hunt.

Stealing blinds alone won't cut it. It's something we have to do, but we're really waiting for a big hand to double up. In the meantime we're just fighting to stay healthy.

Action: You fold. The button limps and wins an uncontested pot when he bets at a flop of 89T.

LET THE BLINDS IN AND SHUT THEM OUT AFTER THE FLOP

You'll see this at the high blinds. If you have a decent M, you don't always have to raise aggressively in position. You can alternate between being aggressive from the button and just limping, betting at whatever flops. The blinds will be less stubborn about releasing the hand after they've missed the flop (which they mostly will).

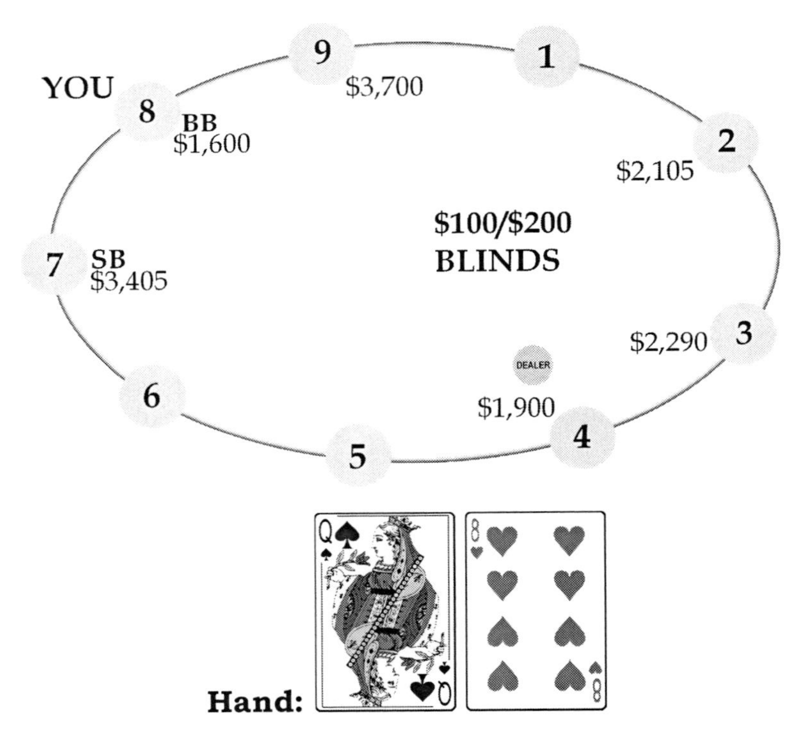

Situation: Next hand and we're in the big blind with fairly average cards. If we're lucky everyone will fold around to us. Always hope for the free pass.

Action: Seat 9 calls. Seat 2 calls. Seat 3 folds. The button calls, and the small blind completes. The pot is now $1,000, and the action is on you.

Analysis: Party in our big blind! Obviously, with four other players in the pot and our short stack, we're not going to move in here. Someone will probably call us down.

A SHORT STACK CAN'T BLIND-DEFEND

You'll see this quite a bit by the way. The other players will take advantage of a short stack by limping into his blind. If we were more critically short-stacked, they'd be hoping to collude in taking us out. This is why it's so important to maintain our arsenal of chips. We don't want to be the weak sister at the table.

Action: You check. The pot remains $1,000, and the flop comes down:

Analysis: Don't even think about getting your hopes up over an inside straight-draw on a paired board against four other players -- especially where the board has paired jacks. If the flop was 99J our hand still wouldn't be anything to write home about, but at least it wouldn't be a death trap.

DON'T PLAY AN INSIDE STRAIGHT DRAW ON A PAIRED BOARD

You're only 16% to complete an inside straight draw. To play this hand aggressively, you have to be able to count on the straight draw being a clean out. If the board is paired, a full-house is possible. Even if you make your hand you could still end up losing. It's not worth investing.

Also, while a paired board is generally a good bluffing opportunity, this is not so if the board has paired aces or jacks. Too many players will play too many combinations of hands with an ace or a jack in them (vs. a king or queen) to bluff here. And with four opponents limping into an un-raised pot, this is much too risky.

Action: The small blind checks. You check. Seat 9 bets $200 into the $1,000 pot, and Seat 2 calls. Everyone else folds. The pot is now $1,400, and two players remain to see the turn:

Action: Well, that's an interesting card. It's curious that Seat 9 bet so little at the pot. While designed to look like a suck bet with a hand like trip jacks, it also looks pretty weak. If he was going to lead out at the pot at all, why would he bet so little? Was he hoping to get raised? How likely is that on a flop of JJ9?

Instead, it looks like Seat 9 was trying to buy the pot cheaply. But he has to be concerned that Seat 2 right behind him could be slowplaying.

Action: Both players check. The pot remains $1,400 and it's heads-up to the river:

Analysis: That card is meaningless, and both players checking the turn means they probably have nothing. With the board paired twice, it's unlikely either player was really dealt a jack or a nine before the flop.

PAIRED BOARD HALVES THE CHANCE OF A PLAYER HOLDING THAT CARD (13:1 AGAINST)

Before the flop, the chance of being dealt a hand containing at least one jack is 14.8% (It's 14.8% to be dealt a hand containing at least one of any card, including ace-high). Since we've now seen two jacks, the chance of being dealt a jack was not 4/52, but rather 2/52 *plus* 2/51 on the second deal. Given this board, the chance of being dealt a jack pre-flop was about half as likely as normal, or 7.75%. The chance of being dealt either a jack or a nine is 15.5%.

In other words, it's over 3:1 against *either* player having a jack or a nine in his hand. But players don't select their hands randomly; how many playable hands contain a nine?

Action: Both players check. Seat 2 turns over:

And scoops with his two-pair: jacks and nines, ace-kicker. Seat 9 had a pair of fours, for two-pair on the flop. He was counterfeited on the turn, and didn't risk a bluff on the river with his three pair.

Analysis: We lost our $200 big blind on this hand, but with a strong ace and a pair of fours out against us and everyone limping into our blind, it was prudent to check-fold here.

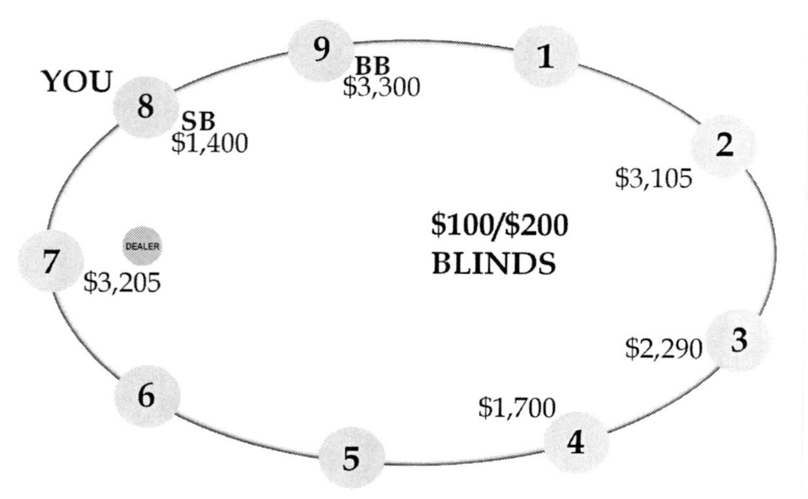

Hand: 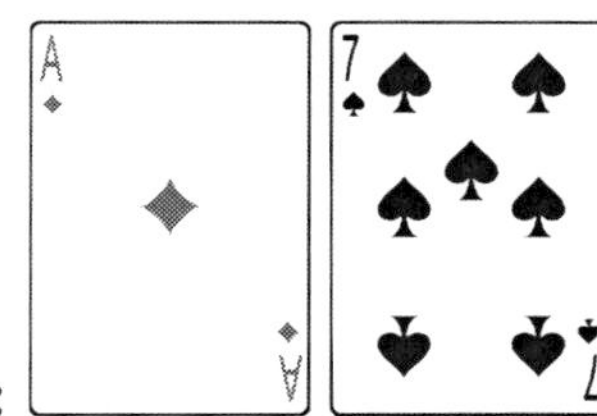

Situation: We're now in the small blind and delighted to see a decent hand. We'll only be dealt an ace 14.8% of the time. In other words, we're 6:1 against being dealt ace-high. At a six-handed table, since we have an ace, it's more likely than not the only ace out there. This is a hand we want to go with in this spot.

Action: Everyone folds to us in the small blind. The pot is now $300, and it costs $100 to call. *What should you do?*

Analysis: You don't need the all-in chart to know this is a hand to push with. It almost always pays to shove against the big blind, even if he has a large stack. With our M under 5 and $100 already invested, good luck to him if he can call. We have an actual hand if he does.

Action: You push all-in, and the big blind folds. You scoop the pot, and your stack is back to $1,600.

Analysis: On the short stack, you want to steal all the blinds you can. You also don't mind gambling if you're guaranteed a heads-up pot. Even if the big blind called here, it'd be a great shot for us to build our stack before we're blinded off.

Also note that our patience paid off. We were concerned about having to fold our big blind, and in effect, just treading water after our earlier steal. By waiting for a better spot, we made up for having to surrender our blind the previous hand.

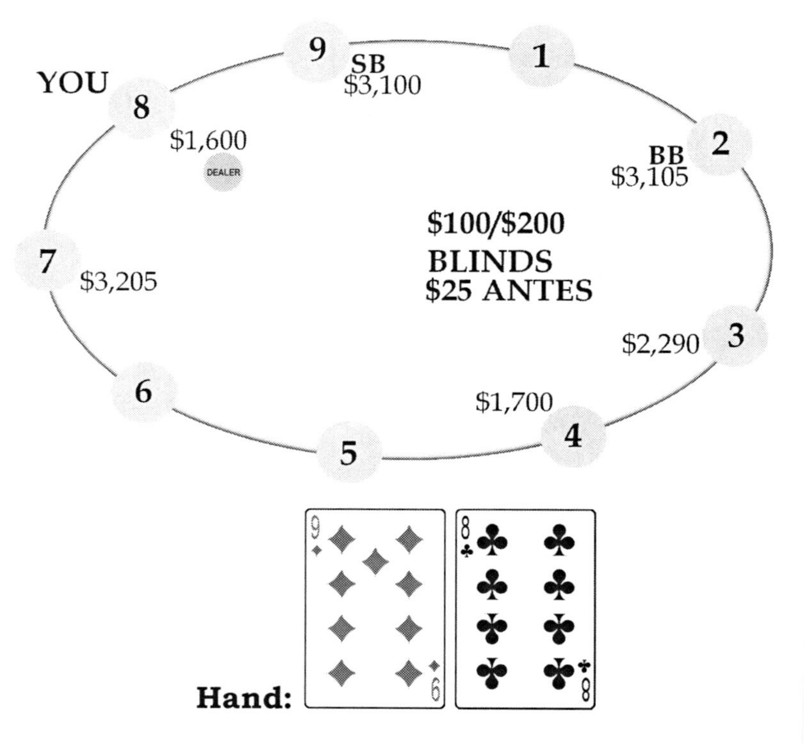

Situation: Still $100/$200 blinds, but now $25 antes have kicked in. This will cost us another $150 per orbit. Even after stealing two pots last round and increasing our stack from $1,300 to $1,600, our M is now down to 3.5. You can never rest in a hold em tournament.

Action: Everyone folds around to you on the button. *Should you push here?*

Analysis: With an M of 3.5 this should be an easy push from the button regardless of how loose the blinds are. Add to that the fact that the blinds have just increased.

EXPLOIT THE HAND RIGHT AFTER THE BLINDS INCREASE

There's something about the hand right after the blinds have ratcheted up. People tighten up enormously right after the forced betting increases. It's as if players suddenly realize it costs money to play. You can profit from your opponents' sudden bout of caution.

Play tightens up the most right after the antes kick in. Online, this may have something to do with the slick animation on the poker sites, showing the antes literally flying out of your stack. This makes players feel poorer (who likes their money flying off?).

Some are even superstitious about the new level, believing it's "bad luck" to play here. Once again, it pays to act contrary to everyone else. It especially pays to attack superstitious, illogical beliefs.

Action: You actually fold, and the small blind folds behind you. The big blind gets a walk, with an extra $150 in antes.

Analysis: Perhaps it's understandable our hero didn't want to jam twice in a row. A raise from the button looks suspicious anyway. And there were two big stacks in the blinds. It's probably a mistake; hopefully it's a relatively small one.

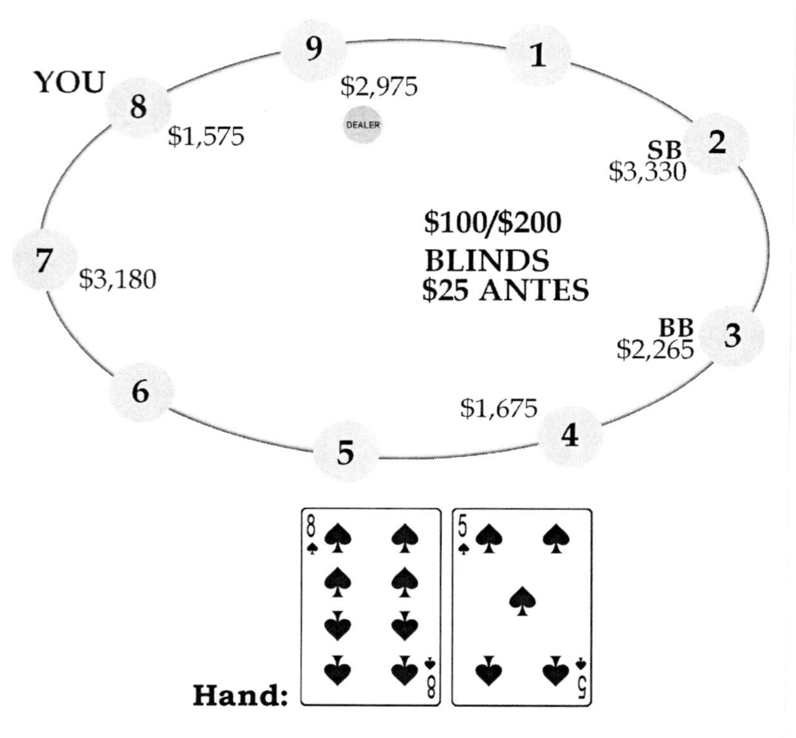

Situation: One hand later. Our M remains about 3.5, and we're in the cut-off.

Action: Seats 4 and 7 folds. *What should you do?*

Analysis: Again we should jam here. Our suited two-gapper isn't a hand to write home about, but our M is so critical we need to take some chances. On the bright side, if we get called down by high cards or a big pair, our hand has a little resilience with its straight and flush potentials.

Action: You actually fold, and the button makes a small min-raise to $400. The small blind folds, and the big blind calls the extra $200. The button takes the pot when he makes a continuation bet at a flop of:

Analysis: Since you would have flopped top and bottom-pair, you know the button was probably bluffing. You'll see a lot of min-raises and continuation bets when the blinds are high.

The big blind feels compelled to call a min-raise with most cards, but misses two-thirds of the time. Even if the big blind hits something, he's never comfortable playing a trash hand in a raised pot out of position. It's a good set-up.

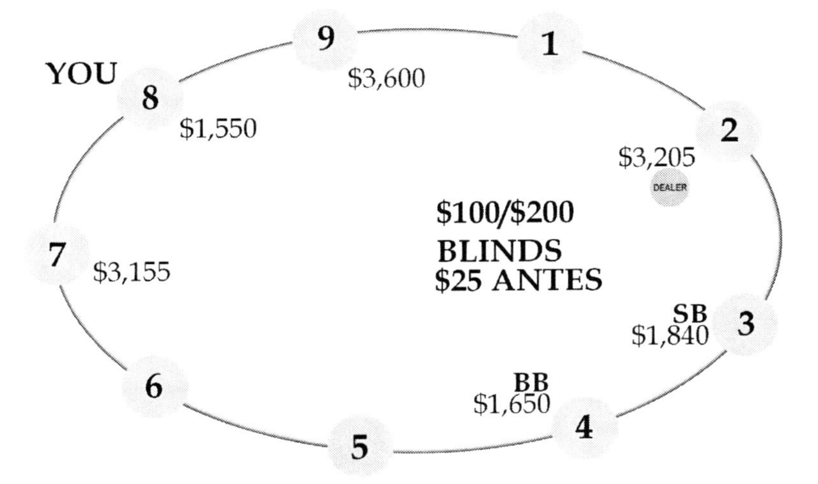

Hand: 

Situation: We're second to act with our J3 of clubs. Our M of 3.5 remains a critical consideration.

Action: Seat 7 folds. *What should you do?*

Analysis: Against four other players with an M of only 3.5, the chart says it's profitable to push even in this spot. This advice probably isn't wrong, mathematically, but this is a situation in which you might use some judgment.

For one thing, our hand is way below average (even though it is suited). The chart assumes that we're not completely dominated if we *are* called. Although we're 36% against AK even with this shabby hand, we'd be in a world of hurt against most pairs and several high card hands.

More importantly, we're not the only short stack anymore. Seats 3 and 4 are about as shabby as us, now. Because of this, we're not quite desperate enough to shove with complete trash here. We may need to go with whatever we're dealt next hand (which will almost certainly be better than this), but we're not the weak sister right now. The rest of the table is in no position to gang up on us, either next hand or if we have to wait until our big blind.

I can't really fault an all-in move here, but our hand is so weak I'd prefer to wait for the next hand. An all-in right before the big blind does look a little weak, but it's better to look weak than to be called down while *actually weak*.

Action: You fold. The hand gets checked down, and Seat 4 wins with ace-high. He had AK in the big blind.

Although you would have been called if you moved in, you actually would have doubled up by hitting a pair of jacks on the turn. The big blind's AK didn't improve by the river. This might have been a favorable result *this hand*, but folding was the better play under the circumstances.

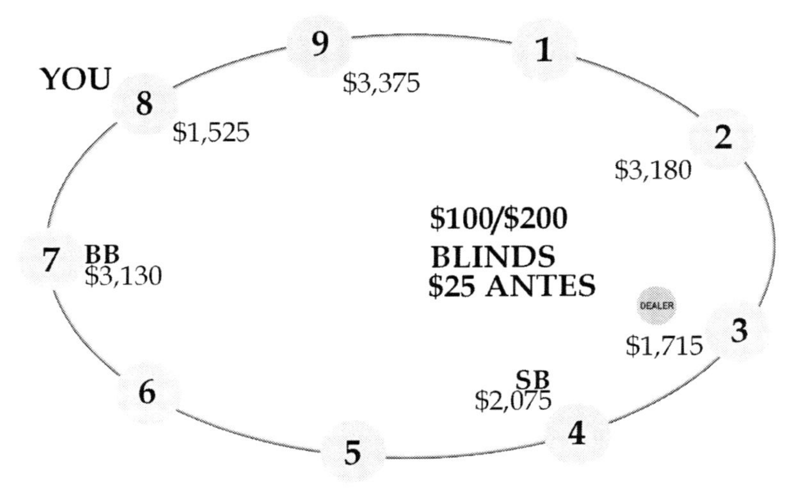

Hand: 

Situation: Under the gun with a critical M of just 3.5, you pick up KQ.

Analysis: Forget about the chart. The push chart merely shows favorable positions to move all-in *with a hand that figures to be a slight dog.* Of course, if we have a good hand in a critical M spot (a pair, ace-high, or king-high) we're going all-in. No point thinking about it for very long either.

Action: You go all-in and everyone folds. This is a good result, but you wouldn't have minded action either. This is a situation where you hope everyone thinks you're moving in with nothing right before the big blind.

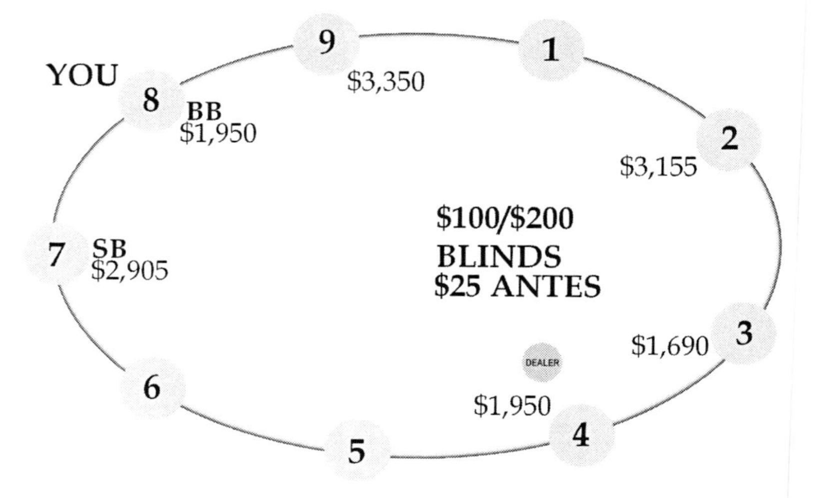

Hand:  

Situation: Back in the big blind again, without much of a hand. Let's see what develops.

Action: Seats 9, 2 and 3 all call. The button and the small blind fold. The pot is now $1,050 and the action is on you.

Analysis: We have no hand and we probably don't have enough chips to force all of these players out. Once again, it's a party in our big blind!

Action: You check, and four players see the flop:

Analysis: Yahtzee! There are darn few flops we'd like with our hand, but here's one. What should we do?

Rarely is there a correct and incorrect move in poker. Usually most moves are debatable. Here, *there is only one correct play*: we check this flop 100% of the time.

We're first to act, out of the small blind, with a short stack. We're never, ever folding this hand.

Our only objective is to get all the chips in. If we lead out against three players, we're signaling a great deal of strength. And on a flop like this, everyone else probably has absolutely nothing.

Don't even think of being tricky by being straight-forward or some other such nonsense. The only play here is to check and hope one of the players behind us bluffs at this pot.

For example, Seat 3 has an even smaller stack than we do, and he's in position. He could have limped with an ace or a small pair, and bet this flop with nothing but position. If that doesn't work, maybe someone will make a pair on the turn and bet it for us.

Let's give them all the rope they need to hang themselves with. We check this flop with trip jacks just as we would check this flop if we hit nothing at all. Any other play is silly *in this spot* – but that doesn't mean we always trap if we hit trips on the flop.

But we're almost always going to trap acting out of the small blind, especially when it's so likely we can sucker someone into betting for us.

Action: You check (give up on poker altogether if you seriously considered any other play). Seats 9 and 2 check. Seat 3 bets the pot, $1,050. The action is on you. The pot is now $2,100, and it costs you $1,050 to call. You have $1,725 left, and your opponent has $415 remaining in his stack.

Analysis: Perfect! Note how incredibly stupid Seat 3's bet is. He probably intended to show he was "serious" by making a full-pot bet. In the process, he has all but committed himself to the hand.

There's no real point slowplaying any more. A check-call here when your opponent has bet so much and committed himself to the hand isn't very believable. It's not very likely you're check-calling 60% of your stack with a flush draw on a paired board. The money is probably going in on the turn, unless Seat 3 can make a very disciplined fold (he's as good as dead anyway if he loses this pot).

So why wait? If we push all-in now, maybe Seat 3 will seize upon the glimmer of hope that we're just playing a flush draw or something. Plus, maybe we can shake one of the other players loose if they have some sort of straight draw, like a QT. Drop the hammer.

Action: You raise all-in. Both players behind you fold, and Seat 3 waits for two-thirds of his action clock to expire before calling his final $415 in chips off with his ace-high:

Analysis: What terrible play from beginning to end. Seat 3 could have made a minimum bet of $200 at that flop and solicited much the same information as he did by betting the entire pot (and committing himself to the hand). He put all his money in needing runner-runner aces.

His critical error was not pushing all-in before the flop. He had a relatively strong hand with a critical M. He may have feared the two limpers ahead of him, but that only made the move that much juicier. *You have to move with your big hands in the late stages of a tournament and hope they hold up.* You can't afford to hand out cheap flops with your premium hands.

Were we "lucky" to flop trip jacks out of the big blind? Were we "lucky" our weak opponent didn't raise us out of the pot with his strong ace?

Perhaps, but you've got to double up somewhere along the line. In a tournament you've got quite a few double-ups to make.

Note that in this series we stole three pots worth $1,050 before we got to this hand. If we hadn't made the moves we did to "tread water" before this hand, we'd have started this pot with $900 instead of $1,950. *In other words, instead of more than doubling up to $4,240, we'd now have about the same number of chips that we started this hand with!*

Was it "lucky" that we aggressively kept our stack in contention, so that if/when we doubled up we'd be the new chip leader?

Chapter Twenty

DEVELOP EQUANIMITY

Maxim 64: Don't worry about what can't be helped.

Neither give nor take bad news unless it can help. Some men's ears are stuffed with the sweets of flattery; others with the bitters of scandal, while some cannot live without a daily annoyance. Worry is a slow-acting poison, and there is no rule of life that you must suffer lifelong trouble in order to give a temporary enjoyment to another, however dear.

Maxim 262: Failure provides useful feedback.

The things we remember best are those better forgotten. Memory is not only unruly, leaving us in the lurch when most needed, but stupid as well, putting its nose into places it isn't wanted. In painful things it is active, but neglectful in recalling the favorable. The only remedy for pain is to forget it.

BAD THINGS HAPPEN: JUST BE SURE BAD PLAY ISN'T TO BLAME

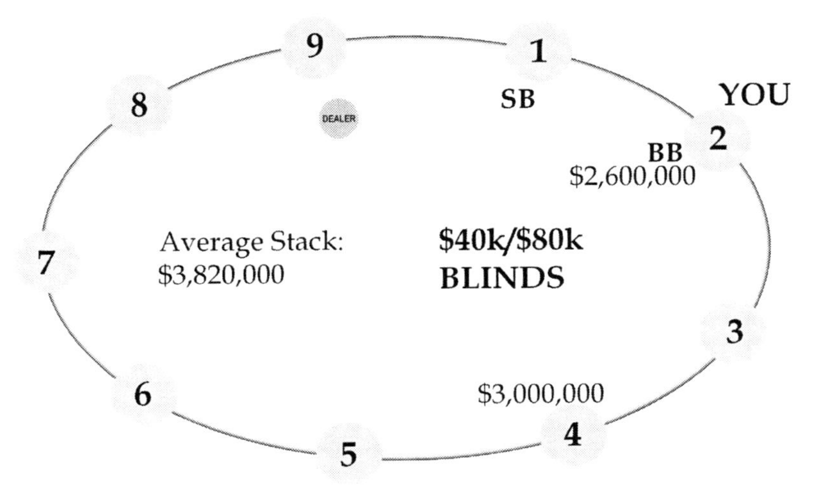

Hand:  

Situation: Final four tables of the World Series of Poker. We're a professional poker player with a reputation for loose, very aggressive play. In fact, we've been playing a very tight, patient game the past two days.

Seat 4, however, has been very loose. He seems to play most aces from most positions, will make small pre-flop raises with almost anything he deems playable, and has been caught bluffing in a few key hands.

We're in the big blind, and both of us are somewhat below the average stack. We'd like to isolate Seat 4 and play a big pot against him.

Action: The player under the gun folds. Seat 4 makes a small raise to $200,000. Everyone folds around to us in the big blind. *What should you do?*

Analysis: Against many opponents, this hand should be played cautiously. Ace-jack is not usually a hand we love to play against an early position raiser. We could well be dominated by AQ, AK, or a big pair.

We have more information here, though. Seat 4 is known to splash around, and ace-jack could well be the best hand right now. Even if it isn't, we've been playing very tight all day. We've shown some big laydowns lately, including a recent hand where we folded ace-king pre-flop.

With the high blinds and antes we're getting great odds to call, which is probably my favorite play here. But a re-raise to up the stakes in this hand against a loose, weak player is a tempting second-best option.

Action: You actually re-raise to $660,000, and Seat 4 shows little hesitation in calling an additional $460,000. The pot is now $1,430,000, and you're first to act after the flop:

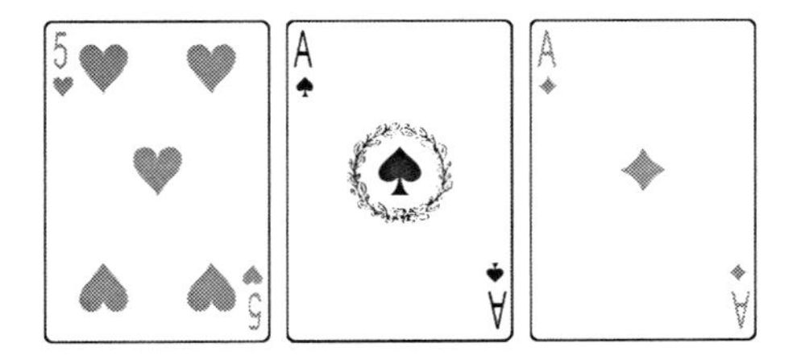

Analysis: That's about the best flop one can hope for. The only way we're beat is if our opponent started with AQ, AK or a pair of 5s. Our objective now is to get as many chips into the center as possible.

Unfortunately, this is usually difficult on a flop like this. Since three of the four aces are accounted for, our opponent would have to be holding the case ace or have flopped a set of 5s for him to legitimately bet. Alternatively, we can try to feign weakness and entice him to make a small bluff at the pot.

It's a cruel twist of poker fate that you can't make much money off your strongest hands. Most big hands (other than hidden sets) use most of the cards on board, so it's unlikely anyone else can have very much.

Here, the ace is an obvious scare card, and it's unlikely our opponent has an ace. A continuation bet here after a strong re-raise pre-flop might scare our opponent away.

On the other hand, we have a loose, aggressive image, and a meek check after a re-raise would look suspicious. Perhaps a bet would actually appear weaker, given our table image?

Action: You actually check, and your opponent quickly checks right behind you. The pot remains at $1,430,000, and you both see the turn:

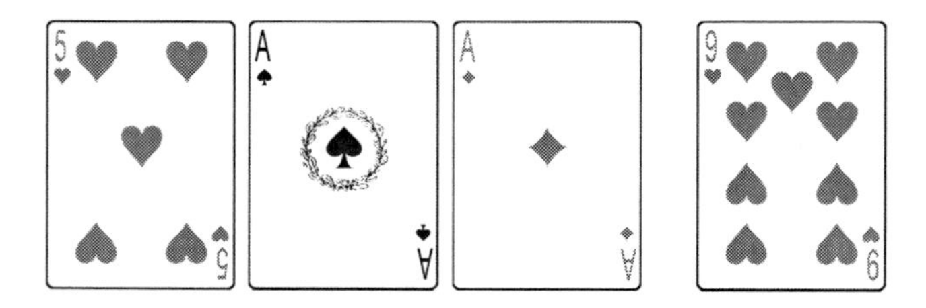

Analysis: Well, that nine of hearts is harmless. We're not too worried about a flush draw either, both because the pot is heads-up and because we're holding the ace of hearts. If our opponent has a better ace, pocket 5s or pocket 9s, he's likely to win a big pot. Otherwise, we might as well try to charge him something now.

Note that a bet here has the added benefit of looking suspicious. Could that nine of hearts really have helped our hand? Are we just betting a small pair, or maybe completely bluffing with a hand like KQ?

Action: You make a small bet of $500,000, and your opponent quickly announces all-in. This is surprising, but the guy has shown himself to be a fairly loose maniac. You're a little afraid he might have turned a full house with pocket 9s, but you can't lay the hand down. You call all-in, and your opponent turns over an unlikely full house:

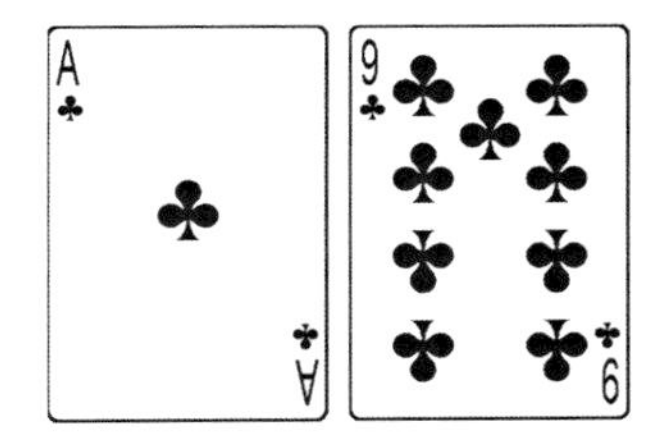

The river brings the king of clubs, and you're eliminated from the tournament when your trip aces lose to aces full of nines.

It's fairly stunning the gentleman in early position was willing to raise, and then to call a re-raise of more than 20% of his chips with A9. Then, rather than being punished for playing ace-rag (*suited*!), he caught an unlikely three-outer on the turn.

The lesson here is that sometimes there is no lesson to be learned. At each step of the way we made the correct play, and simply could not have gotten away from the hand after the flop. Our opponent was obviously committed to the pot after the flop as well.

If there is one thing that could have changed the outcome in this hand, it's our table image. We've been branded as a loose, aggressive wild man, and the advertising has paid off well. Unfortunately, here it meant that our pre-flop raise wasn't given nearly enough respect. This shows there are advantages and disadvantages to being seen as either tight or loose.

But we didn't make any mistakes in this particular hand, and we shouldn't worry over what cannot be helped. Sometimes stuff just happens, and there's no particular reason you should try to find in it.

Chapter Twenty-One

RELATIVE CHIP POSITION

Maxim 84: Make use of your enemies.

You should learn to seize things not by the blade, which cuts, but by the handle, which saves you from harm: especially is this the rule with the doings of your enemies. A wise man gets more use from his enemies than a fool from his friends. Their ill-will often levels mountains of difficulties which one would otherwise face. Many have had their greatness made for them by their enemies. Flattery is more dangerous than hatred, because it covers the stains which the other causes to be wiped out.

When you have a big stack, there's a temptation to single-handedly finish off the other players at the table. This is a mistake. You don't win extra points by scoring death blows against your opponents, and if you start gambling recklessly you'll leave yourself vulnerable.

Don't take unnecessary chances with your chips. You're better off standing aside and letting the small and medium stacks duke it out. You win either way: if the small stacks bust out you advance up the pay scale; if they double up through the medium stacks, you have two relatively weak opponents to face.

Slip in between the big confrontations and steal pots where no one wants to fight. You should be the aggressor, betting and raising pre-flop. You should not be in a reactive mode, calling other player's bets. Do so only with solid hand values.

STEAL POTS WHERE NO ONE WANTS TO FIGHT

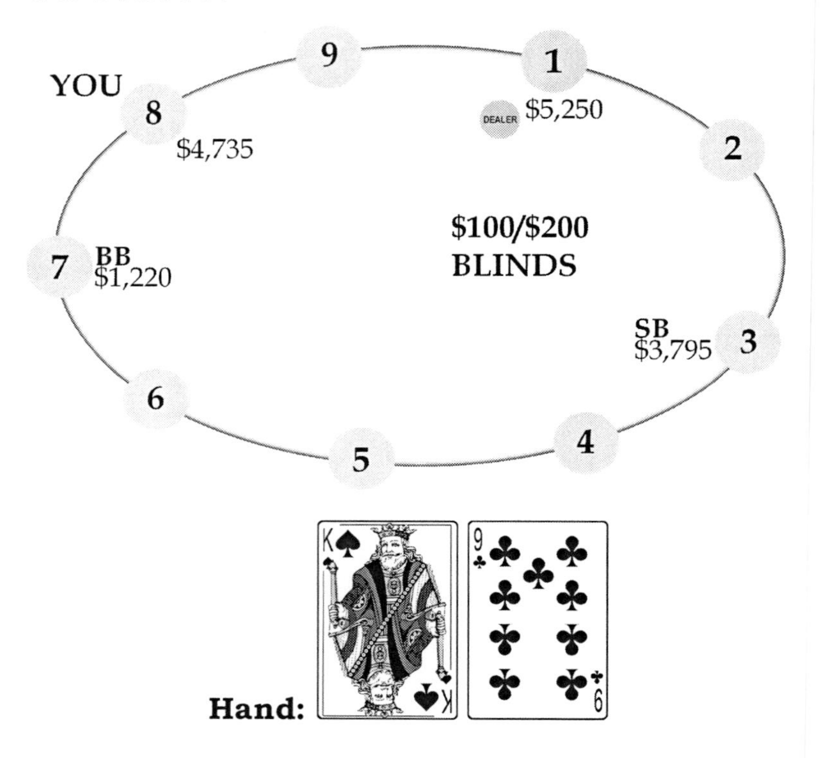

Situation: Final stages of a single table sit and go. There is one short stack at the table in Seat 7 (currently in the big blind). With the blinds costing $300 an orbit, he has only four rounds left before being whittled down to nothing. Nevertheless, he's playing a rock solid conservative game. He hasn't made any moves lately. We're first to act.

Analysis: We're short-handed, so hand values increase. Four-handed, any ace or a decent king (K8 or better) is worth a raise. Besides that, we'd like to keep putting pressure on Seat 7 to force elimination and secure one of the final three places.

If Seat 7 were a savvy player, he'd recognize he has just enough chips left to fold a mediocre hand in the big blind and wait for a better spot. With something like Q8 or better, he might consider making his stand right here. With nearly a sixth of his stack invested in the big blind, he's being paid a premium to take a chance.

Fortunately for us, Seat 7 is a rock. He's aware of his dwindling stack but hopes to hang on for a premium hand. He probably won't go in this spot without a strong ace or pocket pair. Since he's a 9:1 dog to get that lucky, let's *take the odds*.

REDUCE YOUR LATE-STAGE RAISING (2-2.5x BB)

How much should we raise? Since this is late in the tournament and the blinds are relatively high, we don't need to make a standard raise. Two and a half times the blind is more than sufficient to get our point across. Just doubling the big blind may work too.

By this point, you're competing against serious poker players who aren't calling big bets with trash hands (though they may aggressively attack your raises with rubbish). The high dollar cost of seeing the flop discourages action on any raises, however small. So throw in 2x – 2.5x the big blind, leaving yourself room to fold if you don't want to go with the hand.

Action: You raise to $500, and everyone folds around to the big blind. He lets the action clock wind down a ways before folding. You scoop the pot uncontested.

Analysis: If the big blind had pushed all-in, we were fully prepared to call. If he had performed a *stop-start* maneuver (calling our bet with the intention of jamming on the flop regardless) we still would have called him down.

Our hand was reasonable, we would have been getting nearly 2:1 pot odds on our call, we could afford to lose without significant damage to our stack, and we'd advance to the final three payouts if we called and won. Our raise committed us to the hand, and everyone was aware of this.

A SHORT STACK PROVIDES COVER FOR AGGRESSION

Notice how the other big stacks quickly cleared out of the way when we raised to attack the short stack. By risking an all-in confrontation, the other players at the table realize what we're saying: *we have a real hand and we're willing to take it to showdown.* If they called, they'd risk being trapped in the middle of an expensive fight.

You'll often find this in the final stages of a tournament: the other players will back off when you're attacking a short stack. They want that player gone just as much as you do. If they call when you raise a short stack, it's usually with the intention of checking the hand down to maximize the chance of elimination.

In the unlikely event that a big stack plays back at you, he either has a monster hand or is completely incompetent: Check the table stakes to see which is likelier.

There are two things to keep in mind when attacking the short stacks in the late game. The first is that you want to avoid going after the *critically* short stacks, who will be forced to take a stand sooner rather than later. A good rule of thumb is that if a player has 20% of his remaining stack invested, you should only go after him with a strong hand or a lot of chips to spare.

The second point is that you should always have some kind of hand when you're attacking a short stack. You don't want to show down anything less than king-high (or high connecting cards like QJ). This will alert the other players at the table that you're making moves with any two cards. Otherwise, your raises may lose respect.

CAPITALIZE ON YOUR TABLE IMAGE IN THE LATE STAGES

The late game is when you need to capitalize on your tight image -- in order to steal the expensive blinds with trash. You should also come over the top of loose raisers; just jam the pot and force them to a decision for most of their chips.

On the other hand, if you've been playing loose, you can show the table you're a "crazy" person willing to take some gambles -- so they at least respect your "madness." In this, it may not hurt to raise with trash and commit yourself to calling an all-in from a short stacked player: your raises may lose respect but you show you're willing to gamble. Your tight opponents will fear that -- and will be less likely to test you.

The loose, aggressive game plan is to take risks earlier in the tournament to build a big stack for the late game. Now you use it before you lose it. Force the action with hands like ace-x, strong suited connectors or small-medium pairs, especially against the medium stacks. Raise in late position with a variety of cards, and re-raise tight players raising in late position. Call in position and put pressure on your opponents after the flop.

Hand values are all relative in the final, high-blind stages. If the other players won't let you steal pots, let them know you won't back down without a fight.

STAND ASIDE AND LET OTHERS HAVE BIG CONFRONTATIONS

While you certainly can't dodge calling an all-in or two, you want to be the first mover. If someone moves ahead of you, it's usually best to get out of the way. This is true even if you have a big stack. Let someone else, particularly the big blind or another player who limped ahead of the all-in mover, call that bet.

You're looking for good opportunities to earn money in the late game. You'd like to avoid expensive coin-flip confrontations without some compelling reason. You can improve your relative position by standing aside and letting the other players go at it. If they refuse to, simply exploit their tightness to your own advantage.

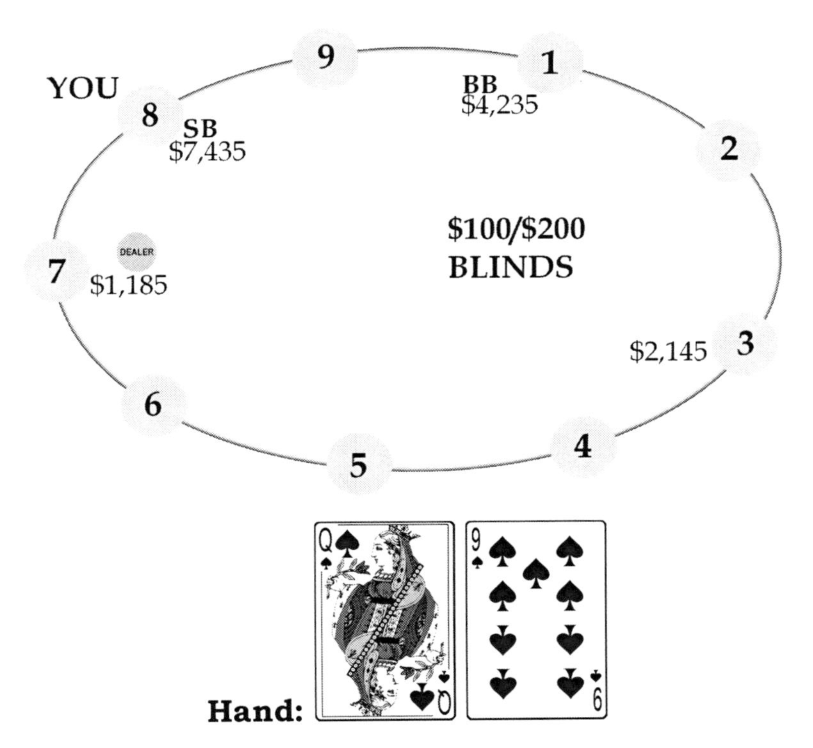

Situation: Same table as before, two hands later. You just took down a big pot against the other two big stacks at the table, substantially increasing your chip lead. Seat 7 is clearly in a must-move situation, but he's been playing extremely tight for the entire game. The big blind is fairly loose and aggressive.

Action: Seat 3 folds. Seat 7 goes all-in for $1,185. The pot is now $1,485, and it costs you $1,085 to call. Seat 1 remains to act behind you in the big blind. *What should you do?*

Analysis: Our hand is reasonable, slightly better than average. We can afford to make this call and lose. But why should we? Let's run through the various scenarios of how our gamble might turn out here.

Maxim 151: Think beforehand.

The greatest foresight consists in determining beforehand the time of trouble. For the provident there are no mischances and for the careful no narrow escapes. We must not put off thought till we are up to the chin in mire. Mature reflection can get over the most formidable difficulty. The pillow is a silent prophet, and it is better to sleep on things beforehand than lie awake about them afterwards.

Many act first and then think afterwards--that is, they think less of consequences than of excuses: others think neither before nor after. The whole of life should be one course of thought how not to miss the right path. With foresight one can envision the line of life.

Consider: the big blind has shown that he has a lot of gamble in him. He just lost more than $1,000 in the previous pot, despite realizing that Seat 7 was playing lock-down poker on the bubble. If he's willing to mix it up with another big stack in a big pot, he may call Seat 7's all-in with a variety of holdings.

Further, we know Seat 7 has been playing extra tight. We're getting about 15:11 on a call here, or 1.36:1; that means we need to win about 37% of the time to break even on a call.

We're getting the odds to call if he has high-card hands like AK, AJ, AT, KJ, KT, or a pair less than nines. We're not getting the odds to call if he has a queen in his hand (AQ, KQ, QJ, or QT), or a pair of nines or better. Given this player's conservatism, we can't count on having the odds to make this call.

Most importantly, Seat 1 is still to act behind us. If we call, it's extremely likely he'll at least call as well. Since he's loose and aggressive, he might take this opportunity to make a power play, raising us all-in and stealing our equity in the pot. If he were to raise behind us, we surely can't call.

NEVER BRING ANOTHER PLAYER BACK FROM THE DEAD

But let's assume that Seat 1 is willing to flat call behind us and check the hand down. Seat 7 almost certainly has a better hand than us, so he'd be the most likely one to win the multi-player pot. If that happens, he'll have tripled up and be fully back in the tournament.

It would be better for us if he just doubled up. He'll still be crippled, along with Seat 3. Then we'd have two short stacks we could aggressively attack; both of them will probably tighten up on the bubble.

NEVER HELP ANOTHER PLAYER BUILD A BIG STACK

But if Seat 1 wins the hand after we call, he'll win an extra $2,200. This will give him a stack nearly equal to our own, after losing an extra $1,100 in this pot to him. This is an even worse scenario than Seat 7 tripling up.

When you have a big stack you never want another big stack at your table, especially a loose and aggressive big stack. Particularly on the bubble, a loose aggressive big stack will sometimes play chicken with another big stack, counting on the tighter player not to risk an expensive confrontation.

If we help another player build a big stack, we'll no longer be the undisputed *table captain*. Here, if Seat 1 calls and wins the hand, it's better that we not shift an additional $1,100 from our stack to his. This is especially so if there's any chance of him raising the pot behind us and shutting us out.

Obviously, we'd like to call, win the pot ourselves, and eliminate Seat 7. But this is an unlikely scenario against two other opponents (it will happen even less than a third of the time, since Seat 7 has a better than average hand).

Calling and losing to either Seat 1 or Seat 7 is a disaster for us: either we make the tournament a four-way race or we've created another big stack that can make life difficult for us. We're better off stepping aside and letting natural selection choose between the short stack and the second-largest stack.

We'll preserve our chip lead whoever emerges from the dust. Even if the big blind folds, we'll still be in a commanding position.

Action: After a long pause, you fold. Seat 1 quickly calls. These are their hands:

Seat 7 doubles up on a final board of:

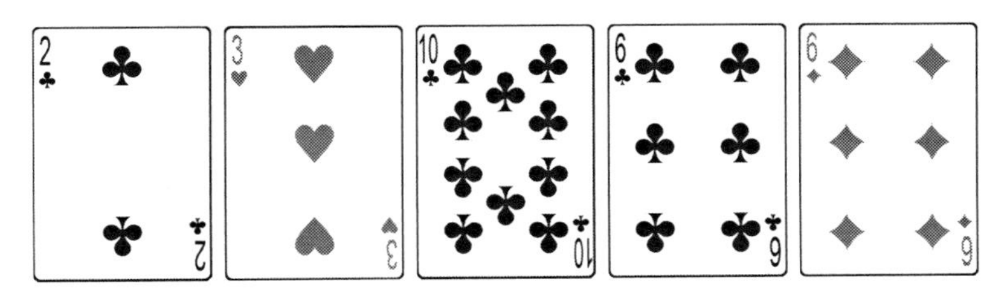

Analysis: We made the right play. Had we called, we would have lost as well, and Seat 7 would have tripled up in the tournament and been right back in contention. As it is, he's still in a weak position (with about a quarter of our chips). Seat 1 is now less of a threat to us as well.

By stopping to consider our relative position in the tournament, we made the smart play. We actually profited from standing aside while the other players clashed. A big stack with three other medium stacks -- on the bubble -- is a surefire recipe for success.

Chapter Twenty-Two

DENY YOUR OPPONENTS INFORMATION

Maxim 3: Keep matters in suspense for a while.

Let your achievements surprise with their novelty. It is unimaginative and unprofitable to play with your cards on the table. If you do not declare yourself immediately, you arouse expectation, especially when the importance of your position makes you the object of general attention. Mix a little mystery with everything, and the very mystery arouses veneration.

Cautious silence is the holy of holies of true wisdom. A resolution declared is never highly thought of; it only leaves room for criticism. And if it happens to fail, you are doubly unfortunate. Make men to watch and wonder.

DENY OPPONENTS INFORMATION BY ROUTINELY CHECKING SOME SPOTS

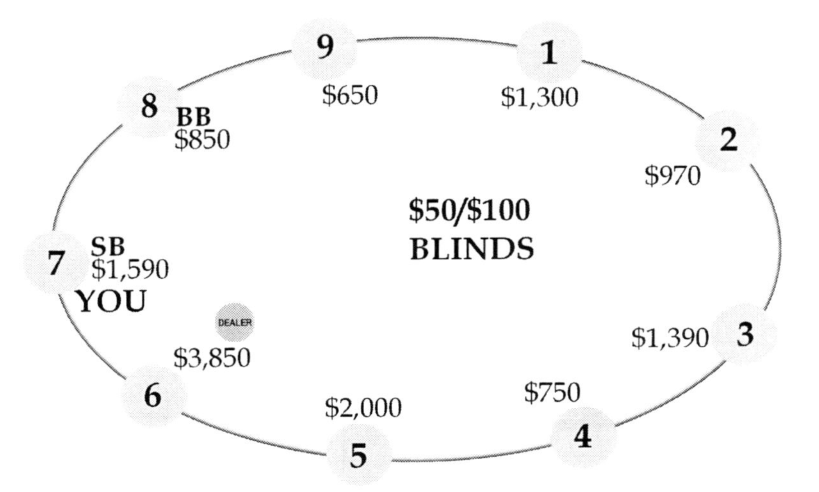

Hand:  

Situation: Mid-level of a one-table online sit and go, with blinds at $50 and $100. The table has been fairly tight and conservative thus far. Player 6 has been loose, wildly aggressive, and has run particularly well. Player 8 is tight and conservative, but suffered a bad beat early on. You're in the small blind.

Action: Everyone folds around to the chip leader on the button. He min-raises to $200. It costs you $150 to call into a $350 pot. *What do you do?*

Analysis: You have a very playable hand, and you know that the loose, aggressive chip leader could be raising with anything on the button. In fact, he's only made a min-raise from the button, which might be a cheap steal attempt against the relatively short-stacked big blind, who can't afford to defend without a decent hand.

All things considered, it wouldn't be entirely unreasonable to consider a raise here. However, it would be risky to make a big move against a loose and aggressive chip leader with just a big drawing hand. I'd tend to favor a call here.

Action: You call and the big blind calls as well. The pot is now $600. Three players see the flop:

Analysis: Well, that's obviously a good flop for our hand: top pair with a decent kicker, and a backdoor flush draw (we'll make our flush with a spade on the turn and river about 4% of the time). We probably have the best hand, but there's little reason to bet here. This is a classic opportunity to check our strong hand out of position and let the pre-flop raiser lead out.

A check here has two advantages: (1) we're likely to earn another bet from the button, who probably missed this flop but will try to represent a queen here; and (2) we effectively "steal the button" here by checking. Since we expect the button will bet out if checked to, the action will ultimately return to us after we've seen what the big blind and button do. Why declare ourselves here, alerting the other players that we have a hand?

Action: You check. The big blind goes all-in for his last $750 (into the $600 pot) and the button instantly calls. The pot is now $2,100, it costs us half our remaining stack to make this call, and the button has us covered. *What should you do?*

Analysis: That was unexpected. One of the many dangers when playing against a loose, aggressive "table captain" who's been running over the table is a natural tendency to focus on him and lose sight of your other opponents. You must fight the urge to tear down the bully. You can earn chips from any of the players at the table. Don't let one bully disrupt your overall strategy.

Looking back at the hand, the tight and conservative big blind called $100 of his remaining $850 pre-flop. While he was getting good pot odds to make that call, he was running low on chips and a conservative player probably would have saved that $100 without some kind of hand. But now he's leading right out and making an overbet at the pot.

A big overbet generally means one of two things: (1) he has a drawing hand and is making a semi-bluff to take the pot down right now; or (2) he has a big hand and is afraid of the diamond or straight draws on that flop. Which scenario is likelier?

Consider the hand from the big blind's perspective. If he had checked here, and the button led out with a standard $400 bet, the pot would be $1000 (assuming we didn't call in the small blind) and the big blind could only raise $350. The loose, aggressive button would instantly call $350 into a $1,750 pot with any hand he could legitimately bet on the flop.

In short, if the big blind check-raises here, he's going to commit the button to the hand. He is leading out here because he wants to give the button (and us) a chance to fold.

But could it just be a semi-bluff with a drawing hand? On a draw-heavy flop like this one, many players are too quick to assume a large overbet is just a semi-bluff with a draw. Always consider the action before rushing to judgment. A diamond draw is unlikely here, because both the queen and ten of diamonds are accounted for. A suited hand with the king of diamonds is unlikely here unless it's precisely the KJ of diamonds, in which case the big blind is a solid favorite with his truly massive drawing hand.

A conservative player likely wouldn't waste valuable, dwindling chips with a small suited connector (like the 78 of diamonds) in this spot, so unless he had a suited hand with the ace of diamonds, this wouldn't fit the action. He might have a hand like KJ with just a straight draw, but the jack in our hand makes this less likely.

If the big blind has a made hand, it almost certainly has to be better than ours. Almost any queen that the tight big blind would have played pre-flop (AQ, KQ, or QT) is beating us. He also could have a set of deuces and conceivably even a set of queens or tens, although he'd probably check-raise the aggressive button with such a strong hand, even with the possible draws out there.

He could have been trapping with a premium pair like AAs or KKs, of course, though he might have re-raised pre-flop with those hands to shut us out. Although we intended to check-raise with our hand, our check has gained us valuable information: the big blind has some kind of big hand that probably doesn't want to see any more cards, and the button has a hand he can call an all-in with.

Conclusion: We're beaten here by one or both players. Even in the unlikely event that the big blind is overbetting the pot with a drawing hand, the button's call of that overbet means he could probably beat top pair, decent kicker. We need to fold here.

Action: You fold, and the big blind turns over two black aces and the button has 89 of diamonds for a flush draw, inside straight draw, and inside straight-flush draw. That gives the button a total of 12 outs from his perspective (9 diamonds and three non-diamond jacks, though in fact we hold one of his apparent outs) so his call is perfectly legitimate given the pot. The turn and the river are blanks, however, and the big blind more than doubles up.

By automatically checking here, we denied our opponents information about the strength of our hand, gained valuable information about our opponents' hands, and saved at least one bet (if not most of our stack). If we had bet right out, we would have basically declared that we had a pair of queens without knowing anything about our opponents' hands.

We saved a lot of money by hiding our hand; note also that the big blind, by smooth-calling pre-flop, also hid the strength of his hand and more than doubled up because of this. If he had re-raised pre-flop, he would not have earned as many chips.

This hand played on the flop as though we had position. Note that this is only true because we could count on the aggressive button to almost always bet at the flop; against more conservative players, we might have led out to deny them a free card.

ADOPT A WAIT AND SEE ATTITUDE WITH LARGE, MULTI-WAY POTS (ESPECIALLY OUT OF POSITION)

There is no surer sign of strength than a player who takes the lead in the betting in a large, multi-way pot, especially when he does so out of position. By leading into several other players, all of whom could raise or re-raise, an out-of-position player is signaling he's serious about the pot. He's also signaling a made hand that doesn't want to give any free cards.

Note this observation applies to *real* bets. Weak or min-bets out of position, unless made by very experienced players, are usually signs of genuine weakness. Such *probe bets* often provide cover for a draw, to head off larger bets from one or more opponents in position. Pay no attention to these tickle bets.

But just as a real bet out of position in a multi-way pot signals strength, so too is it a great way to get one's head cut off. Too much can go wrong in a multi-way pot; and leading right off in the betting raises the stakes too quickly. This is why it's prudent to routinely check out of position in these pots and see what develops.

Large multi-way pots played out of position easily present the greatest opportunity for disaster in no limit hold 'em. There's simply no telling what you're up against. Play these hands with the greatest caution; if in doubt, simply fold the hand and wait for a better spot. You're often better off shoving all-in on the next hand with any two cards than investing too much in these multi-player pots (especially *un-raised* pots).

Chapter Twenty-Three

THE RISK OF RUIN

Maxim 207: An instant of passion can undo hours of careful planning.

One has to consider the chance of a mischance. Passions' impulse causes prudence to slip, and there is the risk of ruin. A moment of wrath or of pleasure carries you on farther than many hours of calm, and often a short diversion may put a whole enterprise to shame. The cunning of others uses such moments of temptation to search the recesses of the mind: they use such thumbscrews as are wont to test the best caution. Moderation serves as a counterplot, especially in sudden emergencies.

Much thought is needed to prevent passion from taking the bit in the teeth, and he is wise who can remain firmly in the saddle. He who knows the danger may with care pursue his journey.

Maxim 214: Do not turn one blunder into two.

It is quite usual to commit four others in order to remedy one, or to excuse one piece of impertinence by still another. Folly is either related to, or identical with the family of lies, for in both cases it needs many to support one. The worst of a bad case is having to fight it, and worse than the ill itself is not being able to conceal it. The annuity of one failing serves to support many others. A wise man may make one slip but never two, and that only in running, not while standing still.

Maxim 261: Do not allow a misstep to become a fall.

Many make an obligation out of a blunder, and because they have entered the wrong path they think it proves their strength of character to go on in it. Within they regret their error, while outwardly they excuse it. At the beginning of their mistake they were regarded as inattentive, in the end as fools. Neither an unconsidered promise nor a mistaken resolution are really binding. Yet some continue in their folly and prefer to be constant fools. There is no strength or wisdom in commitment to a mistake.

EVERY HAND YOU PLAY AT NO LIMIT CARRIES A RISK OF RUIN

At any moment, no limit poker can leave you down to the felt. Unless you start with a substantial chip lead, this risk of ruin should be a major factor in all your decision-making.

The overwhelming majority of the time neither you nor your opponents will be strong enough to play for all the chips. Without big hands or expensive blinds forcing the action, there's no reason to take big risks. In a cash game, especially, all-in confrontations are rare.

Ring games are like featherweight boxing matches. There's a lot of dancing around and maneuvering to land jabs, but few if any power punches. The match is usually decided by who lands more shots while keeping himself protected. Tournament players switching to cash games need to learn patience in order to survive and prosper.

But in tournament poker, the threat of elimination is a major thumbscrew used by aggressive players. If their opponent isn't pot-committed, they can often force him to throw away medium-strength hands with big betting. Of course, they're also betting big when they actually have a hand, too.

BIG MOVES NEED PERFECT TIMING

The timing of such moves is critical. Competent opponents will not allow you to steal pot after pot with crazy all-in moves: you will find yourself getting looked up before too long. If you're trying to force your opponent to make a big laydown, the following factors all need to line up:

(1) **You have a big stack** – You don't have to have your opponent covered (though this would improve your chances of success), but you must have enough chips to cripple your opponent if he calls and loses

(2) **Your opponent is not pot-committed** – Another way of saying this is that your opponent can fold the hand and still have enough chips to seriously compete; do not try to bluff a player who has put anywhere near half his stack into the pot

(3) **Your bets must make sense** – Your actions must be consistent with a big hand that's been trapping until the turn or river

(4) **You have to be equally aggressive whether you have it or not** – If this bet is out of character with how you've played this session, your opponent will be suspicious and likely to call; you can't bet big only when you're bluffing (and don't want action) and make small *suck bets* when you have it

(5) **The board is scary** – Your opponent must put you on a likely hand he can't beat -- while flopping a set with a wired pair is a

powerful hand, it's practically invisible to your opponent (and hence difficult to represent); it's much easier to bluff on a board like AKT than it is A82, no matter how convincingly you try to sell the idea you really hit your set of deuces

(6) **Your opponent cannot stand the pressure** – If you're going to make a big move, select a tight opponent capable of folding and have a solid read that he has a medium-strength hand at best

It may be torture for their more conservative counterparts, but the occasional big move is a loose, aggressive player's premier weapon. As with any dangerous weapon, though, there are risks for those who employ it. When you swing for the fences, you're more likely to strike out.

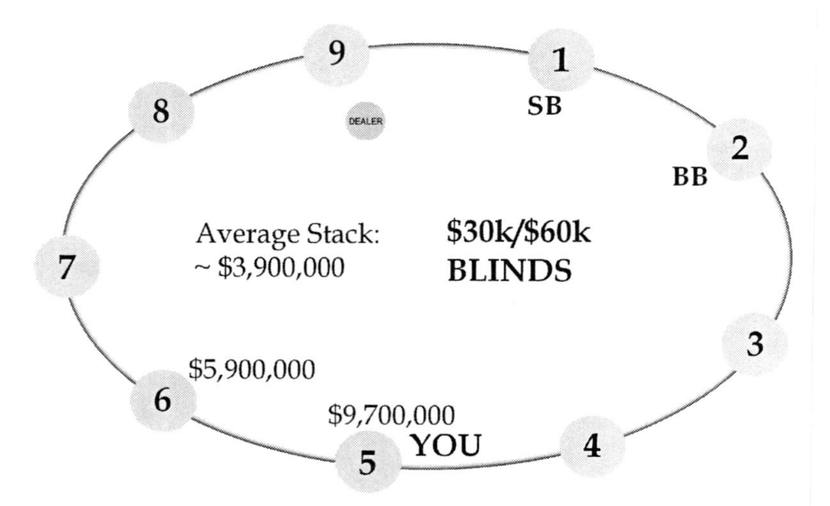

Hand: 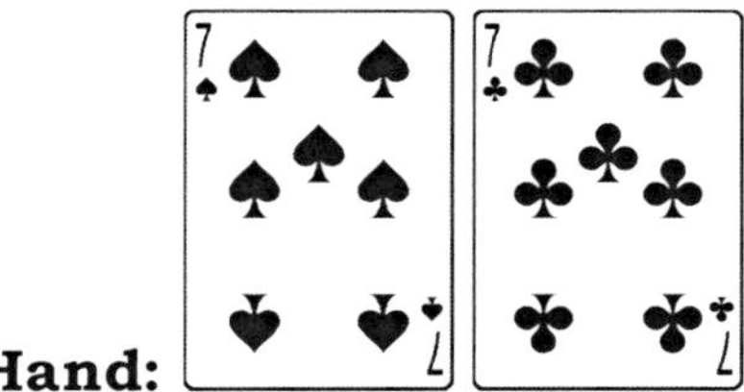

Situation: Final four tables of the World Series of Poker. We're playing along with Brandon Cantu in Seat 5, a loose, extremely aggressive, and successful young player. We're in the enviable position of tournament chip leader.

Seat 4 is playing a tight, weak game in the final stretch here, clearly happy to advance up the money ladder. Seat 6 is also playing tight, perhaps because we've been raising ahead of him so aggressively.

Action: Seat 3 folds, and Seat 4 limps for $60,000. *What should you do?*

Analysis: Against most players in many situations, we'd be happy to call and see a cheap flop with our sevens. But this isn't our style, and there are so many other advantages in favor of raising here:

(1) We have position against our opponent;

(2) We have a substantial chip lead which we can use to bully Seat 4 around (he knows we can easily eliminate him from the tournament);

(3) We probably have the best hand right now, but the flop will almost certainly bring over-cards to our sevens;

(4) We can clarify the hand – if Seat 4 is trapping with a big hand, better to find out right now;

(5) We ***set the tone in the hand*** – we're the aggressor right from the get-go, and players are more likely to fold to the pre-flop raiser if/when they miss the flop; and

(6) We can *isolate* a tight, weak player to ourselves – few of the other players will want to get involved after a limp and a big raise from the chip leader.

Those are a lot of advantages, and consistent with our style of play, we should usually raise here.

Action: You raise to $250,000. Directly behind you, Seat 6 re-raises to $750,000. Every folds around to the initial limper, who also folds. The action is on you. The pot is now $1,280,000, and it costs you $500,000 to call. *Do you call, fold, or raise?*

Analysis: So much for isolating the weak tight player in position. Now we're out of position against a tight, aggressive player with an above-average stack. Although we have him covered, he can do considerable damage to us, and he's already committed 12.7% of his stack pre-flop. Re-raising a limper and a raiser with that kind of investment indicates he's pretty serious about the hand.

We should generally fold here. Our opponent could have a hand like AK or AQ, but he could just as easily be re-raising with jacks or better. Unless we hit our set, we'll have no idea where we stand on the flop.

If we just call hoping to hit our set, we're 7.5:1 underdogs. Expressed as a percentage, that's an 11.8% chance. Since we've been forced to invest 12.7% (just over an eighth) of his stack to see the flop, we have *negative expected value* in this hand even if every time we hit our set we're able to capture his entire stack.

It's true we've already invested $250,000, and therefore to call at this point would require just $500,000, or roughly 10% of our opponent's stack. The initial limp, with the blinds and antes provide another small incentive. The call might appear justified on that basis.

But it's far from certain we can stack our opponent if we hit. What if he has a big pair and overcards flop? What if he has AK and misses completely? Can we still count on a big payoff on our investment here?

Mostly, the flop won't help us, and we'll just have a pair of sevens and no idea what our opponent has. If we call here and it costs us one or two more bets to decide we're really behind, a call here actually carries *negative implied odds* for us.

Raising here is just as problematic. Pushing all-in might work if he holds AQ or a pair less than queens, but otherwise we've committed almost two-thirds of our stack on a pair of sevens.

If we re-raise to something like $2,000,000, can we really fold if he pushes all-in, getting 2:1 on a call? If we do that, we'll have surrendered more than 20% of our chips without a fight, and Seat 6 will now be the tournament chip leader.

If you're not getting good odds to call, and raising will commit you to the pot in a murky situation, folding is your best option.

Action: You actually call the extra $500,000. The pot is now $1,780,000, and you're first to act in this heads-up pot:

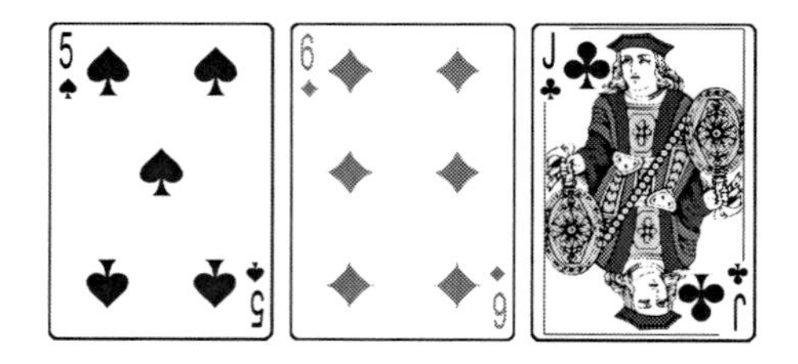

Analysis: That's a great flop for your sevens, with only one overcard to your pair. It's also important to notice which overcard flopped: a jack. This means it's less likely he was holding a pair of jacks pre-flop. More importantly, if he had two big cards, it's unlikely he hit that jack: would a tight player really re-raise a limper and a raiser pre-flop with just AJ? KJ? QJ? JT?

There are now only three hands we're really worried about: QQs, KKs, or AAs. Remember, there's only a 0.45% chance of being dealt a particular pair, or about a 1.35% chance of holding one of the hands we fear. It's much, much more likely we're ahead in the hand.

We should generally bet right here. We're not the type of player that "checks to the raiser", and we want to see how committed he is to the hand. If we check and he bets, then we'll have to make a big raise to see if he's serious or just making a continuation bet. We'll be pretty deeply committed to the hand at that point.

If we bet into him, he'll be forced to either raise or fold. If he does raise, it might be enough to commit him to the pot, and then we can decide if we want to call. But our bet gives him the chance to get away from the hand with plenty of chips remaining. If he doesn't have much, he'll probably go away, especially since he knows we're aggressive enough to force a big confrontation.

The final concern is that if we check he could check right behind us. Seat 6 is much more conservative than us. Playing against the chip leader, he may try to keep the pot fairly small. He can also read the board as well as us, and knows that a continuation bet here would represent AAs, KKs, or QQs, all of which are fairly unlikely. Checking could give our opponent a free turn card to hurt us.

Action: You actually check, and Seat 6 quickly checks behind. The pot remains $1,780,000, and the turn comes:

Analysis: That is literally the worst possible turn card for our hand. How could we be ahead now? There's a small chance our opponent could have KKs, QQs, or TTs and fear that ace as much as we do.

But if that's the case, why didn't he bet the flop – especially with QQs or TTs? That board would have looked good for him, and too many threatening cards could come on the turn. The pot was already big enough to take down at that point (a third of his remaining stack). It's generally not a good idea to try trapping with a single, vulnerable pair in a big pot against the chip leader.

No, it's much more likely he re-raised pre-flop with AK or AQ and that turn just made his hand. We should realize it was a mistake not to bet the flop, and cut our losses.

But if we really wanted to test whether our opponent has an ace, we should make a small $400,000 - $500,000 bet. If he's still interested in the pot, we're surely beaten.

It's a much better idea to check here and see what develops. Remember: you should have a good reason to bet, rather than just throwing away chips to be aggressive. What can a bet here achieve?

Do we think we have the best hand? No, we probably don't. Can we force a better hand to fold by betting here? We probably can't, given our opponent's likely range of hands. Even if he had a pair of kings or queens, he will probably call an average bet here: he knows we're aggressive enough to bluff when an ace hits the turn.

Since a bet here can't achieve either objective, we should check.

Action: You check, and your opponent bets just $200,000. The pot is now $1,980,000, and it costs you $200,000 to call. *What should you do?*

Analysis: I don't like that bet at all. If this were amateur hour at the $4 sit and go tourney, a tiny bet like that might mean our opponent was weak and trying to cover a draw. But these are high stakes and our opponent has shown himself to be a tight, dangerous player. Why would we he make such a tiny bet in position, risking a raise?

He knows we're very aggressive, and that bet looks like he's waving a red cape in front of a bull. He's probably trying to lure us into making a big raise. We shouldn't oblige him, especially given how the hand has played.

But we might consider calling. Unless our opponent is sucking us in with a set of aces or jacks, there are two sevens left in the deck that should be clean outs. With six cards seen (the four on board and two in our hand), there are 44 non-sevens and the 2 remaining sevens. Those are odds of 44:2, or 22:1 against.

Our opponent is offering us odds of 10:1 on our call. But the *implied odds* could be twice that if we hit our miracle card on the river. Plus, it's still theoretically possible we could have the best hand -- our opponent really could be drawing with a hand like KQ. It's a Hail Mary call to make, but given the enormous odds, the size of the pot, and our huge stack, it's a justifiable call.

Action: You actually raise to $1,000,000. Your opponent thinks for about two seconds before quickly moving the chips to the center. The pot is now $3,780,000. Your opponent started the hand with $5,900,000 and now has $4,150,000 in chips remaining. You started with $9,700,000 and now have $7,950,000 in your stack. You have your opponent covered by $3.8 million, and you're first to act on the river:

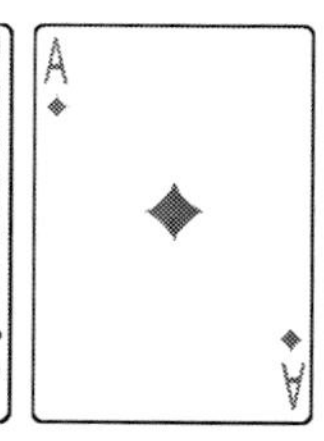

Cantu's Analysis: In Brandon Cantu's mind, that card just opened up a lot of possibilities. Now there are six hands he can plausibly hope to represent: AJ, AT, JT, KQ, or a set of fives or sixes. Any of those hands would now give him a straight, a set or two pair.

The KQ possibility is probably the most frightening to our opponent, since it's entirely possible Cantu was fooling around with a bluff on the turn and caught an unlikely inside straight draw. Now KQ would give Cantu the absolute nuts, and any player could be expected to push that hand with maximum aggression.

On the other hand, you don't have to be Daniel Negreanu to read our opponent's hand: he has either AK or AQ, for a pair of aces, good kicker. He wouldn't have raised pre-flop, bet the turn, and been able to stand our raise with anything else.

With the board like it is, that's only a medium-strength hand. Six entirely plausible hands could beat a single pair of aces. A loose, aggressive player like Cantu believes he can force a fold here. And against many tight opponents in other situations, he might be able to.

If we're going to try to take down the pot, a medium-sized bet isn't going to do the job. The pot is now nearly $3.8 million and our opponent has $4.15 million left. If we only bet $2 million or so, he's unlikely to fold top-pair, top-kicker after investing so much in the hand.

A bluff here can only work if it puts his tournament life on the line. If we're serious about forcing a big laydown, we need to bet the pot. And if we're betting that much, we should just set him all-in right here and put him to the ultimate test.

Action: You push all-in, and your opponent thinks for just a few seconds before calling. Our heart sinks as we realize our big river bluff failed. He turns over the:

And his pair of aces beats our pair of sevens. He doubles up to $12,080,000 (the new tournament chip leader) and we're back down to an average stack of $3,800,000. We've got some work to do in order to climb our way back to the top.

What went wrong here? Quite a lot actually, and the blunders piled on top of another until we were fully committed with a losing hand. There were several opportunities to eject before losing 60% of our stack:

- Although raising pre-flop to isolate the weak, tight limper was a good move, when a tight, above-average stack came over the top of our raise in position it would have been prudent to fold the hand and wait for a better spot; if we're going to play a big pot, we'd rather play in position against weaker, smaller-stacked players with a hand that holds more potential to improve

- Not betting the flop was a modest mistake; we were planning a check-raise, but we should have anticipated our opponent would check a variety of hands rather than make a continuation bet at a jack-high flop

- Raising the turn when the ace hit was a big mistake; at this level of play, we're facing skillful opponents who will not make teaser bets in position with absolutely nothing

- Trying to steal the pot on the river was the boldest (and biggest) mistake of all; we shouldn't have expected our opponent to fold after he enticed us into raising the turn; furthermore, half the hands we were trying to represent would have been made on the river *after* our check-raise on the turn (JT, AT, or KQ), which makes them unlikely – did we bluff the turn and get very lucky? Our lousy table image (loose, aggressive cannon) is not going to help sell this story.

- Finally, it's never a good idea to force a big move against a player who could be holding top-pair, top-kicker (our opponent here actually had second-kicker), ***particularly when he has a pair of aces***

CRACKED ACES PRINCIPLE

Although skillful players can lay this hand down in the right spots, many players are quite reasonably stubborn about folding aces, particularly in a heads-up pot. At a certain point, players will simply say, "If you really cracked my aces, I guess I'm going home -- but show me!"

TIGHT PLAYERS DON'T WANT TO GO BROKE WITH SECOND PAIR

Notice the situation would be different if we weren't up against aces. Imagine our opponent held KQ instead of AQ, and hit a king (instead of an ace) on the turn. If an ace then came on the river and we made the same all-in move, we'd almost certainly be scooping the pot right now.

Tight players do not want to look foolish. They don't want to bust out with a marginal hand. They may be willing to take their chances with top pair, good-kicker under the right circumstances. But they don't want to go out with second pair.

To bluff conservative players, look for situations where they flop big (jacks, queens, or kings) and the turn and river bring scare cards. Don't risk being called down when it's obvious they hold top-pair, strong kicker.

The main lesson is not to get stubborn about a pot merely because you've invested some money. If the situation isn't good for a bluff, then don't make it. Don't throw good money after bad. Walk away from a move gone bad.

Chapter Twenty-Four

STAY OUT OF TROUBLE

Maxim 138: Do not get swept up in the tempest of excitement.

It takes a wise doctor to know when not to prescribe, and at times the greater skill consists in not applying remedies. The proper way to still the storms of the vulgar is to hold your hand and let them calm down of themselves. To give way now is to conquer by and by. A fountain gets muddy with but little stirring up, and does not get clear by our meddling with it but by our leaving it alone. The best remedy for disturbances is to let them run their course, for so they quiet down.

DON'T PUT YOURSELF IN THE MIDDLE OF A BAD SITUATION

If you're seated between loose, aggressive players going to war with each other, it is foolish to get involved without a big hand. Similarly, it's a big mistake to invest a lot of money in a dangerous hand. You want to save your chips for a situation where you're comfortable you have the best hand, or at least a big draw.

If you find yourself making a lot of ambitious calls in the mere hope that your opponent is bluffing (or hoping for a big suckout), you're playing too loose. Against the right opponent, a hand like second pair is worth a call. Against a fairly tight opponent, who plays few hands, second pair is an easy fold, depending on the texture of the board.

Don't think to yourself, "I have a bit of a hand here so I should call." Instead ask, "What are the odds I have the best hand here? What can I gain if I'm right, and how much will it cost me if I'm wrong?"

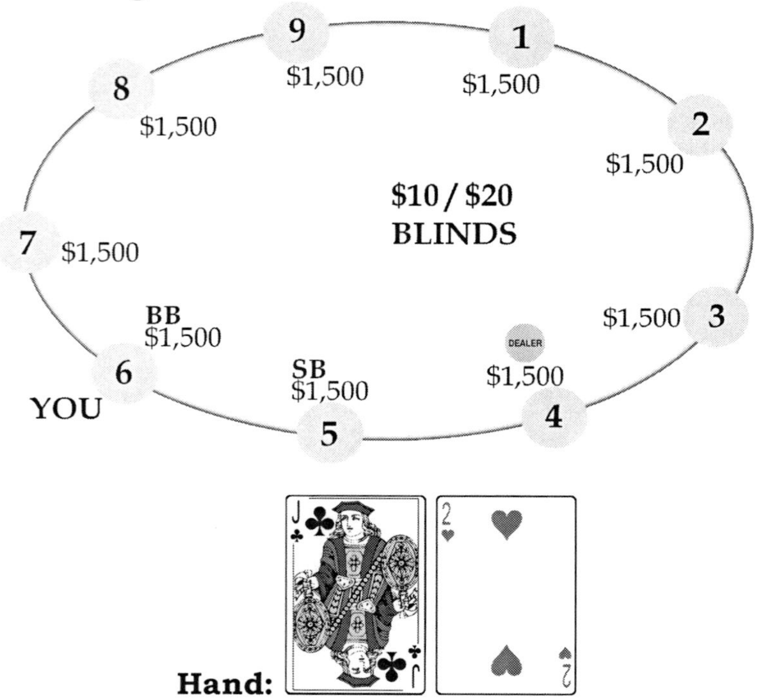

Situation: First hand of a single table online sit and go. The top three players will be paid. You're in the big blind.

Action: Players 8, 1, 3, and 4 all limp for $20. Seat 5 completes the small blind. You check your useless hand in the big blind. The pot is $120 and six players see the flop:

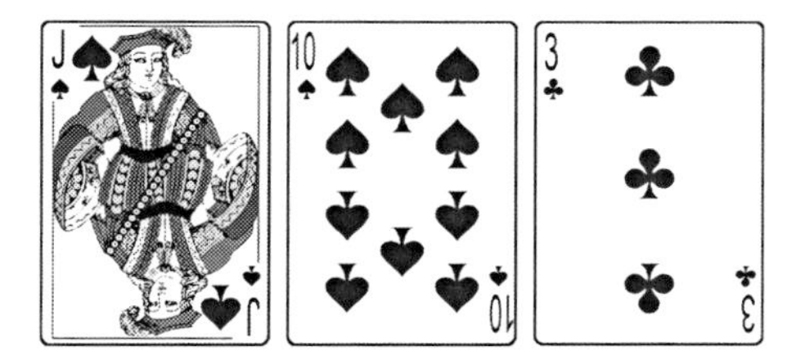

Analysis: The small blind has checked to us. The first thing is to evaluate our hand and the texture of the board. While we have top pair, we have absolutely no kicker whatsoever. Unless the turn or river bring a deuce, we're playing a pair of jacks plus whatever the board brings. That's simply not a very good hand, and this is why we avoid playing big cards with no kicker (e.g. A2 or K3), even if suited.

Our second thought should be that the texture of the board is extremely dangerous, with straight and flush draws threatening. Even if we have the best hand at the moment -- which is by no means certain -- we will get action from all kinds of draws. If we do, we won't know whether we're being called by a set, two pair (perhaps JT), a better jack, a flush draw, or a straight draw (KQ, AQ, or 98 can easily call a substantial bet on the flop). There are many made hands or drawing hands that will raise us here.

Our final thought should concern the number of opponents we're facing, and the price they paid to see the flop. Here, we're up against *five* other players, all of whom invested barely 1% of their stack. Since this is the first hand of the game and loose players will limp with anything in the early stages of a tournament, we're in mystery land here.

When you're facing a lot of opponents who could have anything, you should proceed with the most extreme caution. *A single pair against four or five other opponents is simply not a big hand you want to invest in.*

"What are the odds I have the best hand here?" Maybe better than even *now*, but with a lot of scare cards by the turn or river. If we play this pot, we'll have no idea where we're at throughout the hand.

"What can I gain if I'm right, and what will it cost me if I'm wrong?" It will cost 5-10% of our stack to make an initial bet at this pot, and we could face a threefold raise.

Even if we're just called, we may get two or three calls, driving the pot up to at least $300. Then any betting on the turn or river could have us investing half our stack or more by the showdown, if we still thought we had the best hand. In short, we might bet out and give up on the pot if there's resistance.

But the odds of taking the pot down without a fight, given five opponents and the variety of hands that can call us, is so very remote that any bet is a waste. Maybe we can call a single bet, depending on the action, but leading out is a dangerous move in this spot.

Action: You check. Player 8 makes a minimum bet of $20. Player 1 calls, but Player 3 raises to $160. Seats 4 and 5 fold. The pot is now $320, and it costs you $160 to call the raise (unless Seat 8 re-raises). *What should you do?*

Analysis: Fold. If you're facing a bet and a raise and you have a single pair, it's rarely correct to do anything other than fold. If there's been a substantial bet and a call, you shouldn't call without a strong draw or a hand that might be best. Perhaps the initial bettor is bluffing or semi-bluffing, but the caller or raiser seldom is.

IF THE FELLOW IN FRONT OF YOU CAN CALL, YOU PROBABLY CAN'T

If there's been a bet and a call ahead of you, and you don't love your hand, think to yourself, ***"Well if that fellow can call, then I sure as heck can't!"***

Here, if Seat 8 can bet, Seat 1 can call, and Seat 3 can make a big raise, one or all of them (especially the raiser in Seat 3) likes their hand a lot better than our jacks, no kicker. We fold and don't look back.

Action: You fold, Seat 8 goes all-in for his last $1,460. Seat 1 folds, and Seat 3 quickly calls. Seat 8 turns over KQ with one spade, for an open-ended straight draw, two-overcards, and a backdoor flush draw. Seat 3 has JT of hearts, for two pair.

From his perspective, Seat 8 has eight outs twice (the four nines and four remaining aces), plus another 4% for the runner-runner flush draw, for a total of roughly 36%. He's nearly a 2 to 1 dog, but he catches a 9 on the turn and takes a quick lead in the tournament when his king-high straight holds up.

I hate Seat 8's play here. Besides the fact he went all-in with just a draw, he already had good evidence that Seat 3 really liked his hand. Seat 8 telegraphed that he had a draw with the lead-out minimum bet; this is often used to provide cover for a straight or flush draw.

Betting a drawing hand is called a "semi-bluff" because at heart it's still a bluff; you don't have the best hand, but you're hoping to make it look like you might, and even if the bluff doesn't work you have outs.

Here, it was fairly obvious that Seat 8 was bluffing with the probe bet and then the huge all-in re-raise. These actions usually scream, "I'm weak, please don't call me!!" Plus, given the action in the hand, it was too likely that Seat 3 had two-pair or a set he wasn't getting away from. Perhaps Seat 3 might have been able to fold QJ or KJ, but the eighth seat knew a king or queen in Seat 3's hand was less likely given his own hand (KQ). This is just a case where bad play was rewarded.

By folding after a bet and a raise, we avoided putting ourselves in the middle of a bad situation. In fact, we might have folded to a single bet and call. Don't get between two aggressive players or invest money in a pot that's being actively contested without a very good reason.

Maxim 172: Never contend with a man who has nothing to lose.

Such a battle is an unequal conflict. The other enters without anxiety; having lost everything, including shame, he has no further loss to fear. He therefore resorts to all kinds of insolent boldness. One should never expose a valuable position to so terrible a risk, for what has cost long hours and hard work to gain may be lost in a moment. The wise man balances his own and the other's position: he only enters into the contest with the greatest caution. For even by victory he cannot gain what he has lost by exposing himself to such risk.

PICK ON THE MEDIUM STACKS, NOT THE (CRITICALLY) SHORT STACKS

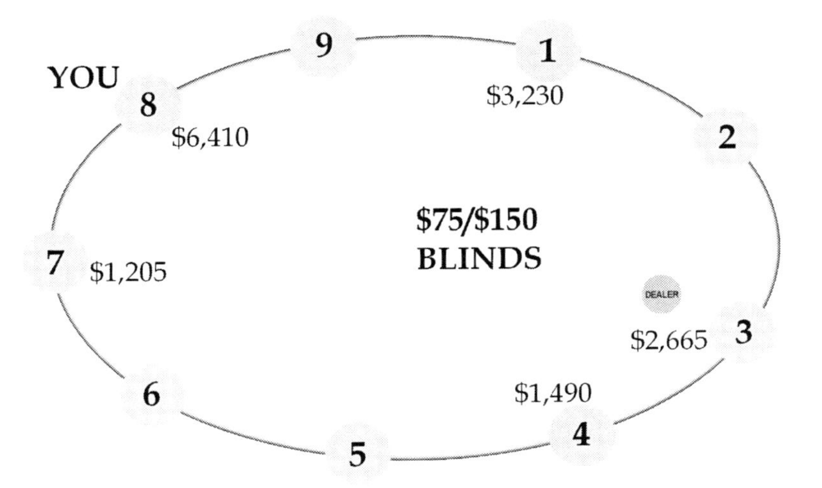

Hand: 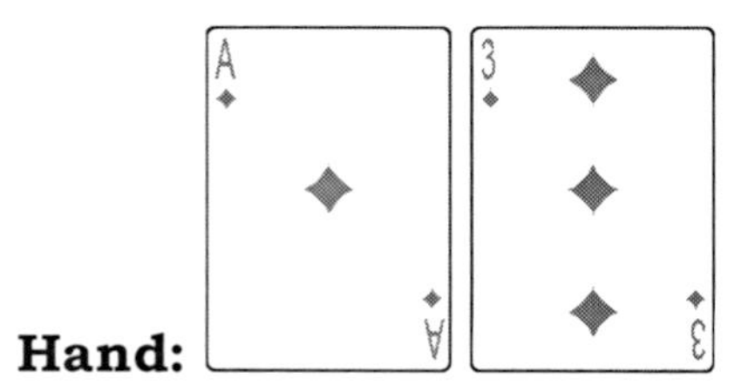

Situation: Late middle stages of a single table online sit and go tournament. You've racked up a substantial chip lead with tight, aggressive play and a few excellent reads. The big blind has been weak and fairly passive throughout the game, playing few hands and folding quickly in the face of aggression. You're first to act with your suited ace.

Analysis: Five-handed, any ace, especially a suited one, is a pretty good hand. You're not looking to play a big pot here, but you've got the kind of hand that's great for stealing. And you have the big chip lead to scare away any competitors. Make a small raise here and see if you can take down the blinds.

Action: You raise to $400. Everyone folds around to the big blind, who calls another $250. The pot is now $875, and your heads up with the short stack. The two of you see the flop:

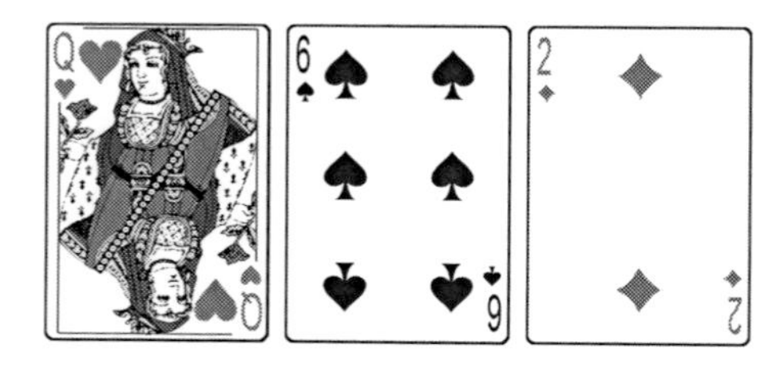

The big blind checks.

Analysis: Well, you have nothing but ace-high and a back-door flush draw (which will only get there 4% of the time). This is not a hand to write home about. On the bright side, unless your opponent has a queen, with a hand like AQ, KQ, QJ, or QT, this flop probably didn't help him either. If he has any of those hands, he's laying a trap for you and he'll soon go all-in no matter what you bet.

In fact, given that he's so short-stacked, he could be trapping here even with a medium pair less than queens. In that case, he called your pre-flop raise with the intention of getting all his money in regardless of the flop.

Think about this: why would a weak, passive player on a short-stack call a healthy pre-flop raise and then check over to us in an obvious spot for us to make a continuation bet? When you're on the short stack with stakes this high, you're either going to be all-in or all-out in a hurry. No competent short-stacked player should be check-folding in this spot.

Action: You decide to use your chip strength to push around the short stack and force him to a decision for all his chips. You bet $1,000 into the $875 pot, enough to set him all-in. He quickly calls, and turns over the AQ of clubs. You're drawing dead to running 3s or running diamonds, and the turn and river bring neither. The short-stack doubles up.

Analysis: What went wrong here? For starters, we didn't have to pick on the short stack in his big blind, when he already had 10% of his chips in the pot. Then, we didn't have to raise $400 to start with, since a minimum raise to $300 might have gotten him to fold if he truly had nothing. But our primary mistake was betting so much on the flop when it was highly unlikely the short-stack was really check-folding after investing a third of his chips.

If we bet the flop at all, a bet of $250 or $300 (followed by the short-stack's all-in check-raise) would've been more than enough information to tell us we were beat. Instead, we came up snake eyes by trying to gamble with a man who had nothing to lose. When you have a big stack, you want to focus your bullying on the medium stacks who are scared of losing their opportunity to advance. You can't push around someone who has to take a stand.

Chapter Twenty-Five

TAKE THE LEAD IN THE HAND

Maxim 164: Use a trial balloon to find out how things will be received.

Throw straws in the air to see which way the wind is blowing, especially when the matter is most uncertain. One can thus be assured of its starting out well, and an opportunity is afforded for going on in earnest or withdrawing entirely. By testing men's intentions in this way, the wise man knows on what ground he stands. This is the great rule of foresight in asking, in desiring, and in ruling.

SET THE TONE OF THE HAND RIGHT FROM THE BEGINNING

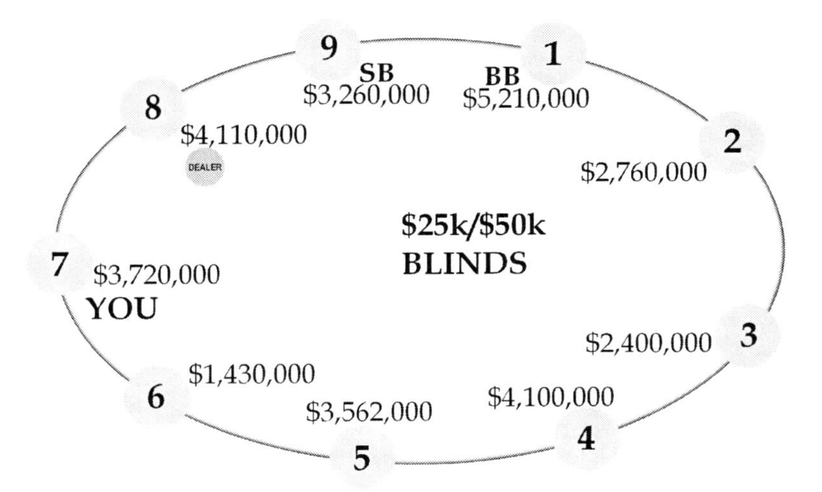

Hand: 

Situation: Final five tables of the World Series of Poker. The pressure is intensifying and the importance of every hand is magnified with big payouts just down the road. You're in the cut-off position with your ace-rag. Seat 4 is a loose, aggressive female player (the last one remaining in the Series). She's been on a big run lately, and splashing around more often.

Action: Seats 2 and 3 fold. Seat 4 makes a standard raise to $150,000. Seats 5 and 6 fold, and the action is on us.

Analysis: The standard play here is to fold. Our ace-rag is a mediocre hand at best. A raise from early position is usually an indication of a better than average hand, and we could easily be dominated by a better ace.

However, to win a tournament you have to make some moves every now and again. We have some advantages here: we're in position against the mid-seat raiser, we have plenty of chips to splash around with, our opponent has shown she's fairly loose and could be raising with a variety of hands, and we do have ace-high (which tells us it's less likely she has a strong ace).

If we play this pot, we need to set the tone right here. To make your moves believable, you have to tell a convincing story from beginning to end. If we want this pot, let's play our A5 like we have a big hand (AAs, KKs, or AK).

In short, we need to either re-raise here to establish we have a big hand or fold and wait for a better spot. Usually this is an easy fold, but occasionally you need to make moves like this and hope your timing works out.

Action: You re-raise to $475,000. The table folds around to Seat 4, who calls the extra $325,000. The pot is now $1,080,000. It's heads up to the flop:

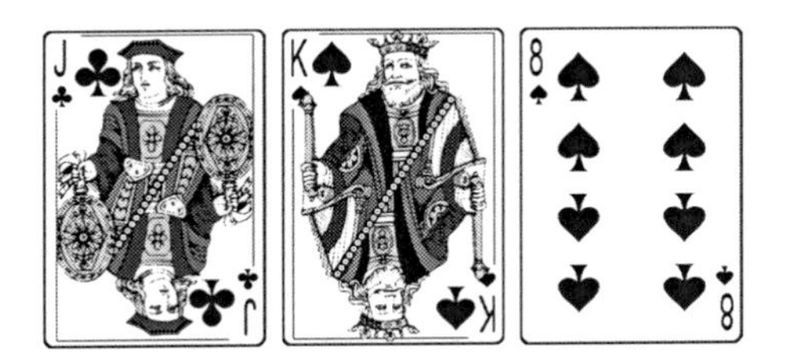

Action: She checks to us.

Analysis: Well, we got action on our pre-flop re-raise. This is to be expected. Many amateur players get spooked when they make a single bet or raise and get called. When you're playing in the big leagues, you have to be willing to make compound moves. We're not just betting or raising at a single point in the hand to see if we can take down the pot. Sometimes making a move requires more than a single bet or raise. We want our actions to tell a consistent story: we started with a big hand pre-flop and this board has helped us.

By making a big re-raise before the flop, we set the tone in this hand. This is why our loose, aggressive opponent "checked to the raiser" (whether or not she had anything). Most players will check to the raiser in a spot like this, and by setting the tone that we're very strong right from the start, we'll take down more than our fair share of these pots.

Action: You bet $525,000. Our opponent waits about eight seconds before hurriedly announcing a raise to $1.6 million, almost jumping out of her seat to shove the chips in. She tucks her hands neatly under her chin, and assumes one of the most obviously confident facial expressions you're going to see at this level of play. Her entire body posture screams that she has it, though she quickly tries to resume her cool.

Analysis: Even without the obvious tells, the betting pattern alone tells the story. Our re-raise before the flop indicated a big pair or AK, and this board (with a king and a jack out there) should make our continuation bet believable. Yet our loose, aggressive opponent has now made a major check-raise and seems to be hoping we have the hand we're representing.

The conclusion is simple: she has a set or two-pair. We, on the other hand, have absolutely nothing, and there's no reason to believe we can take this pot away. We fold, and don't look back.

Action: We fold. Our opponent actually flopped a set of 8s, and we were nearly drawing dead. We're lucky we didn't have AK in this hand. Which raises an interesting point: *when you bluff, you can contain your losses; you know what you really have and can decide how much you're willing to bet in order to steal the pot.*

You usually won't go broke on failed bluffs; most of the time you'll be felted when a legitimate hand runs into a better one.

Some people will review this hand and decide it was a mistake to play the A5 at all. Although it turned out badly in this case, it was not a bad move.

Consider if the board would have come down JK7 instead of JK8. Our opponent would have had a lonely pair of 8s with two face cards out there. Even though she still had the best hand, would she have been able to call $525,000 at that point? We could have AK, AJ, AAs, QQs, TTs, or a set of kings or jacks.

We actually just got unlucky in this hand. By re-raising aggressively before the flop, we set a tone of strength. Our opponent's body language after the flop indicated she expected to be called – in short, our pre-flop aggression worked. It was only because our opponent actually flopped a big hand (which she was 7.5:1 against hitting) that we lost this pot.

DON'T MAKE DEFENSIVE CALLS

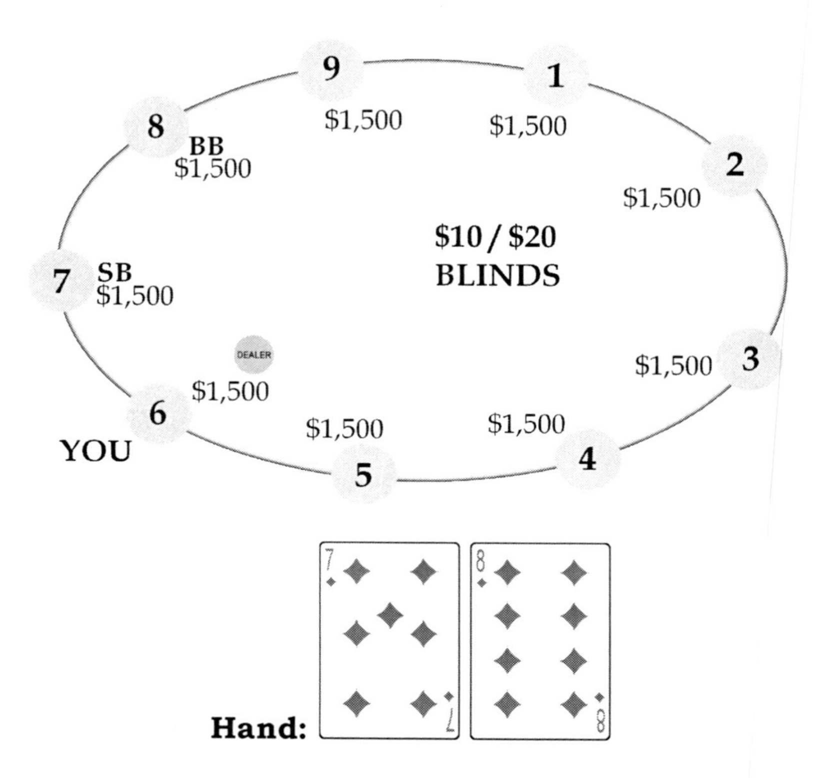

Situation: First hand of a single table online tournament.

Action: Seat 1 folds. Seat 2 makes a standard raise to $60. Seats 3 and 4 fold, while Seat 5 calls. *What should you do?*

Analysis: A call isn't bad here. We have the button with a very playable suited connector. It costs us very little of our stack to see a flop and go from there. Plus, we have two other opponents, and one or both of the blinds may still come in. There could be five-way action if we call here. With a drawing hand, we *want* to see more players in the pot so we can draw cheaply and get paid if we make our straight or flush.

We shouldn't always make this call; but a little speculation is fine in this spot. Of course if one of the blinds decides to re-raise behind us, we're quickly folding.

Action: You call, the small blind calls, and the big blind checks. Five players see the flop, and you're in position:

Analysis: Although we hit a pair of eights, we're done with this hand. When you call with a suited connector like the 78 of diamonds, you're hoping to flop a straight or flush draw, or two-pair if you're very lucky. We might even stick around with a single pair on a non-threatening board, where no one else is likely to have much.

This is a very threatening board. With four other opponents, our eights are worthless. It's much too likely we're drawing dead, and even if a 7 or another 8 would help us, we then have just 5 outs, or a less than 20% chance of improving by the time the river comes around.

A SMALL PIECE ISN'T ALWAYS ENOUGH

It's true we have a made hand. We caught a "small piece" of the board, and many players will automatically call with any made hand.

But consider: sometimes bottom pair is just unplayable, especially if you're up against more than one opponent. If we're behind right now (this is very likely given the texture of the board), we may not even have five clean outs.

What if the initial raiser has pocket kings or queens? We're dead to running eights (a less than 0.1% chance). What if one of our opponents holds KQ? Then a seven won't help us, and we're dead to one of the two remaining eights (roughly 4%).

What if we're up against a straight draw? How long can we stay in this hand if another face card, a ten or an ace shows up? What if someone has two clubs? A club flush draw would eliminate the seven or eight of clubs as legitimate outs for our hand.

In short, sometimes you can connect with the flop and still not be able to play. Don't invest good money in an uncertain and dangerous situation just because you paired one of your hole cards. You don't want to be forced to call bets without having any idea where you're at in the hand.

You can't be aggressive if you're in the dark!

Chapter Twenty-Six

—

VALUE BETTING

Maxim 185: Avoid staking your full credit on a single cast.

It may easily happen that a man should fail once, especially at first: circumstances are not always favorable: hence they say, "Every dog has his day." Always link your second attempt with your first: whether it succeed or fail, the first will lay the groundwork for the second. Be sure you have considered the deficiencies of the first attempt in putting forward your second.

Maxim 189: Make use of others' wants and desires.

The greater his wants the greater the turn of the screw. Philosophers say privation is non-existent, statesmen say it is all-embracing, and the politicians are right. Many rise to great heights on the backs of others' wants. They make use of the opportunity to tantalize the appetite. The energy of desire promises more than the inertia of possession. The passion of desire increases with every new obstacle to its enjoyment. It is a subtle point to satisfy the desire and yet preserve the dependence.

Maxim 242: Push every advantage to its maximum.

Some put all their strength in the commencement and never carry a thing to a conclusion. They invent but never execute. These are vacillating spirits. They earn no fame, for they sustain no game to the end. They sweat away till one key obstacle is surmounted, but content themselves with surmounting it: they do not know how to push the victory home. If the undertaking is promising, why not finish it? If it is bad, why undertake it? Strike down your quarry, if you are wise; be not content to flush it.

EXTRACT MAXIMUM VALUE FROM YOUR HANDS

Inexperienced players believe their profit at the poker table comes primarily from bluffing. It's true you have to make some moves every now and again. You'll certainly remember an audacious bluff *that turns out well.* A well-executed (and successful) bluff is a huge ego boost.

But if you stop and analyze your wins and losses over an extended session, you'll notice that bluffing is not by itself the most profitable part of your game. It plays a key role, but bluffing is not your greatest source of profit.

YOU PROFIT MOST FROM YOUR VALUE BETS

In fact, most of your money comes from legitimate hands. This is true even if you're playing a loose, aggressive style: in that case, you're giving a lot of action when you have the worst of it, in order to get action when you have the best of it. In effect, your loose aggressive bluffs help you earn more from your real hands.

Many players believe they'd be a great, winning player if only they could perfect their bluffing. The reality is they'd be far more dangerous and effective if they knew when to push with a medium-strength hand and how to snap-off other players' bluffs.

WINNING POKER MAXIMIZES WINS AND MINIMIZES LOSSES

The difference between a winning and losing session is often a few key value bets. Too many players are happy just to win, as though being dealt a winning poker hand has something to do with skill. If you have a strong hand and your opponent is second-best, your ability didn't have much to do with the end result.

But if you earn an extra bet or two that most players wouldn't, that is skill. And if you save an extra bet or two when you're second-best, that is even more skillful.

A talented poker player will question how he could have earned (or saved) extra money on each of the hands he plays. If he could have earned an extra bet by doing something differently, he'll make adjustments to tighten up his game.

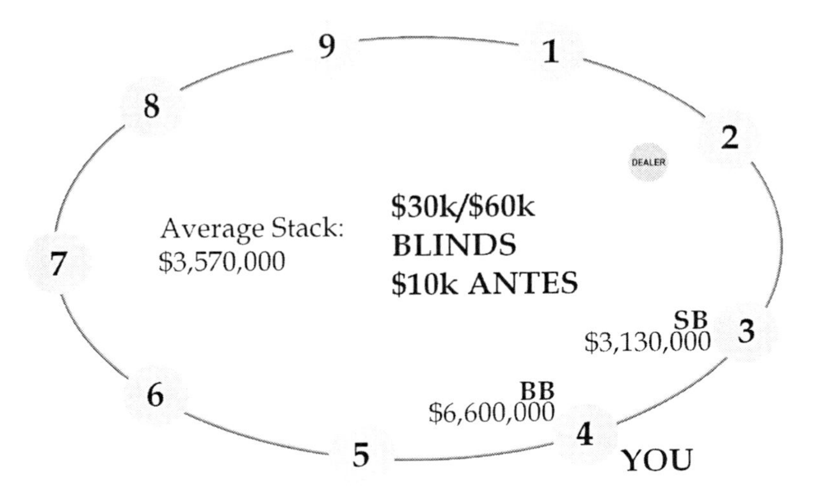

Hand:  

Situation: Final five tables of the World Series of Poker. We're the last woman remaining, and our loose, aggressive game has produced some wild swings in our chip stack. At the moment, with nearly twice the average number of chips, we're in very good shape and feeling confident.

Our opponent in the small blind has not won in a while, and looks pretty frustrated. He's also flat-out told us he hates playing against women. This is useful information: he won't feel good about folding to a woman after losing so many pots in a row.

Action: Everyone folds around to the small blind, who limps in. *What should you do?*

Analysis: Well, we should always start by considering a raise. We're in position against the small blind, and we have a slightly better than average hand. Why shouldn't we raise?

(1) Our **table image** – We're seen as a loose, aggressive player, and a raise from us in this spot is not likely to earn much respect.

(2) The risk of being re-raised out of the pot – If we raise here and the small blind comes

over the top (a move he is fully capable of executing), we won't be able to stand the pressure. We could raise ourselves right out of the hand.

(3) We **don't want to build a big pot with small cards**. Since our hand is unlikely to connect hard with the flop, we should try to keep the pot small. The easiest way to do that is by checking.

(4) Our opponent is not likely to fold to us. He doesn't seem to respect our play and is in no mood to go away. A raise here wouldn't take down the pot. All we'd achieve by raising is to invest a lot more money with a Q8 off-suit.

On the other hand, we are in position. This is an important factor to consider in evaluating whether to raise or fold.

BUILD A BIGGER POT WHEN YOU'RE IN POSITION

When you are in position you'd like to have a bigger pot, since you're at such an advantage. Acting last after each betting round provides you with additional information about the strength of your opponent's hand. If he bets into you, you can raise or fold; if he checks, you can check behind and see a free card.

All things considered, the advantages of checking significantly outweigh the benefits of raising pre-flop. Our loose image, mediocre hand, and lack of respect mean that a standard raise probably won't succeed in taking down the pot.

ALWAYS HAVE A REASON TO BET

If you can't think of a good reason to bet, just check. Being aggressive does not mean making mindless bets. Always bet with a specific objective in mind. If you don't know what you hope to achieve by betting (other than "being aggressive"), don't put your money out there.

Action: You check behind. The pot is now $210,000, and you see the flop heads-up:

Action: The small blind bets $125,000.

Analysis: We have top-pair, very good kicker. But we're vulnerable to a variety of cards on the turn and river. There's a better than even chance a card higher than our pair of eights will hit the turn, and we won't know if it helps our opponent.

What could our opponent have? Most likely he has nothing at all, and is simply betting a ragged board to take the pot away from us. Perhaps he has middle or bottom pair.

It's unlikely he has us beat with two-pair or better, since calling with 82 or 62 would be unusual at this level of play. If he was playing complete trash like that, it's more likely he would have raised pre-flop to steal.

Mostly, I would favor raising here. But our opponent is aggressive and is desperate to finally win a pot: he may continue betting into us on the turn if we check-call. If the turn isn't threatening, we can drop the hammer at that point.

Another important consideration is that this is blind-on-blind action in an un-raised pot. These situations can get fairly wild, and you shouldn't open a bidding war with just a pair of eights.

GOING BROKE IN BLIND-ON-BLIND ACTION

Nothing good comes from massive all-in confrontations between the small and big blinds. When everyone folds around to the blinds, raw aggression kicks in and hand values go right out the window. Suddenly, a weak top pair (with any kind of kicker) can trigger huge raises and re-raises. A ragged board can give one of the blinds an unlikely two-pair. Peculiar six and seven-high straight draws can hit on the turn.

In short, in blind-on-blind action, you usually have no idea where you're at in the hand. Did the small blind raise because he was strong, or just trying to steal? Did the small blind limp because he wants to see a cheap flop, or is he trapping with a monster? Did the big blind check a big hand just to rope us in? Or did he raise just because he has position on us?

Blind-on-blind action is one of the most treacherous parts of no limit hold 'em. If you step out of line, you could find yourself committing your entire stack with a single pair, perhaps not even top pair. That is not a winning formula. Instead, stay calm, try to keep the pots small, and proceed with sensible caution.

In many ways, blind-on-blind action mirrors heads-up play. The difference, though, is that in a heads-up match you have many hands to observe the flow of your opponent's style. You have time to test his level of aggression, his betting patterns, and when he may be making a move.

Blind-on-blind action at a full table is a sporadic episode of raw heads-up aggression. Unless your fellow blind is conservative, it's usually not a good idea to let too many fireworks fly without a big hand. A weak top pair (jacks or lower) doesn't qualify.

Action: You actually just call the $125,000, announcing that it's a "friendly call."

GOING HOLLYWOOD AT THE POKER TABLE

While many professional actors dabble in poker these days, that doesn't mean the reverse should hold true. You're not a professional actor, and there's no reason to "fool" your opponent with speeches, gestures, or strategic shifts in posture.

It's a bad idea to say or do anything suggestive in the middle of a hand. Competent opponents will not be fooled by deliberate "trickiness." As professional poker player and author Mike Caro has noted, ***strong means weak, and weak means strong***.

In other words, players who act strong are usually weak, and those who act timid are almost always strong. Amateur actors invariably employ such "reverse psychology", and they're as easy to read as small children fibbing.

In fact, saying anything about how strong we are is a mistake. We can imagine we're being extra tricky by using reverse-reverse psychology (which is either psychology or plain-old straight-forwardness?); but we're still giving away information to experienced readers of people. Our changing blink rate, voice stress, tone and rhythm of speech can all provide indications of deception. The best rule of thumb is to remain silent and play the fool:

Maxim 240: Make use of foolishness.

The wisest play this card at times, and there are times when the greatest wisdom lies in playing the fool. He is no fool who affects folly, but he is who suffers from it. No one will suspect any danger from he who is disguised as the simplest of creatures.

IT PAYS TO PLAY THE FOOL

If someone stares you down, you go blank. If they ask you what you have (after the hand), you say you forgot. If someone criticizes your play as foolish, you agree. If you're going to act at the poker table, it's better to be severely underestimated as a random fool. The alternative is to be respected as a tight rock; that will earn some folds, but acting the fool will earn some bets.

Here, we have a classic case of reverse psychology from the Rocco School of Bad Acting. Announcing we want to play "friendly" with a mild call is portraying weakness. In fact, we feel good about our hand. We're playing at the World Series of Poker; our experienced opponent is unlikely to be fooled by this cheap ploy.

The pot is now $460,000, and you're last to act after the turn:

Action: Your opponent bets $175,000.

Analysis: That's pretty much the worst possible card for us. This is why we might have raised with our pair of eights on the flop, to avoid seeing an ugly card like this on the turn.

At this level of poker, many players are capable of limping out of the small blind with a strong ace, hoping to trap. We're somewhat less concerned about that possibility here, however, because our opponent is aggressive and has been on a losing streak. He also knows that we're loose, and that we might have called him pre-flop if he raised with a good ace.

While it's possible our opponent limped with an ace, then bluffed ace-high on the flop and connected with the turn, we can't fold to a single scare card. We need to call and see what develops on the river.

Action: You call the $175,000, announcing to your opponent that he should "keep betting!" Again, it's a bad idea to play Hollywood in the middle of a hand at these stakes. Our statement that we *want* him to keep betting into us is designed to feign strength.

In fact, we didn't like the ace at all. By acting strong, we're likely to be read for weakness. We are indeed weak, and if he makes a big pot-sized bet on the river we have a tough call.

Do not attempt to use reverse psychology at the poker table. For some reason, even top-notch players think they can get away with bad acting.

The pot is now $810,000, and you both see the river:

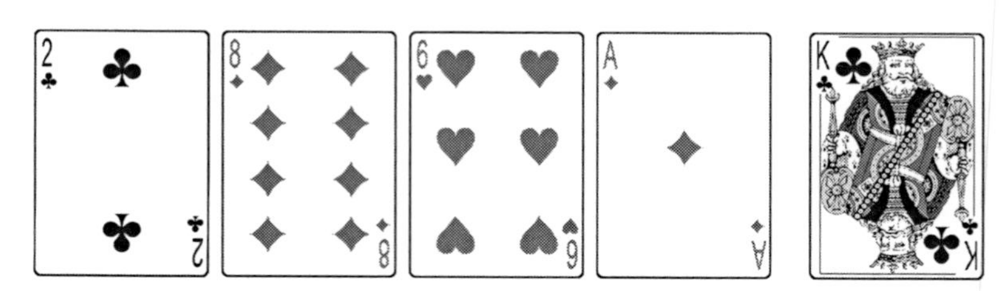

Action: He checks.

Analysis: That king is another unhelpful card. At this point, we have a pair of eights with a queen kicker. The board has turned a strong hand on the flop into a relatively weak one.

This result also shows why we don't like to play high card/low card combinations (like Q8 or K3, etc.) in Texas hold 'em: you can be dominated if you pair your top card, or face a wide range of overs to your low card. Even your ideal flop (top-pair on the low card) could get you in a lot of trouble: your opponent may be trapping, or else not believe you and get lucky with one or more overcards.

The vast majority of the time, against most opponents, we should check behind here. Our now-modest hand is being offered the chance to see a free showdown. If we bet our pair of eights and get raised, we would probably have to fold.

The safe, conservative play that preserves our equity in the hand is to check and see if our hand is still best. Remember the rule: ***don't bet a medium-strength hand on the river***.

However, we might consider making what would be a very aggressive value bet here. This is an advanced play that depends entirely on the unique texture and action of this hand.

To see why we can value bet here, let's step back and consider the small blind's perspective:

The aggressive small blind limped and we checked behind. He could have anything. The flop came down 2 8 6 rainbow. He made a decent bet at the flop, either with a small piece of it (perhaps sixes or deuces) or else thinking it's unlikely we had much of anything.

Then the ace comes on the turn, and he makes a substantially smaller bet given the size of the pot ($175,000 into a $460,000 pot). He knows it's unlikely we have an ace, since we're loose and aggressive and probably would have raised him pre-flop. His bet is designed to signal that he may an ace, and is just sucking a bit more money into the pot.

We're not in love with that card, but if he really had an ace he probably wouldn't have limped out of the small blind pre-flop. So we call. And then the river brings a king, and he checks.

What does it mean when a player fires two barrels, gets called down twice, and then checks the river? There are two possibilities:

(1) He was bluffing all along, fired two barrels, and has decided that after being called twice, a final river bet is unlikely to be successful.

(2) He was betting a made hand all along, and is now checking a medium-strength hand on the river. He may even have been bluffing and all of a sudden hit something on the river which might legitimately win in a showdown. In either case, his check now is not a white flag of surrender: it's just that he wants to minimize any further betting. In other words, the pot is big enough for the strength of his hand.

There are relatively few players who will attempt an elaborate check-raise bluff (or trap) on the river. And even those players who could make that play would only do so when they expected their opponent to bet into them on the end.

Here, we've been passively calling the entire way. Our opponent probably expects us to check behind him. He isn't giving us credit for either an ace or a king, and perhaps not even an eight. Our actions make it appear we were calling him down with second or third pair on the flop, and have refused to release the hand.

Our conclusion: the small-blind is not planning on check-raising us. He's either been bluffing all along with nothing, or now has a medium-strength hand looking for a cheap showdown. If he has a medium-strength hand, what could it be?

He can't have aces, because he'd bet those for value. He probably doesn't have kings, because he either would have raised pre-flop with king-high or would now bet that pair of kings he caught on the river for value. A good rule of thumb is ***if you catch an unlikely card on the river, you should bet it; your opponent will not give you credit for that hand***.

Notice that we can beat almost every other made hand that wouldn't bet for value. If he has a pair of eights, we have a better kicker (since otherwise he would have two-pair and would certainly bet that for value). If he has sixes or deuces, he might call a moderate bet, especially since he's lost several hands recently.

The only realistic threat is a pocket pair greater than eights. If he's that strong, he certainly fooled us by limping. But we know the odds of being dealt any pocket pair is just 5.9%, and a pair higher than eights less than 3%. We can discount aces or kings; in fact, any of these pairs would probably make a smallish bet for value here.

If *we* make a value bet, he'll either fold or call us with one of several hands we can beat. The chance he'll call us with a hand that beats us is unlikely. A check-raise is also unlikely, since he shouldn't expect us to bet after passively calling.

A value bet here is a bold, aggressive move, a borderline incorrect play in fact. But you need to think about earning an extra bet with your hands, especially on the river where the bets are largest.

Action: You muse to yourself (and the rest of the table), "What are you going to call here?" Then you bet $500,000. That makes the pot $1,310,000, and he's getting over 2.5:1 to call. Another advantage in making this aggressive value bet is that we've only invested $800,000 of our $6.6 million stack, even after this move. Our greater than 2:1 chip lead means our opponent must be fairly cautious in dealing with us.

He says he needs to "win one", and we goad him by saying he'd be a "sissy" to fold. He shouts that he's not folding, and can't believe it when we turn over our Q8. He shows a T8, and our pair of eights ace, king, queen kicker beats his pair of eights, ace, king ten kicker.

At the end, our opponent wonders aloud whether we were value betting or bluffing on the river. If he were in our shoes, he clearly would not have bet his 8s on the end. Most players wouldn't. Our value bet here was so aggressive it almost looks like a bluff, as though we were trying to represent aces, kings, or two pair.

Chapter Twenty-Seven

TAKING CHANCES

Maxim 51: Know how to choose well.

Most of life depends thereon. It needs good taste and correct judgment, for which neither intellect nor study suffices. To be choice, you must choose, and for this two things are needed: to be able to choose at all, and then to choose the best. There are many men of fecund and subtle mind, of keen judgment, of much learning, and of great observation who yet are at a loss when they come to choose. They always take the worst as if they had tried to go wrong.

Maxim 53: Be diligent and intelligent.

Diligence promptly executes what intelligence slowly ponders over. Hurry is the failing of fools; they know not the crucial point and set to work without preparation. On the other hand, the wise more often fail from procrastination; foresight begets deliberation, and lack of action often sets aside good judgment. Decisiveness is the mother of good fortune. He has done much who leaves nothing over till tomorrow.

Maxim 194: Aim high and be prepared for whatever comes.

Everyone has a high opinion of himself, especially those who have least ground for it. Every one dreams of his good luck and thinks himself a wonder. Hope gives rise to extravagant promises which experience may not fulfill.

The wise man anticipates such errors: he always hopes for the best, but always prepares for the worst, so as to receive what comes with equanimity. If a man knows the true sphere of his activity and position, he can reconcile his ideals with reality.

There is such a thing as a no-win scenario in poker. The cards can fall in such a way that the hand will all but play itself (KKs vs. AAs, AK vs. QQs, etc). At other times your relative chip position forces you to make a move, and you run into a stronger hand.

This is part of the game. You have to play the odds, trusting that these no-win situations are relatively rare. It is a much bigger mistake to avoid taking chances when you need to. Aim high, hope for the best, and be prepared for whatever comes. If you come up short this time, there's another tournament or cash game you can buy into soon enough.

SOMETIMES YOU HAVE TO TAKE A SHOT

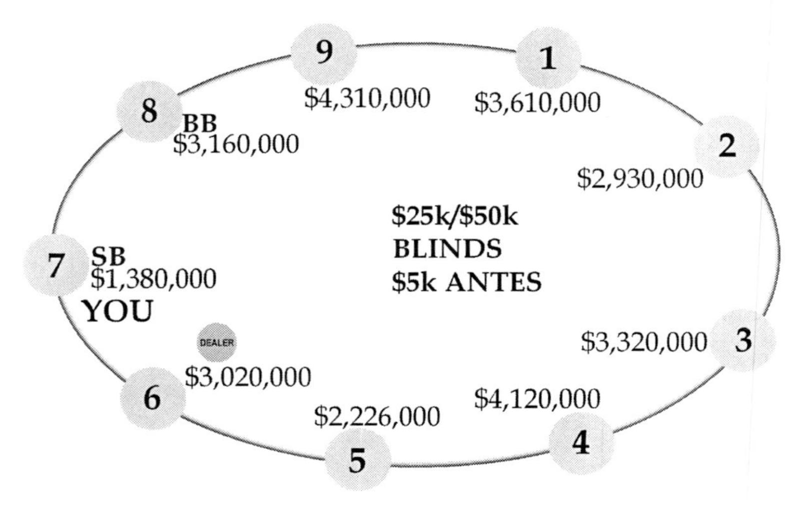

Hand:  

Situation: Final four tables of the World Series of Poker. You're one of the shortest stacks remaining in the tournament. Seat 1 is fairly loose, willing to limp from any position and calling raises with suited connectors down to 76. The average chip stack is nearly $3.5 million in chips, and you have just 40% of that.

With $25,000/$50,000 blinds with $5,000 antes and an increase to $30,000/$60,000 soon, you need to make something happen to stay in contention.

Action: The under-the-gun player folds. Seat 1 raises to $225,000. Everyone folds around to you in the small blind. The pot is now $345,000, and it costs you $200,000 to call. *What should you do?*

Analysis: This is a very tough situation. Obviously you at least want to call with your ace-king. The probability of being dealt any pair is 5.9%, and being dealt AK is 1.2%. Those are the two strongest classes of starting hands, meaning this hand is in the top 7% of all hands.

On average, we'll have to wait one and a half more orbits (at a cost of $140,000, or $155,000 if the blinds increase) to see a hand this strong again. If we get "unlucky", it could be three orbits or more, with our stack dwindling while we wait.

But if we decide to play this hand, can we just call? If we call, we're going to miss the flop nearly two-thirds of the time. And we can expect Seat 1 to bet whether the flop helps him or not.

Unless we hit our ace or king, we won't have any idea if we're ahead or behind after the flop. We'll have invested 15% of our stack, out-of-position, against a loose and aggressive opponent with no idea where we stand.

The alternative (and better play) is to push all-in and capitalize on AK's *fold equity*. If we push here, we can raise Seat 1 an additional $1,130,000, or roughly five times his initial raise. Unless he has a big hand, he'll have to fold. Most early position raisers will have a fairly big hand and will probably make this call.

But this loose, aggressive opponent has shown a propensity to play small pairs and drawing hands, and he should fold those hands in the face of our all-in re-raise.

Action: You re-raise all-in. The big blind folds, and action returns to Seat 1. You're an experienced tournament poker player, so you don't want action if this is a coin-flip. You try to play mind games by telling him you can beat his AQ, but in the process you confirm that he's facing a coin flip with his pair of jacks.

He calls the additional $1,130,000, and the following board does not improve your AK:

His full-house, jacks full of nines, beats your ace-king high.

A great poker player usually won't call all-in with ace-king for his tournament life, unless he feels confident he's got much better-than-even odds. But sometimes you simply have to push with a hand like ace-king (or significantly worse), even if you know you're forcing a 50/50 situation.

When the time comes, don't shy away from making a big move. You must win a few races to win a tournament.

This hand may have been a no-win scenario for you, but you played it correctly under the circumstances. Next time, you'll try to build a better chip position earlier, before reaching the point where you have to make this play.

BEWARE BROOMCORN'S UNCLE

Never let yourself get blinded off! While we said before that you shouldn't take ***unnecessary risks***, there is such a thing as a ***necessary risk!*** Sometimes you should be happy to get your money in with *any competitive hand at all.*

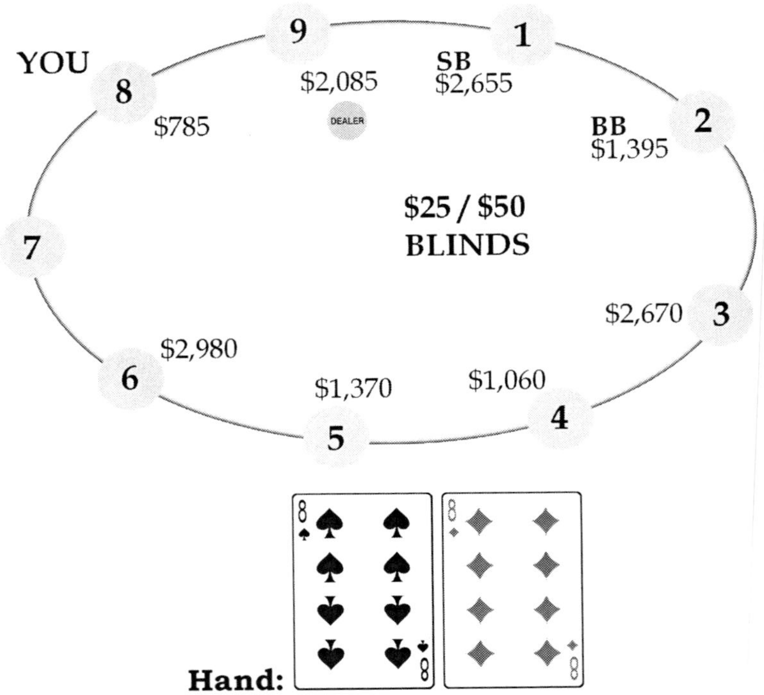

Situation: Late early stage of a single table online tournament. After a strong early start, a bad beat has left your stack crippled. The blinds, currently at $25/$50, will rise to $50/$100 in minutes.

Action: Seats 3 and 4 fold. Seat 5 raises to $175. Seat 6 folds. Action is on you.

Analysis: This is an all-in or fold situation. With the blinds set to rise, you'll have an M of 5. You're in critical condition, and you can't afford to call and fold this hand. Are your eights good enough to push here? With $250 to be earned in this pot, you bet they are! It may be a coin flip if he calls, but that's a risk you need to take right here, right now. You're all-in! (Your opponent actually folds).

Chapter Twenty-Eight

PLAYING THE RIVER

Maxim 82: Drain nothing to the dregs, neither good nor ill.

A sage once reduced all virtue to the golden mean. Push right to the extreme and it becomes wrong: press all the juice from an orange and it becomes bitter. Even in enjoyment never go to extremes. Thought too subtle is dull. If you milk a cow too much you draw blood, not milk.

DON'T BET A MEDIUM-STRENGTH HAND ON THE RIVER

David Sklansky, in his *Theory of Poker*, says there are only two fundamental reasons to bet a hand: (1) to get a stronger hand to fold; or (2) to get a weaker hand to call. In the former case you profit by winning when you otherwise might have lost, and in the latter you profit by getting more money in the pot when you're ahead. You have no reason to bet if you aren't aiming at one of those two objectives.

This concept is particularly critical on the river. By this point, there have been three prior betting rounds: pre-flop, on the flop, and on the turn. You and your opponent have one of three types of hands: (1) a **big hand** (such as two-pair, trips, or a completed draw); (2) a **medium-strength hand** (a single pair), or (3) a very **weak hand** (such as a busted draw). By betting and raising in the earlier stages of the hand, you should have an idea which of these your opponent is most likely to hold.

To play the river effectively, it is critical to evaluate how our hand strength compares to that of our opponent's. If we have a big hand (or the nuts), we should generally check to our opponent if he is very weak (so he can bluff), but lead into him with a value bet if he has a good, but second-best hand. Making a value bet is critical if our opponent has a hand he can call us with, but which he is unlikely to bet if checked to.

Conversely, if we have a weak hand on the river, we should bet if our opponent is weak also. This can happen on a board full of low cards and possible draws where both players missed. In that case, he may have something like ace-high that would win a showdown. Usually these are small pots that no one has shown much interest in, often in blind on blind or button vs. blind action. We must win our fair share of little pots when no one has much of anything to remain competitive.

Whether we should try to bluff an opponent who may be holding a medium-strength hand depends on the texture of the board (are there three or four to a straight or flush?), the tightness of our opponent, our table image (conservative or aggressive?), the relative stack sizes, and the action in the hand thus far.

DON'T GO FOR THE LAST-MINUTE KAMIKAZE BLUFF

The last factor is particularly crucial: if you played the hand passively all along it's usually a bad idea to try a big bluff on the river. *If you're going to bluff, your actions should tell a consistent, believable story.* Nothing is more suspicious than a series of checks followed by a last-minute bet when a blank comes on the river.

If in doubt, err on the side of not bluffing the river, even if you think your opponent could potentially make a laydown.

A BLUFF IS MOST EFFECTIVE ON THE TURN

By the time the river comes, if your opponent is still hanging around he may feel committed to seeing the hand through. He knows calling will ensure a showdown at a fixed price (the amount of your one bet). Because of this, a bluff on the river is usually less effective than a bluff on the turn, with the *implied threat* of another bet to follow.

If we hold a medium-strength hand on the river, our primary objective is to see the showdown without investing much more money. By this point, most of the time a hand like one pair (even top pair) should be considered a medium-strength hand. This does not mean that we should meekly fold top pair – this would be disastrous to our bottom line. We just want to avoid a bidding war with a hand that could be vulnerable.

This means we should generally check if first to act, or check behind if checked to in position. By checking out of position, we can profit either from drawing a bluff from a weak hand or avoiding a raise from a strong hand. By checking in position, we avoid losing our chance to see the showdown if our opponent is trying to trap us.

To summarize: you almost never bet a medium-strength hand on the river. You can bet a strong hand for value or a weak hand to bluff. You'll also mix in some checks when you have a strong hand to encourage bluffing and to earn extra value with a check-raise.

BET A MEDIUM-STRENGTH HAND ON THE RIVER DEFENSIVELY

The only time you should consider betting a mediocre hand on the end is to prevent an even larger bet from a very aggressive opponent. In other words, if an aggressive player will bet the whole pot if checked to, we try to head him off by betting something like half the pot. This may work; but if your opponent is very aggressive he's just as liable to make a big raise and cost you more than check-calling. Use this play sparingly.

Note that this defensive betting does not change our objective. With a medium-strength hand, we still want to see the showdown *as cheaply as possible.* In rare circumstances, leading out with a bet against an aggressive player who's in position may be the cheapest way to see the showdown. Let's see how this principle works in practice.

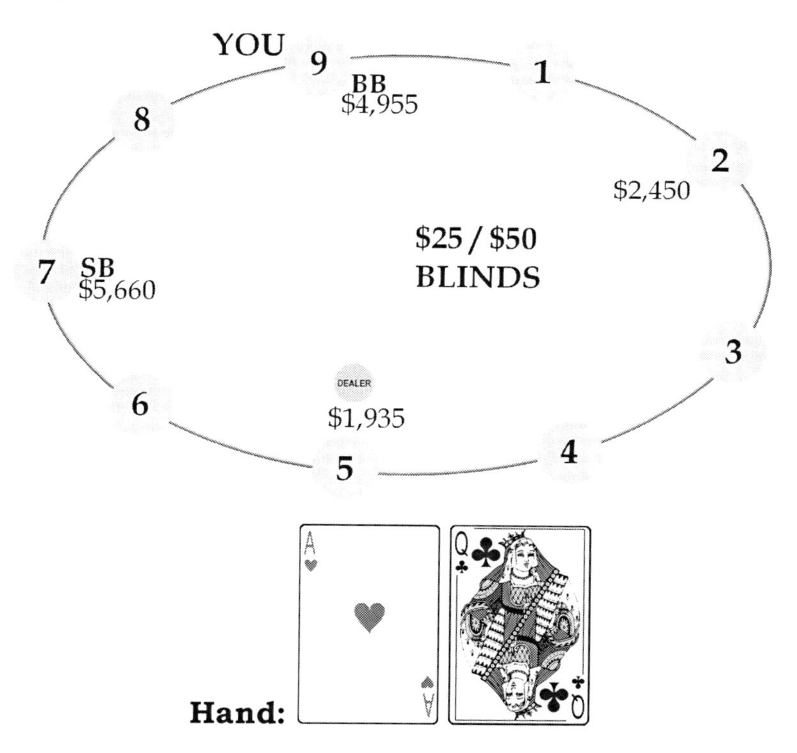

Situation: On the bubble of a single table online sit and go tournament. We're one of two large stacks at the table. All the remaining players have demonstrated tight, competent play thus far. We're in the big blind with our AQ off-suit.

Action: Seat 2 limps into the pot. The button folds, and the small blind completes. *What should you do?*

Analysis: There may be an argument for checking here to disguise the strength of our hand, given that the blinds are still relatively low and no one can limp in behind us. It's not a terrible play.

But I don't like checking here because of the presence of the big stack in the small blind. We shouldn't let the only guy in the tournament who can knock us out limp into the pot cheaply with two random cards. If we don't raise here, we'll have no idea how strong the small blind or Seat 2 is. We should raise here for two reasons: (1) to define the strength of our opponent's hands and whether they're serious about the pot; and (2) to isolate Seat 2 (a relative small stack) in a heads-up confrontation.

Action: You raise to $260. Seat 2 calls, but the small blind folds. The pot is now $670 and the two of you see the flop heads-up:

Analysis: Our pre-flop raise succeeded in knocking out the big-stacked small blind and isolating the relatively short-stacked second seat. Regardless of how the hand goes, we've dramatically improved our overall chance of winning the hand and no longer face the threat of elimination – we have Seat 2 covered.

At each stage of the betting it's important to try to narrow down our opponent's likely holding. We know that Seat 2 initially limped under the gun and then just called a healthy pre-flop raise - but did not re-raise us. This betting pattern is consistent with either a small to medium pair or a drawing hand like a suited connector.

It's possible that Seat 2 has a weak ace. This is less likely, though, both because we have an ace in our own hand and because Seat 2 might have initially raised. It's extremely unlikely he's slowplaying a premium pair, since he probably would have sprung that trap pre-flop rather than merely calling our raise, giving odds to the small blind to call behind him.

Of course, we've flopped top-pair, top-kicker here and we're clearly going with the hand. Our best-case scenario is that Seat 2 has a drawing hand like KQ or QJ and was unlucky enough to flop top-pair with a weaker kicker. Our worst-case scenario is that Seat 2 flopped a set of deuces or eights, but *when the game is short-handed we stop worrying about hidden sets*. That 5% possibility we discussed earlier has been cut to something like a negligible 2% probability.

We're going to bet here, and I'd favor an amount that looks like a standard continuation bet. The continuation bet is only effective if made whether we have a hand or not. A standard half-pot continuation bet has become such a textbook play that it is often read for weakness today.

Ideally, we'd like to entice a raise from a skeptical opponent here.

Action: You bet $380 into the $670 pot. Your opponent calls. The pot is now $1,430 and you both see the turn:

Analysis: It's interesting that our opponent just called. Our best guess for Seat 2 was that he had either a drawing hand (i.e. suited connector) or a small-to-medium pair. If he missed entirely he would have folded or come over the top of our bet. If he hit the queen he probably would have raised. In the very unlikely event he flopped a set, his call makes sense: he's just stringing us along in case we're very weak.

Many players are tempted to assume our opponent must be drawing at the flush. But we're playing a heads-up pot in a short-handed game. When you're playing with half a table or less, you need to substantially discount the possibility of drawing hands or hidden monsters.

It's still possible we got lucky, and he paired that queen with a lesser kicker (perhaps QJ). Remember, we're close to the money here, we've got a big stack, and our opponent may be playing very conservatively. But if he is drawing at the flush, we still need to charge him. In fact we need to charge him here regardless. If we're beat, he'll be doubling up on this hand.

Action: You bet $600 into the $1,430 pot, and Seat 2 quickly calls. The pot is now $2,630, and you're both going to the river. You have $3,715 left in your stack, while your opponent has $1,160, having invested just over half of his stack in this pot.

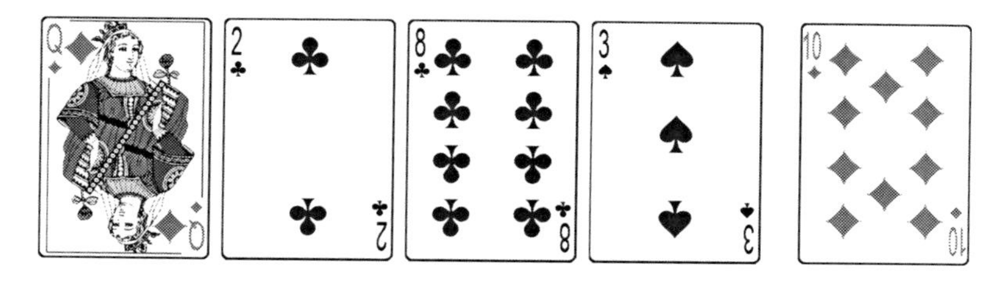

Analysis: We're first to act, and we've reached the river. We have top-pair, top-kicker, and we played this pot at a short-handed table heads-up against a single opponent. We're not folding here, especially since we'll still be in contention even if our opponent goes all-in and has us beat. We probably have the best hand, but it's just one pair (medium-strength), and there are three very good reasons to check in this spot:

(1) Our opponent may be very weak – All of our opponent's actions here are consistent with a flush draw. He could have something like an Ax or KJ of clubs and missed everything by the river. If we feign weakness here, he might go all-in on a

kamikaze move to try to steal the pot. We will of course be calling him.

(2) Our opponent may be very strong – All of our opponent's actions are also consistent with a very strong hand, such as a flopped set. Why has he invested half his stack by passively calling along this close to the bubble? If he's been trapping all along, if we bet any amount at all he's coming over the top of us all-in. He may go all-in even if we check to him.

However, it's also likely he'll interpret our check as weakness and decide to make a smaller value bet here, saving us money and allowing us to retain a decent chip lead over the remaining small stack.

"IS THE POT BIG ENOUGH FOR MY HAND?"

(3) The pot is big enough for our hand. You should have a big hand to play a big pot; with a small hand, work to keep the pot small. Here, we've built a pretty big pot for a one pair hand. Checking here is probably our best chance to minimize this pot.

I know many players will want to go for the jugular here and try to eliminate Seat 2 from the tournament. While this aggressive instinct is admirable, we need to concern ourselves primarily with maximizing our potential win and minimizing our potential loss on this hand.

If we win here, Seat 6 will be in bad shape regardless. We don't need to take any unnecessary risks and diminish our own tournament chances to achieve a "knock-out" blow.

Action: You check, and Seat 2 bets $600. The pot is now $3,230 and it costs you $600 to call.

Analysis: Of course we're calling. We're getting better than 5:1 and we have top pair/top kicker. Plus, we fully intended on calling any bet when we checked over to Seat 2. By checking to him, we signaled weakness, and now his bet could indicate anything from a suck bet with a monster to a complete post-oak bluff. We're obligated to at least call.

Should we raise him his last $610? Again, a lot of players would try for the knock-out here, but consider: most competent players would never bet a medium-strength hand (which we could beat) on the river. He's probably got either two-pair or better and is sucking us in for a little bit more, or he's making a weak post-oak bluff. If it's the former, saving $610 translates to another twelve big blinds which could make all the difference to our chances in this tournament.

Action: You call the additional $600, and your opponent turns over KQ of hearts, for top-pair, king kicker. Your top-pair, ace kicker takes the pot. Seat 2 is left with $560, and is effectively crippled.

Analysis: I don't like Seat 2's bet on the river. We telegraphed a strong hand from beginning to end, and there was no good reason to bet top pair at the end. He got a bad deal for sure, but his poor decision to bet a medium-strength hand on the river cost him an extra $600 he didn't have to lose.

The difference between $1,160 and $560 on the bubble of a sit and go tournament is like night and day. He no longer has enough chips to intimidate any of the other players with an all-in shove, and is probably doomed to bust out before the final three because of this one mistake. He should have checked behind us, because there were few hands that could have paid off his extra $600 (perhaps only a QJ or a few medium pairs less than queens). We either had him beat, or else we were bluffing and couldn't call him anyway.

CONCLUSION

Poker is a game that takes minutes to learn and a lifetime to master. In fact, the game can never be "mastered": you're only as good as your competitors' mistakes. The key to becoming an expert poker player is to encourage others to make mistakes, while avoiding errors of your own.

Poker is a competitive game - you win by forcing your opponents to lose: calling bets when they should have folded, and folding hands they would have won.

It's a game of information: the player who has a better idea of his opponents' likely cards can escape from trouble and maximize the return on his own hands.

Finally, it's a game of chicken: even if you have perfect information about your opponents' cards, you still have to gamble, and bluff, and understand how far to push every possible advantage. Sometimes you have to take chances and make things happen. Sometimes you need to swerve away at the last second *before* the head-on impact.

The best teacher is experience, and that is why I have focused on real-life hand examples to illustrate the elements of winning poker play. Hopefully you have taken from this analysis several interesting points you can add to your own game. At the end of the day a book's value is often found in one or two key ideas you hadn't considered before.

Since this is an age in which even the newest books show their age by the time they roll off the presses, I have dedicated a section of my author's website to additional tips, strategies, and hand examples that couldn't be included here. You can view this information (and more) at

JonathanGelling.com

I hope you have found some ideas that will improve your game at the table. I look forward to seeing you there!

INDEX

ABOUT THE AUTHOR

Jonathan Gelling was born and raised on Long Island, New York. He graduated from Binghamton University in upstate New York and earned his JD from Vanderbilt University Law School in Nashville, Tennessee.

A long-time student of the game of poker, Jonathan specializes in online cash games and single table sit and go tournaments. He has won hundreds of online tournaments and has never had a losing year playing poker.

His winning style of poker play is geared toward the everyman working their way up the low and medium stakes games. With the right effort and experience, anyone using these techniques can be a winning poker player.

CPSIA information can be obtained at www.ICGtesting.com
Printed in the USA
LVOW071957081012

301997LV00029B/125/P